Bouldering
USA

Bouldering
USA

A Complete Guide to
25 Selected Destinations
Around the Country

Alli Rainey Wendling

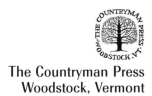

The Countryman Press
Woodstock, Vermont

WARNING: BOULDERING IS A DANGEROUS SPORT IN WHICH YOU MAY BE SERIOUSLY INJURED OR KILLED.

Safety is a vital concern in all outdoor activities, particularly in bouldering. This book is not a substitute for professional training and sound judgment. Your climbing safety depends on your training and your commonsense judgment as you acquire skills and begin bouldering on your own.

Bouldering is a technical sport. Practicing it safely depends on employing the correct techniques and deploying the right gear for the respective conditions. If you make errors on any of these fronts, serious injury or death could result. It is strongly recommended that you learn skills from professional instructors (see *Online* and *Other* resources in the Lowdown section of each locale mentioned in this book). This book is intended to introduce you to bouldering and offer you a foundation on which to build your skills.

Copyright © 2004 by Alli Rainey Wendling

First Edition

All rights reserved. No part of this book may be reproduced in any way by any electronic or mechanical means, including information storage and retrieval systems, without permission in writing from the publisher, except by a reviewer, who may quote brief passages.

Library of Congress Cataloging-in-Publication Data
Wendling, Alli Rainey.
    Bouldering USA : a complete guide to 25 selected destinations around the country / Alli Rainey Wendling.—1st ed.
        p. cm.
    Includes bibliographical references and index.
    ISBN 0-88150-651-6
    1. Rock climbing—United States—Guidebooks. 2. United States—Guidebooks.
    I. Title.

GV199.4.W47 2004
796.52"23'0973—dc22

                                                                                                    2004052719

Cover design by Johnson Design
Interior design and composition by Faith Hague Book Design
Front cover photo © Matt Wendling
Back cover photo © Phil Mislinski
Interior photographs by the author unless otherwise specified
Maps by Ed Faherty, www.fahertydesign.com

Published by The Countryman Press, P.O. Box 748, Woodstock, VT 05091

Distributed by W.W. Norton & Company, Inc., 500 Fifth Avenue, New York, NY 10110

Printed in the United States of America

10 9 8 7 6 5 4 3 2 1

*Dedicated to nourishing
and inspiring the spirit
of the vagabond
in all of us.*

NORTHWEST

1 Sinks Canyon–Lander, WY
2 Cody–WY
3 Dierkes Lake–Twin Falls, ID

CALIFORNIA

4 Castle Rock State Park–Saratoga
5 The Buttermilks–Bishop
6 Joshua Tree National Park–
   Joshua Tree

UTAH AND COLORADO

7 Ibex–Delta, UT
8 Joe's Valley–Orangeville, UT
9 Little Cottonwood Canyon–
   Salt Lake City, UT
10 Flagstaff Mountain–Boulder, CO
11 Castlewood Canyon State Park–
   Franktown, CO

SOUTHWEST

12 Priest Draw–Flagstaff, AZ
13 Box Canyon–Socorro, NM
14 City of Rocks State Park–Deming, NM
15 Hueco Tanks State Historic Site–
   El Paso, TX

MIDWEST

16 Mount Baldy–Keystone, SD
17 Rock City–Minneapolis, KS

NORTHEAST

18 Rumney–NH
19 Hammond Pond Reservation–
   Newton, MA
20 Lincoln Woods State Park–Lincoln, RI
21 The Gunks–New Paltz, NY

SOUTHEAST

22 Horse Pens 40–Steele, AL
23 Sandrock–Leesburg, AL
24 Rocktown–LaFayette, GA
25 Boat Rock–Atlanta, GA

contents

preface

SINCE I WAS FIRST INTRODUCED to rock climbing more than a decade ago, I've long thought that if more people would just rock climb, the world would be a much happier and healthier place. Perhaps that's a naïve assumption, but given the current state of our nation, where obesity has reached epidemic proportions and millions of people take antidepressants, I can't help but think there's still a grain of truth in it. If the population at large could experience joy in movement and exercise instead of viewing working out as a loathsome task, then I think that we as a nation wouldn't be so overweight. After all, it's much easier to exercise if you actually enjoy what you're doing. And if people could experience the bliss of complete mental, physical, and emotional unity experienced via a regularly undertaken physical activity like rock climbing, then far fewer people would feel the need to turn to prescription medications to enhance their moods. Believe it or not, I've found that rock climbing can both enhance people's moods and provide them with a fun and social physical activity that makes exercise something to look forward to—which is why I think that everyone should try it!

Alas, the biggest problem with this nonmedical prescription of mine is that many people are terrified at the prospect of climbing high off the ground and of trusting their very lives to another person or to the climbing equipment—all understandable and valid concerns.

That's where bouldering comes in. Bouldering is the perfect solution for those who've always wanted to try out rock climbing but are scared of heights or of dealing with the equipment. By its very definition—the climbing of small rocks sans ropes and harnesses—bouldering allows the participants to control how far off the ground they climb. You do not need to learn about ropes, harnesses, knots, belaying, or other such technicalities involved in rock climbing to become a boulderer. Bouldering is rock climbing at its simplest and most accessible, making it the easiest way for

Kenneth McGinnis, Horse Pens 40, Alabama. PHOTO BY MATT WENDLING

people to try their hand at rock climbing.

Realizing these truths and spurred by my strong belief that everyone should try climbing at least once, when the opportunity arose to write a book aimed at introducing bouldering to a wide audience, I couldn't resist. Thus *Bouldering USA* came into being. I hope this work inspires you to start bouldering and motivates you to continue bouldering, and ultimately, I hope to meet you out on the rocks someday!

Acknowledgments

I AM GRATEFULLY INDEBTED to every climber and boulderer I encountered in my travels to research this book who provided helpful beta, the local tour, words of encouragement, transportation, and/or lodging, including Dan Dewell, Mike May, the Chenvainus (Kristi, Alex, Andreas, and Mattias), Joe McLoughlin, Dino Tsidavis, Jackie Chiddo, Tim Kemple, the Maine guys (Greg and David), Christine Balaz, Alana Hanks, Ward Smith, Ivan Greene, Scott Pettitt, Bob Broilo, Eric and Beth Johnson, Kate Reese, the Schultz family, and the many others I'm failing to recall.

I also owe a huge thanks to the entire Wyoming crew, especially John Abel, Tad Anderson, Heidi Badaracco, Steve Bechtel, Luke Decker, Mike Decker, Leif Gasch, Charlie Kardaleff, Reid Leslie, Leslie Paul, Julia Reese-White, Emily Robins, Rio Rose, Jeremy Rowan, Micah Rush, Todd Skinner, Meg Snyder, Mike Snyder, BJ Tilden, Trevor Turmelle, Tarris Webber, and Vance White—not only did they provide an endless supply of beta, camaraderie, belays, spots, and laughter, but also, many of them appear in photos throughout this work.

Thanks, too, to all of my supporters in the outdoor industry who have been there through the years—Sterling Rope, Petzl, Boreal, Flashed, Clif Bar, Native Eyewear, Rocky Mountain Sunscreen, Acopa USA, and Megalith. I'd like to acknowledge the following individuals as well—Paul Niland, Carolyn Brodsky, Dale Bard, Scott Hinton, John DiCuollo, John Bachar, Steve West, Julie Pearson, Walson Tai, Lev Pinter, Dylan Seguin, George

Schott, Tawny Hurter, Sean Zimmerman, David Erickson, and Bart Groendycke, as well as all the other folks I'm definitely forgetting.

Thanks to all of the boulderers who have taken the time to lovingly craft impressive catalogs of problems—or to provide any beta, for that matter—at one or more of their favorite areas (in particular those areas included in this work). Whether for the Internet, a published guidebook, or just themselves and whoever happens their way, they deserve a huge amount of recognition and gratitude, for truly such endeavors are a labor of love that provide an invaluable resource for all those who visit those areas. Many of these works aided me both in finding my way around the bouldering areas with which I had less familiarity and in providing me with one or more resources I could recommend to readers who are interested in knowing the full beta on the areas included. See Appendices B and C as well as the *Guidebooks to area problems* and *Online resources* sections for each destination for the full rundown of guides and sites that I feel are particularly helpful and interesting.

Random appreciation goes to all of the people through the years who have impacted my climbing in a positive way, including the person who introduced me to the sport, Bowie Hillberg; all those guys at the Arches (Norm and Leon in particular) who loaned me their gear and gave me belays; Dan Nguyen, who loaned me a pair of shoes for my first multipitch route; the Boston Rock Gym and all of the people there who supported me, especially Soon, who gave me countless rides to and from the gym; my past climbing coaches, Robyn Erbesfield-Raboutou, Didier Raboutou, and Chris Wall, all of whom helped me make remarkable leaps forward in my climbing; and everyone else I've climbed or bouldered with throughout my tenure as a climber, whether once or many times—the fantastic people in the worldwide climbing community are undoubtedly one of the top reasons why I've continued climbing for so long.

I'm grateful to the fantastic team of folks at W.W. Norton and The Countryman Press who aided me—a lowly first-time book author—throughout this entire process, particularly Dale Hetsko, Kermit Hummel, Jennifer Thompson, and David Corey.

I appreciate the support of my family as well—Cindy Rainey, Bill Rainey, Joel Rainey, and Valerie Chanlot, as well as my dog, Maple, and my enduring companion of the past 15 years, my cat, Sassy. Finally, this book would not have been possible without the loving support of my patient and wonderful husband, Matt Wendling, my companion through many of my travels, my bastion of sanity, and my soul mate.

INTRODUCTION

I'VE COME TO REALIZE that it's all a matter of perspective.

You could say that bouldering is the purest form of rock climbing out there. Many people do. Bouldering distills a traditionally equipment-intensive activity—rock climbing—into such a simple form that it's rendered almost as accessible as buying a pair of running shoes because you've always wanted to start running. Without ropes, knots, fixed or removable pieces of protection, or required dependence on a partner (though bouldering with another person is highly recommended), boulderers attempt to scale or traverse small rocks via lines of naturally occurring hand- and footholds—cracks, depressions, pockets, bumps, edges, and so forth. Often boulder "problems" (specific routes, using specific holds, by which a climber can ascend or traverse a boulder) present short and savagely difficult sequences of moves. Such sequences would be virtually impossible to execute in the middle of an 80-foot rock climb because the climber's power and stamina would already be too depleted from the climbing required to approach the difficult section. This is one of the many aspects of bouldering—along with the social component and the lack of technical training and equipment required, among others—that have made this form of rock climbing increase dramatically in popularity in recent years.

You could also say that bouldering is the most absurd form of rock climbing out there. Instead of seeking peaks, walls, or even cliffs to scale, grown people seek out little rocks to climb, often ignoring the easiest way to the top and preferring to select specific holds or lines of holds, designating them as a problem. These adults will then spend an afternoon, a week, a month, or even years attempting to ascend or traverse this particular small rock using these particular small holds. Sometimes they even ignore the bigger holds right next to the small holds if this problem happens to be what's known as "an eliminate"—a problem that disallows the use of certain handholds and/or footholds that the climber could potentially utilize to make ascending or traversing the rock easier. A huge amount of effort goes into this process— maybe fingertips will get so worn by the abrasive holds that they will bleed (a common occurrence at some bouldering areas), maybe the boulderer will continue the onslaught through inclement weather conditions, maybe a fall will result in a twisted ankle or bruised heel—or worse. All so that the boulderer can have the satisfaction of knowing that he or she ascended some random little rock using some randomly appointed holds that make a problem. Does it get any sillier than that?

So you see, it really is all a matter of perspective . . . but I'm guessing that if you picked up this book, you have some interest in bouldering or maybe even rock climbing, despite the absolutely inane component of the activity that I fell in love with as a teenager and haven't been able to stop doing since. You see, those little boulders are so beguiling, so tantalizing, so perplexingly attractive—from the beauty of the stone, to the incredible formations that enable me to climb on

Simply put, climbing just feels good.

them, to the artistry required to effectively execute movements utilizing those features—that I can't seem to help myself, I just keep on climbing. And every once in a while, I turn into the obsessed boulderer I described above, attacking a problem until my fingers bleed, until all I can think about are the moves on that problem, until I'm re-creating the problem with plastic holds in my local gym to train the moves. Why? I don't really know. It's like full-body, three-dimensional Tetris, I suppose . . . a game or puzzle that requires my physical, mental, and emotional parts to operate in unity and harmony, enabling me to perform a brief dance on the face of a rock—all so I can move on to the next problem, attempt to solve the next puzzle.

Simply put, climbing just feels good. That's why.

You may want to try out bouldering as a stepping-stone to getting involved in other forms of rock climbing—or maybe bouldering will be enough for you. In any event, bouldering is a great way to get acquainted with rock climbing without making a tremendous monetary investment, since the equipment requirements are much more basic than those required for safe roped climbing. Other benefits of bouldering include a terrific overall body workout, an extremely social scene in which you can easily meet other folks who are interested in bouldering, and the fact that once you do know what you're doing, you can go to your local gym or outside area and create a circuit of problems that are safe for you to do solo—just like going for a run over familiar ground.

About This Book

In the first chapter of this book, you'll be introduced to the basic nuts and bolts of bouldering, including equipment requirements, safety concerns, and other pertinent issues you should know about before you head for the rocks or the local climbing gym for your first bouldering experience. The second chapter delves more deeply into the facets of actually becoming a boulderer, helping you to develop a more comprehensive understanding of some of the many aspects of bouldering, from training tactics and techniques to comprehending bouldering guidebooks.

Chapters 3 through 9 should prove useful for beginning and experienced boulderers alike. Here you'll find profiles of 25 selected bouldering areas around the country—a personally chosen assortment of areas that range from world-class destinations to local, urban hangouts. While the information offered by no means provides a complete guide to each area's boulder problems (I'll leave that to the local guidebook authors), where this book can really help you out is with the detailed information that reaches beyond just the climbing itself. Listings for each area include specific access concerns and suggestions for nearby places to camp and shower, check your e-mail, eat, climb indoors, and much, much more. I hope that you also get a feel for the singular characteristics that render each and every area I've selected a worthwhile destination in its own right, and that you find your way to some great boulder problems to get you started.

After mulling it over for a while, I decided to organize the 25 destinations in this book in a way that makes sense to me. Since all of my travels begin and end in Wyoming, the destinations described begin in Wyoming and then take you on a loosely west-to-east and north-to-south loop around the country. You should know that I've recently visited all these areas as a traveling rock climber and boulderer doing firsthand research for this book, and they have struck a chord with me for one reason or another. This accounts for the distinct holes in the fabric I've woven of the bouldering areas available across the nation, for I could not in good conscience recommend that you visit bouldering areas where I've never been, nor could I create an adequately researched guidebook to such areas. Nonetheless, these are holes that I ultimately would like to fill in, perhaps in a future edition, with greater attention to the Pacific Northwest and the Midwest in particular. Suggestions for new areas that I should explore and corrections or additions to the current information are more than welcome.

The appendices offer useful information that will help you familiarize yourself with the sport of bouldering and plan your adventures. The Glossary (Appendix A) provides you with a full rundown of bouldering lingo to help you understand what all those boulderers are talking about. Appendices B and C provide reference lists of the comprehensive guidebooks and general Web resources that I recommend, having consulted many of them myself in putting together this work.

Please note that mileages can differ due to variations in different autos' odometers, and I've done my best to ensure the accuracy of the directions I've given, which is the best I can do. Suffice it to say that I'm truly sorry if you get lost or frustrated because of me—I know how angry I've been when other guide-book authors have misguided me in the past, but I now have a much greater appreciation of how hard it is to ensure 100 percent accuracy. (Be aware as you read that Web sites in particular seem to go in and out of functioning on a nearly daily basis.)

In any event, this is not your normal guidebook, and it is in no way intended to be a replacement for the comprehensive and painstakingly compiled guide-books containing detailed information about each individual boulder problem at an area that are already available for many of the areas included. Rather, this work should be viewed as a motivational resource to get you started as a boul-derer, and as a helpful supplement to the available comprehensive resources and guidebooks, providing you with enough information to find each area and get started, but not enough for multiple visits.

How to Use This Book

Chapters 1 and 2 should be basically self-explanatory. The headings throughout both chapters should help you find the information you seek with relative ease.

Chapters 3 through 9, detailing the 25 selected bouldering areas, all begin with a detailed write-up of my impressions of the areas. This is followed by a section called *The Lowdown*, which provides you with itemized information as follows:

➤GETTING THERE

This section provides you first with **driving directions,** since in my experience it seems that most boulderers reach their destinations via car rather than plane. This section also lists the **nearest major airports** and information about **public transportation** to the boulders, if this is available.

●▶CLIMBING CONCERNS

Here you'll find a comprehensive collection of information about the climbing area itself, starting with basics—the **entry fee, hours,** and **land** manager; verbal directions on **how to find the boulders** (often only a few key boulders to get you started), and the **type of rock.** This is followed by **five good problems** I've chosen to recommend for the area, based on input from other boulderers (local and nonlocal), as well as my own opinion from sampling a number of problems in each area. After this, you'll find the **prime season** to visit the boulders; whether or not your dog is welcome; and any **special notes** about the area, which most often address access concerns, so please be sure to read them. Also included in this section are listings for the **guidebooks to the area's problems,** should you wish to further your exploration and knowledge of the area; **online resources** that can also help you further your exploration and knowledge; additional **local, climbing-related resources,** where you'll find listings for guiding services and climbing clubs, among others; **local climbing gyms,** in case it rains or you just want to climb indoors; and **nearby bouldering and climbing areas of note**, should you want to explore elsewhere.

Welcome to the vertical world . . .

●▶OTHER IMPORTANT STUFF

This section provides you with other key information that you're likely to need for planning a bouldering trip to each destination, starting with suggestions for **camping** areas, usually those that appear to be most popularly used by boulderers. You'll also find directions to a **nearby phones, showers, water, hospitals, and Internet hookups,** all of which could be important to you during your stay. Finally, there are suggestions for restaurants (and other eateries) near the bouldering, complete with directions, price ranges, and most important, hours, since I know from experience that sometimes after a long day of climbing, all I want to do is sit down and have someone serve me a hot, delicious meal. So I've chosen the restaurants based solely on merit and/or proximity to the climbing, and I've indicated whether they are expensive (more than $15 per person), moderate ($10 to $15 per person), or inexpensive (less than $10 per person) to help you fit them into your budget if that is an area of concern.

Have fun exploring, support your local guidebook authors, and welcome to the vertical world . . . I hope you stay for a lifetime!

chapter 1

THE BASICS

A Very Brief History of Bouldering

When my friend Dave purchased a crash pad in 1993, we—all of my climbing friends and me—laughed at him for spending $100 on the silly little thing, deeming it useless and a waste. Little did we realize that Dave had purchased what would, in a few short years, become a standard item of equipment for many rock climbers, and the sole form of safety equipment for those folks who only boulder—a choice that a mere decade ago was almost unheard of.

What my laughing friends and I didn't realize then, however, was that bouldering traces its roots way back, having long been used by rock climbers as a practice tool for bigger climbs, as a rainy day activity, as a rock climbing activity when bigger rocks and cliffs were unavailable—and even just as an activity to pursue for the sake of bouldering itself, like so many boulderers do today. Though most climbers seem to believe that bouldering as an end unto itself is a relatively modern development, the fact of the matter is that rock climbers have practiced bouldering for just that purpose—as well as to practice for the bigger rocks—since the late 1800s. Britain appears to be the site of the sport's origin, and in the United

Matt Wendling bouldering at Rocktown, Georgia.

States bouldering has been around for at least 80 years, and possibly much longer than that.

If you want to read more extensively about bouldering's history both internationally and in this country, you should look to John Gill, one of the sport's legendary, historic figures, who has been responsible for developing and promoting bouldering in the U.S. since the mid-1950s. Gill has compiled a wonderful resource on the history of bouldering, which you can find online at www.johngill.net. The site includes photographs of folks bouldering since the 19th century, a comprehensive history of the sport, and a fantastic, in-depth discussion of the validity (or lack thereof) of distinguishing "historical bouldering" from "modern bouldering."

Despite its lengthy history, bouldering's true explosion in popularity didn't occur until it became far more accessible to the masses in the 1990s with the advent of crash pads like the one purchased by my friend Dave. Crash pads (or mats, as some folks call them) lower a boulderer's potential for getting seriously hurt when falling off a boulder problem. Since the first crash pad hit the market, pads have grown beefier, bigger, and cushier, making for even softer and wider landing surfaces—and drawing more people into the fray. With the addition of a padded landing surface, many, many more people have embraced bouldering as a low-commitment, low-cost, non-gear-intensive, and extremely social way to move around on rock surfaces. Quite often, boulderers travel in flocks and work problems together, as well as helping guide one another to safe landings on the crash pads (known as "spotting"). In fact, a whole new climbing culture has grown out of the extremely social bouldering scene.

So how many boulderers are out there today? Unfortunately, no one seems to keep tabs on such statistics—at least, I couldn't find any. But given the rapid development and notoriety of formerly little-known bouldering areas and the proliferation of bouldering-oriented companies, bouldering gyms nationwide, annual bouldering competitions (notably the American Bouldering Series, www.rockcomps.com, and the Professional Climbers' Association (PCA) tour, www.pcatour.com); bouldering guidebooks, bouldering Web sites, bouldering fashions, bouldering chalk bags, and boulderers flocking to bouldering areas leading to bouldering-related access issues, it appears that any estimate of the number of boulderers in this country, or even the world, would be out-of-date the moment I typed it. Let's just assume that the sport is big, it's growing, and there is no end in sight to the bouldering boom.

In response to this, indoor climbing gyms dedicate entire sections to bouldering, and some gyms even devote their entire facility to it. This allows boulderers to boulder at night or in poor weather, to train for competitions (which are often held indoors), to train on specific angles or grips, to socialize and climb with a regular bouldering group, or just to climb indoors because they prefer to climb inside. This phenomenon occurs more often than you might think, as indoor climbing—with its sculpted plastic hand- and footholds bolted onto variably angled, sometimes textured walls to create human-engineered boulder problems—presents different sorts of climbing challenges than those presented by natural rock surfaces. Indoor bouldering also allows novices the opportunity to check out bouldering in a controlled, relatively safe environment in which the entire floor usually serves as one giant crash pad. Some facilities offer bouldering instruction to help novices get started or even to help more experienced boulderers improve.

Bouldering's popularity shows no signs of waning, as more and more people discover the simplicity and social nature of this form of rock climbing. Oftentimes, you'll find a crowd of five, ten, or even thirty boulderers of all ages, sexes, and walks of life hanging out, sharing beta (information), spotting each other, and taking turns trying the same problem or problems together. Sound like fun? It is . . . and it's never too late to get started!

Equipment and Start-up Costs

As far as rock climbing goes, bouldering is just about the cheapest way you'll find to get involved and decide whether the activity suits you.

Shoes

Shoes are the first item you should acquire—but you don't necessarily need to buy them in order to try out the sport once or twice. A local climbing gym or shop will likely rent a pair to you for $5 to $15 a day and let you take them for a spin. Just be aware that the shoes most places have for rent are the vintage 1970s station wagons of the climbing-shoe world—durable, bulky, worn, and designed to take a real beating. You'll be lucky if they fit your feet, since most climbers find only one brand or a few particular shoe designs from different companies that they feel conform to their feet best, thus yielding top performance on the rocks. But for your initial foray into bouldering, a pair of rental shoes should do just fine, and if you like it enough, you'll be ready to go shoe shopping in a couple of weeks or even days.

Once you've decided to invest in a pair of climbing shoes, be picky. Don't just buy what's on sale. The general rule is that you'll want to go at least a half size down from your street-shoe size, and many climbers go a full size, a size and a half, or even two sizes down from theirs. The reason for this foot-binding torment stems from the higher performance you'll experience if the shoes have as little dead space as possible, making for greater sensitivity in all areas of the foot—a necessity for standing on dime-size edges or balancing on a polished slab of granite. So you want your shoes to almost suction onto your feet, fitting like a second skin or a glove. I always take it as a good sign if I can hear the air escape as my foot displaces it from inside the shoe when I slide (or forcibly wrestle) it onto my foot. Some people will try to tell you that one brand makes better, more durable shoes or has better sticky rubber (the specialized rubber that allows modern climbers tremendous purchase on the most improbable features) than another, and while this may be partially or wholly true, ultimately such concerns are secondary to the bottom line—does the shoe fit your foot?

Once you've narrowed down your selection to shoes that fit your feet, if you've found more than one option, you can bring in those other concerns, such as the company's reputation for shoe construction (asking a salesperson or a couple of experienced climbers you trust can help here), rubber thickness and stiffness of the soles (beginners generally want thicker rubber than more ad-vanced climbers, since their feet tend not to be as strong and the stiffer, thicker rubber provides added support), and price. Climbing shoes are expensive, ranging from $50 to $150 or more for a pair, but with a little creativity and shopping around you're likely to find a pair that you like on sale if cost is an issue to you. Just don't let price be your main criterion for shoe selection, or you could end up throwing your money away on a pair of shoes that ultimately will be a source of frustration, pain, or lackluster performance.

Chalk Bag

You'll probably want to pick up a chalk bag and some chalk once you've decided you're going to pursue bouldering, since most modern climbers subscribe to the belief that chalking up their hands before trying a problem helps decrease the chances of hands slipping off holds (much like gymnasts who chalk before grab-bing the bars and such). You can likely rent a chalk bag along with shoes the first couple of times you go bouldering, but buying a chalk bag and some chalk won't put you in the poorhouse—and unlike shoes, chalk bags are honestly more of a fashion or personal statement than a piece of high-tech performance equipment. This is especially true in bouldering, since most boulderers don't even wear their chalk bags while bouldering (rock climbers who use chalk usually have an open chalk bag strung around their waists for easy access while en route). If you wear a chalk bag while bouldering, when you fall, often the contents—loose chalk chunks and chalk dust—explode wastefully and messily all over the ground, crash pad, or gym floor. Another reason to avoid wearing a chalk bag while bouldering is that repeatedly dipping your hands into the bag while contemplating a move can become a crutch and ultimately lead to failure, since most boulder problems require rapid decision making and movement, not contemplative hanging out on the rock and problem solving. In fact, many chalk bags designed specifically for bouldering do not even have a belt loop on them, and some are so huge that they are called "buckets." Most boulderers choose to just leave their chalk bag or bucket on the ground while they climb, dipping their hands in the chalk before attempting the problem. What I'm trying to say is that you should just buy whatever bag suits your fancy, and you can probably find one on sale for as little as $5 to $10 if style isn't an issue.

Chalk to fill your bag is really inexpensive, too, whether you go with basic gymnastic chalk (a block costs a bit more than a dollar) or one of the fancier climbing-specific chalks with additives that supposedly increase the chalk's effectiveness.

Toothbrush

Though it is small and not essential, due to its inexpensiveness you may want to grab a toothbrush to add to your arsenal of bouldering gear—not to keep your teeth clean, but rather to brush off holds when they become caked with chalk from repeated grabbing, or to brush dirt off them. This is a common practice in bouldering.

Crash Pad

If you plan to spend time bouldering outside—and you really should, if you like bouldering—you'll probably want to invest in a crash pad, unless slamming into the ground in weird positions and potentially busting an ankle, heel, or other body part sounds like fun to you.

The crash pad is your line of defense when you fall, cushioning your landing area and covering up potential hazards like uneven ground or rocks that could cause an injury if you fell onto them. Though crash pads vary greatly, your basic crash pad will be made of a durable fabric shell encasing a 2- to 4-inch piece of relatively firm foam designed to cushion your fall. A landing area of 3 feet by 4.5 feet is fairly common and certainly adequate for most purposes, though much larger pads (such as a 4-foot by 6.5-foot pad) are available as well. But the larger pads cost much more and also are that much heavier to tote around. Crash pads generally fold up into weird-looking backpacks in which you can carry all of your bouldering gear, food, water, and clothing, and they are therefore equipped with backpack straps and usually with a waist belt as well.

You can pick up a pad for as little as $100, give or take a bit, but I'd suggest that you research the market and get some feedback from folks who already have pads, since there are definitely inferior and superior types and brands of crash pads. What should you look for? Test the pad by jumping on it at the store, preferably off a climbing wall, should they have one for shoe demos, and see how it cushions your fall. Like porridge, some pads are too mushy, some too stiff, and some just right—but you must be the judge of that, since your size and personal preference will determine how the landing surface feels to you. Since crash pads double as backpacks for boulderers, you should also put the pad on and check out the suspension system for carrying it. Will the straps dig into your shoulders? Will the pad be unwieldy or uncomfortable to hike with? Can you fit your bouldering gear—shoes, chalk bag, clothes, food, and water—easily inside the pad? Some boulderers use their crash pads as sleeping pads, too, so if you plan to do that, test how it feels as a sleeping surface as well.

Clothing

Climbing-specific clothes are unnecessary for bouldering—and climbing, for that matter—and they can be really pricey. You'll do just fine with any sort of loose-fitting and/or stretchy clothes that allow your arms and legs unrestrained range of motion. Nonetheless, as with all sports, there is a definite fashion in climbing, so if style is important to you, you'll want to check the selection at your local climbing outfitter or online retailer. If money is tight but you simply must have clothing labeled as "climbing clothing," you should try to buy it at clearance prices, since it's a real downer to put a hole in the knee of a $50 pair of pants the first day you wear them.

Grades

Difficulty grades for all forms of rock climbing—not just bouldering—are totally subjective and at least as arbitrary and political as the ratings given by gymnastics and figure-skating judges appear to be and are to some extent. This will seem especially true when you're first starting out, until you start to get your own sense of how hard a one-move V1, a five-move V1, a one-move V5, or a five-move V5 generally feels. Then you have to add all of your strengths and weaknesses into the equation, as well as stuff like your familiarity with the type of rock, holds, and angles. Given all of these variables, it's amazing that we ever come up with consensus ratings for anything, but somehow, most boulder problems and climbing routes seem to eventually settle in at a particular rating, once enough people have done them and given their feedback. And no, there is no official body or registry that keeps track of grades of routes or problems—in fact, some areas have no written record of the problems that have been done, much less specific grades for them.

For better or worse, with the growth of bouldering came a commonly used grading system (the V—or "Vermin"—scale) entirely separate from that commonly used to grade rock climbing routes in this country (the Yosemite Decimal System). The V scale evolved from one man's attempt to grade problems at one specific climbing area (John Sherman in Hueco Tanks), allowing boulderers to evaluate their climbing ability based purely on the small rocks. Currently, boulder problems range from V0 to V15 (with each number representing a step up in difficulty from the one before it) on an open-ended scale that allows for the addition of higher-end grades should people boulder harder than V15 in the future. Problems that are considered easier than V0 are given a grade of V0- or VB to indicate their difficulty level as beneath V0.

Like porridge, some pads are too mushy, some too stiff, and some just right.

To give you a sense of how ratings will feel when you start out, you should expect VB/V0- to present plenty of challenge your first time bouldering if you're a total beginner. A V5 boulder problem would likely be somewhat difficult for at least 75 percent of all boulderers out there today. A V10 boulder problem would be untouchable by at least 95 percent of boulderers, while bouldering V15 is unimaginably difficult for 99.9999 percent of boulderers. It's good to be aware as well that bouldering tends to isolate a given climber's particular strengths and weaknesses, probably because boulder problems tend to be short and to the point, containing hard individual moves compressed into a short distance. This explains why a climber might flash (do a problem on the first attempt) a V5 and then spend the rest of the day struggling on a V2. This also is a very good scenario to keep in mind when you're out on the rocks getting frustrated by a problem that, according to the grade, is "supposed" to be easy for you. In the succinct words of a friend of mine, "Grades are dumb." Don't fall into the thankless mire of embracing grades as the one true method to measure your achievement; think of them merely as guides to help you find appropriate problems that will challenge you.

You should know that in addition to this grading system, many other grading systems (for both routes and boulder problems) exist in the U.S. and in other countries, making for a world full of grading confusion.

BJ Tilden, Ibex, Utah. PHOTO BY MATT WENDLING

Safety Concerns

Bouldering is simultaneously one of the safest and one of the most dangerous forms of rock climbing. Your chances of dying from a bouldering accident are quite slim, since you're not likely to be high enough off the ground to hit with enough force to do that kind of damage, unless you get into attempting death-defying highballs (problems that take you high enough off the ground that you could be injured even if you have the best spotters in the world in the event of a fall) or climbing on chossy (fractured, loose, and dirty). Nevertheless, you will be high enough off the ground at times to hit with enough force to shatter bones. I've seen several boulderers break their ankles by missing the crash pad, and I've witnessed many other minor injuries as well, from bruised heels to gouged hands. This is why you should make it a habit to boulder with a crash pad and a spotter—another person who can help guide your flailing, falling body into the crash pad when you pop off the rock unexpectedly.

Don't, however, place the responsibility for your safety in your spotter's hands. If you decide to try a problem and you get hurt, it is never your spotter's fault. I loathe it when boulderers screw up on a problem, fall, and then turn to berate their spotter for not providing the perfect spot that they desired, since usually fallen boulderers are simply frustrated at their failure on the problem and choose to lash out and take it out on the hapless spotter. Spotting can be a challenge—think about catching another flailing adult body, limbs akimbo, falling from 15 feet up, and you'll get the picture. So take responsibility for your actions, and realize that you are the one who decides whether or not to attempt a potentially dangerous movement on a boulder problem. If you go for it and come off, there may be little, if anything, a spotter can do to prevent your getting hurt. Realize, too, that some people are better spotters than others, and judge your decisions about attempting potentially injurious moves accordingly.

Ethics

With bouldering comes a responsibility for taking proper care of bouldering areas and helping to preserve and protect the surrounding environment. With the sport growing so rapidly, the negative impact from hordes of boulderers flocking to popular areas is growing. For details on how to have a minimal impact on your natural surroundings, please visit the Leave No Trace Web site (www.lnt.org). The following are 10 general guidelines for ethics and etiquette at the boulders, most of which involve plain common sense. (For the 25 areas throughout the book, I've reiterated some of these concerns in the *Special notes* section where appropriate; however, these rules should be observed without exception at every bouldering area.)

1. Use the established trails. Don't trample the vegetation. Don't cut vegetation or hang off it. Don't put your crash pad on top of vegetation.
2. Pack out all of your trash and the trash of others. This includes banana peels, orange peels, cigarette butts, tape, and chalk spills.
3. Do not chip, aggressively brush, or otherwise alter the rock's surface. Do not climb on or anywhere near petroglyphs or pictographs. Brush tick marks and excess chalk off the rock when you're done trying a problem.
4. Interact maturely with land managers and other officials. Be a positive and conscientious ambassador for the bouldering community. Obey all posted signs, speed limits, and traffic laws. Pay user fees. Respect camping limits and restrictions and campfire regulations.
5. Keep numbers low; if you are in a large group, consider splitting up into smaller groups to minimize potentially negative impact. If an area is already packed or a parking lot is full, choose a different area to visit or park elsewhere and walk.
6. Keep noise levels low, particularly at areas where other groups are present. Families out for a hike don't want or need to hear boulderers screaming expletives as they fall off problems. Leave your boom box at home or save it for the gym.
7. Use established sanitary facilities, or if there are none, remove yourself from trafficked areas to do your business. Do not poop anywhere near the boulders or near water. Dig a hole at least 6 inches deep and bury what you produce, disguising the hole when you're done.
8. Keep your dog leashed if required or if it is not *truly* manageable with voice and sight control. Pick up after your pet. Do not bring dogs into areas where dogs are not allowed.
9. Respect other boulderers and their efforts, both on and off the rocks. Don't put others down, intimidate them from trying a problem, hog a particular boulder or line, or spray unsolicited beta. Keep in mind that just because you boulder harder than others or others boulder harder than you do doesn't make their bouldering or yours any more or less valid or important, nor does it make any of you better or more respectable human beings.
10. Check in advance to be sure that you have the most up-to-date information about an area before planning a visit there.

Access

If you're not a boulderer or rock climber, you're probably not yet aware of the gravity of the term "access" in the climbing community—but you will be soon. Access to climbing areas—or rather, the legal or official permission to climb or boulder at individual areas around the country—has become an increasing source of concern and distress for the nationwide climbing community in the past 20 years. More and more areas have come under scrutiny by land managers and officials, sometimes resulting in restrictions and closures. With the explosive growth in popularity of climbing in general, and bouldering in particular, doing everything possible to help maintain and preserve access to bouldering areas should top every boulderer's list of priorities.

In addition to developing and adhering to a strong system of personal ethics, starting with the guidelines given in the preceding section, boulderers can take this commitment to securing access for both themselves and for future generations of boulderers to the next level by becoming involved in nonprofit organizations that strive to secure access and/or minimize the negative environmental impact of outdoor enthusiasts. For climbers and boulderers, these organizations include, first and foremost, the Access Fund (www.accessfund.org), "a national, nonprofit organization dedicated to keeping climbing areas open and to conserving the climbing environment." Since 1989, the Access Fund has done wonders for the climbing community at large, rescuing many threatened crags and bouldering areas from the jaws of closure, often by working to establish positive relationships between land managers and climbers, among other achievements. The Access Fund recently launched the Boulder Project in recognition of the growing popularity of this sport and the need to address the specific access issues and concerns that come with its growth. Boulderers of all abilities and ages should consider jumping on board with the Access Fund and becoming part of the Boulder Project to help secure access to threatened areas, to promote sound bouldering ethics, and to foster positive relationships with land managers.

In addition to the Access Fund, numerous other local, regional, and national bouldering- and climbing-related organizations exist that you might consider joining. These include the American Alpine Club (www.americanalpineclub.org), "a nonprofit organization dedicated to promoting climbing knowledge, conserving mountain environments, and serving the American climbing community," and Leave No Trace (www.lnt.org), "a national nonprofit organization dedicated to promoting and inspiring responsible outdoor recreation through education, research, and partnerships." There are many others, some of which you'll find listed in the *Other resources* section of the 25 different areas profiled in this work.

chapter 2

Becoming a Boulderer

THOUGH I'M CERTAINLY NOT the best boulderer out there—not by a long shot—I have managed to achieve moderate success in bouldering, despite my body's propensity for doing well in endurance events. In this chapter, I offer some helpful tools, tactics, techniques, and training methods to enable you to experience greater success in your bouldering efforts a little bit faster than you might without any such guidance.

A word of caution before I offer the following training and performance advice: Be aware that I hold no degree, much less an advanced degree in body sciences, nor am I a certified personal trainer. Therefore, the following information represents simply my own personal opinions and advice, garnered from my 12-plus years as a devoted training junkie and sometimes climbing coach, for you to take or leave as you will. You many think I'm full of it, or you may find some of my observations earth-shattering (I hope you experience more of the latter). Just be careful when embarking on any new activity or exercise regimen, and consult with a physician or qualified professional before attempting any of the activities I describe—in other words, use your common sense and pursue bouldering at your own risk.

Alan Pirie, Sinks Canyon, Wyoming. PHOTO BY MATT WENDLING

Thinking It Through—Is This Sport for You?

Before you start bouldering seriously, or at all, you should contemplate first what sort of role you want this new activity to play in your life, keeping in mind that this decision can be modified at any point in the future. Such reflection, though not necessary, will help you make informed decisions about issues such as how much money to invest in bouldering initially, how much time to allot for it on a weekly basis, and how you want it to fit in with other physical activities in which you may already be involved.

Probably the first of these concerns—the monetary one—is the most important consideration for the novice boulderer. Before you run out and purchase shoes, crash pad, chalk bag, chalk, and a gym membership, you should make sure that this is a sport you want to pursue (unless dropping several hundred dollars isn't a big deal for you). Rent a pair of shoes at your local gym—most gyms will allow people to play on their bouldering walls (for a day-use fee) even if they can't pass the belay test required for roped climbing. Try out bouldering a few times indoors, and get a feel for whether this is something that might be fun to pursue more seriously. Alternatively, if you don't want to climb indoors or there is no facility available, you might be able to rent a pair of shoes from a local outfitter and try bouldering outside—but be extra careful if you choose this route, and consider hiring a guide or hooking up with an experienced boulderer who has a crash pad and can spot you so that you don't jeopardize your safety. The last thing you want is your first or second time out on the rocks to end with a broken ankle!

You Want to Be a Boulderer—So Now What?

Okay, so let's say you've spent a few days bouldering, and you've decided that this is the sport for you, that it's more than just a way to recreate on the occasional weekend. You want to become a "real" boulderer now!

As a total beginner, the best way to experience success is simply to boulder a lot, so that you add to your repertoire as many of the climbing-specific movements and motions necessary for success as possible, as rapidly as possible. A great way to enhance your learning is to seek out bouldering partners who are stronger or more advanced than you are, because they can offer helpful advice and beta for specific problems or movements, as well as provide you with visual examples of ways to succeed on specific problems as

. . . the best way to experience success is simply to boulder a lot . . .

they climb them themselves. If you have some extra money to invest, you should also consider hiring a bouldering trainer or coach, though this service may or may not be available, depending upon the popularity of climbing in your area. Even if you sign up for only one or two sessions, an experienced coach can help guide you and create a healthy program designed to improve your bouldering without causing you injury or burnout.

As any coach will tell you, you must include ample amounts of rest in your personal training program, since rest is when muscles rebuild, grow, and strengthen. Adequate rest usually means not bouldering more than two days in a row and taking off at least two days in a row at least once a week—more if you are feeling fatigue or residual pain on days when you had planned to boulder, which is a likely scenario if you're just starting out. Keep in mind that bouldering is a power-intensive activity—you are lifting and pushing your own body weight up a variety of angles utilizing all sorts of handholds and footholds that stress different muscles and tissues accordingly. If you've never done this before, it will take your body some time to adapt to the new loads and stresses being placed on it. Be aware and extra attentive to your body, since many climbing injuries, such as finger injuries and shoulder injuries, can come on gradually and then linger for months or even years. The best way to avoid them is to listen up and stop bouldering when your body says to stop.

By putting together a program involving days of bouldering coupled with days of total rest—and perhaps a few days that involve a more aerobic activity as well—you should be well on your way to improving your bouldering at a steady pace.

10 Body Basics for Boulderers

From the tips of your toes to the top of your head, every part of your body plays a crucial role in propelling your movement up the face of a rock. Beginners often approach climbing with the erroneous idea that it's all about upper-body strength or simply arm strength, while in reality, success in bouldering requires much more than bulging biceps and six-pack abs. Although tremendous upper-body strength can certainly make a difference once you're knocking on the door of the elite echelons of bouldering, for the beginner and intermediate boulderer, the greatest gains are usually made by improving technique and coordination—and gains in upper-body strength will come about as a by-product of practicing. Attention to the following 10 areas will prove helpful in developing sound and effective bouldering technique.

1. **Feet**. Like a ballerina, you will learn to use parts of your feet that you probably never realized had so much to offer before you started climbing. Try to use the very front, inside portion of your shoe most of the time, avoiding the common novice tendency to place the ball of your foot on holds—just imagine how clumsy *The Nutcracker* would look if all of the dancers slapped around on the balls of their feet! You will gain way more control of your motion and add to your reach and versatility on almost every foothold by stepping delicately onto the hold with the inside edge of your big toe or the outside edge of your shoe around your pinky toe (see *backstepping*, #7 on page 42). Try it—choose a hold and see how mobile you are and how far you can reach moving off it with the ball of your foot, and then with your big toe, and then with the area around your little toe. Make an effort to keep your feet "quiet," too, choosing footholds with care and stepping onto them deliberately instead of smacking your feet around while you grovel for the next handhold.

2. **Legs** are the source of much of the strength that you need to succeed. Climbers often forget that they simply need to stand up on or step up on a hold or holds in order to reach the next set of handholds, becoming overly focused on what to do with their hands while neglecting to recognize the untapped power and ability in their legs. As you advance as a boulderer, this becomes particularly true when you attempt *dynos* or *deadpoints* (see #6 on page 42), in which your legs will play a crucial role. Learn to use your legs now—your arms will thank you.

3. **Hips and butt** are often the parts of the body that start to drift away from the wall, pulling the rest of you with them. Instead of climbing straight on with your butt hanging off and your knees pushing you away, focus on keeping your hips in tight to the wall when you can, turning and pivoting on your feet in order to swivel your hips closer to the wall. Turn from side to side as you climb, moving your right hip and then your left hip in toward the wall. This will enable you to experience greater fluidity of movement. Turning your hips into the wall according to the type of handhold you are using can make an enormous difference in the rate at which your arms and hands fatigue as well. Ask an experienced boulderer to demonstrate this to you if necessary.

4. **Core,** or more specifically the muscles in your abdomen and lower back, will do a ton of work when you climb, particularly when you're on steeper terrain. You'll find at times that if you consciously tighten up your core muscles, it can make the difference between failing and succeeding on a specific move. Doing a million crunches probably isn't the best way to increase your core strength, so if you're weak in this area, consider a supplemental activity

like Pilates, which will help you gain more active core strength, or consult with a personal trainer for bouldering-specific core-strengthening exercises.

5. **Lungs** must be working in order for you to perform at your best. "Of course my lungs work," you're thinking. And I'm sure that they do, but you'll notice soon enough that when attempting difficult series of movements, many boulderers will stop breathing and hold their breath for the entire sequence, letting it out explosively when they're done—or, more likely, when they fall. Focus on breathing while you boulder, starting to breathe consciously before you begin and maintaining your breath as a rhythmic background beat throughout your attempt to climb the problem.

6. **Heart.** Your heart rate will increase noticeably after a serious effort, and you should listen up. Don't jump right back on the problem. Allow your heart rate and breathing to drop back down to a level that makes them unnoticeable, and spend that period of rest visualizing the moves you want to execute on your next attempt or on the next problem.

7. **Arms** should be kept straight at all times until you must bend them to make a move. This helps avoid the dreaded pump, saving valuable energy and enabling you to have more power and endurance to complete a problem. Practice climbing with your arms as straight as you can keep them, bending them only when necessary. Learn-ing to keep your arms straight early on will make a world of difference in the difficulty of the problems you will be able to send (complete successfully with-out falling).

Learn to use your legs now—your arms will thank you.

8. **Hands** should hold on to each hold with as little effort as is necessary to maintain a solid grip. Otherwise you are overgripping, or using more strength than is necessary to stay on, and this will make you pump out and fail much faster than if you were using each hold efficiently. Another component of efficient hold use is to make sure you have found the most positive portion of the hold to grip. If you can, feel around with your hands to see whether there is perhaps a sweet spot on the hold where you have better purchase and power to pull, and then grip the hold accordingly, turning your body if you can to maximize the ease and efficacy of this way of gripping the hold. Also try to avoid regripping holds once you take them in the sweet spot. Often in bouldering you must move on and off holds quickly to maximize efficiency, even if you miss the sweet spot. Try to close your hand on each hold only once, or twice at most, if you need to readjust your grip according to the shape of the hold. Every time you regrip after that, you are simply asking the

same muscles to fire all over again, thus decreasing your stamina at a much faster rate.

9. **Eyes** should be watching each body part as you place it on a hold. This means watching your foot as you place it on each individual foothold and looking for other options for feet and hands—both from the ground before you start to climb and while on the rock. Too often boulderers allow their footwork to become messy and imprecise, and this is usually due to a lack of attentiveness (often induced by fatigue) in observing each foot placement to ensure it connects with the desired hold.

10. **Mind** is likely to be the most limiting factor for almost every boulderer, from the novice to the superelite. Believing in yourself and your ability will take you farther than strength or technique ever can. Don't be daunted by grades, by other boulderers, by angles, or by holds. Keep your mind open to all possibilities at all times and reject any negative self-talk that invades your psyche when you're trying something hard. Persistence and patience usually yield the desired results, and if not, you should always keep in mind that we learn far more from our "failures" than we do from our "successes."

Believing in yourself and your ability will take you farther than strength or technique ever can.

10 Helpful Bouldering Techniques—Illustrated

To enhance your learning curve, following are photos illustrating 10 techniques often utilized in bouldering (and rock climbing, for that matter), complete with an explanation of each one. Every couple of weeks pick one technique and focus your bouldering efforts on finding problems in which that technique is useful. Then put it into effect, asking for feedback from your partners about your execution of the given move and the applicability of it in the situation you are using it. If you can, rope a partner into playing this "game" with you, and see how many different ways the two of you can come up with for using the new technique. By the end of a couple of weeks, I'll bet that technique has become part of your climbing repertoire, and you'll be ready for the next one!

1. **Sit-down start.** Often you will read in guidebooks that a problem has a "sit-down start," or simply "sds." This means that to do the problem correctly, you must start with your rear on the crash pad (or the ground, if the pad is in the way), place your feet on the footholds of your choice, and pull your body

Leslie Paul demonstrates a sit-down start in Cody, Wyoming.

off the ground in this manner. Choosing which handholds to use depends on the problem itself—sometimes the handholds you must start on are specified and sometimes not, and sometimes there is only one set of holds possible to start on anyway. (This can be problematic if you're too short to reach them from a sitting position, though most folks are kind enough to credit you with a send if you stack the pads up to create a booster seat so that you can reach the starting holds.) Sit-down starts almost always increase the difficulty of a problem, sometimes by several grades.

Tarris Webber mantling on the Rubber Blanket, Sinks Canyon, Wyoming.

2. **The mantle** is like getting out of a swimming pool without the helpful buoyancy of the water. When you encounter a mantle while bouldering, most of the time it will be part of topping out the problem (summitting onto the top of the boulder, so that you can stand up and then walk off or down climb). Sometimes mantling can be the crux (the most difficult portion) of the problem. As you pull up on the holds to top out the problem, at some point you will need to transition from pulling on the holds to pushing them down, while at the same time bringing up a foot that you can rock your weight onto. It can take a while to figure out the coordination required for mantling, so try not to get frustrated.

3. **Open handing** a hold maximizes the surface area of hand touching rock and utilizes a grip that is not as injury-provoking as crimping. Many climbers open hand almost every hold they grab, as they find that this works best for them in terms of both performance and injury prevention. In the open-hand grip, your fingers and usually as much of your hand as possible make contact with the hold, and you do not curl your fingers. This means that your finger joints are bent only to the extent necessary for them to conform to the shape of the hold and for you to hold on—they are not curled or balled up into

Kate Reese uses the open-hand grip to ascend the classic problem Great White at Horse Pens 40, Alabama.

almost a fist or even half of a fist (hence the "open hand" name). Think of how you hold on to a baseball or a glass of water, and you'll get a visual of an open-hand grip. This is hard to explain, so look at the photo and ask for a demonstration from a more experienced boulderer if it's still not clear.

4. **Crimping** on a hold can sometimes garner you a little bit more purchase and power than open handing it can—but the price to pay can be serious if your fingers are fragile, untrained, or injury-prone, since crimping places great stress on your joints. Unlike open handing, in crimping you *do* ball your fingers up and bend your finger joints, often closing your hand almost into a fistlike position—hence the stressful nature of this grip. Wrapping your thumb across the tops of your pointer and middle fingers to help keep them on the hold adds the strength of the powerful thumb musculature to the equation. Experiment with crimping by choosing a hold that can be pulled on with both an open hand and a crimp grip, and see if you notice any strength difference. Most people find that they need to crimp only every so often to gain a bit of extra strength on a specific hold. You can also vary your grip to a half-crimp, half-open hand, and everything in between.

The crimp grip is both powerful and stressful on the fingers.

5. **Heel hooking** (and its cousin, **toe hooking**) is a versatile technique with many uses. It helps take the weight off your arms, thus making moves off less-than-decent handholds possible or easier. To heel hook, you place one of your heels on a feature of the rock—often a large shelf, pocket (hole), crack, or even the top of the boulder—and pull your body upward (or in whatever direction you need to go) toward the next handhold with your heel, bending your knee in the process. Sometimes you use a heel hook just to take the weight off your arms for a couple of seconds, just holding the position while you rest and then dropping your foot back down to another foothold to move. Other times you use the heel hook to take some weight off your arms so that you can advance them to the next handholds without really pulling with your heel—just having your heel take some of your weight off your arms makes your hand movements possible. Heel hooking can also allow you to employ mostly your leg muscles to pull you to the next hold. Look for protruding or in-cut rock features or holds to practice levering off

Reid Leslie heel hooking in Cody, Wyoming.

your heel. You can heel hook on improbably small features sometimes, once you have mastered the technique.

Toe hooking works much the same way, only you hook features with your big toe and pull with it. Practice both of these techniques together and figure out in which circumstances each is more appropriate.

6. **Dynos**—or **deadpoints**—are often the most efficient way to go from one hold to the next on boulder problems. Using momentum and explosive power from your legs, you push off the footholds and surge upward with your leading hand (or occasionally both hands) to catch the next hold. If your feet come off in the process (and you catch the next hold), it's a true dyno. If not, it's a deadpoint—the point where your upward momentum stops and before your downward momentum starts. Two keys to succeeding in dynamic movement are timing and using your legs, though many boulderers, even experienced ones, tend to muscle too much with their arms, especially when they dyno or deadpoint, forgetting the powerful legs that can help propel them to their destination.

Tad Anderson winds up and dynos on the Rubber Blanket, Sinks Canyon, Wyoming.

7. **Backstepping** can be a useful way to position your body on footholds, and it can extend your reach as well. To backstep, step on a foothold with your foot and knee turned inward, a position that will naturally pivot the hip of that leg toward the wall. The point of contact between your climbing shoe and the foothold on the backstepping foot will be in the vicinity of your little toe. Think of positioning the backstepping foot as if you were pigeon-toed, but allow the rest of your body to turn into a comfortable position as dictated by your turned foot. Often the other foot will be positioned with the inside

Tad Anderson backsteps with his left foot at the start of Jeremy's Traverse in Sinks Canyon, Wyoming.

edge of the shoe on another hold, allowing you to push with both legs. Sometimes, though, you will find it more effective to backstep with one foot and flag (see #8) with the other.

Matt Wendling flagging in Sandrock, Alabama.

8. **Flagging** is an excellent way to learn about balance and is often an effective tactic when you're looking to solve a problem but can't seem to find an effective foothold for one of your feet. Often there are no additional footholds available, or those that you have to choose from put you in an off-balance or awkward position. In such a situation, instead of forcing yourself to keep both feet on the wall, it can actually be more efficient to simply flag with that troublesome foot (and the leg attached to it). To flag, place one foot on a good foothold and then drop the other one off the wall entirely, moving it to the side or even behind your other leg to find a good balance point. Think of the leg that is off the rock as a cat's tail, swinging to find the perfect balance point to help you ex-

Kate Reese uses a drop knee to her advantage at Horse Pens 40, Alabama.

ecute the move. To learn how to employ this technique effectively, practice climbing with one foot always flagged at the gym or on problems that are easy for you.

9. **Drop knees** can make otherwise impossible moves possible. But beware—many climbers damage their knees by doing this move, as it puts tremendous stress on the joint, especially if you're doing a "hard" drop knee, where your knee is turned all the way down and pointing toward the ground. To do a drop knee, usually you have one foot stably positioned on a hold with your big toe. The other foot is then placed on another hold to the side of the stable foot, toe up. You then pivot that toe so that it is partially or all the way turned downward, depending on the drop knee that is necessary, and you sometimes can push off it, as there is a ton of power stored up in that bent leg.

10. **High steps** require great active flexibility. To high step, you step your foot up to a foothold close to your waist or your hands (or even "match" your hand and foot, or place them on the same hold), often rocking your weight onto

Matt Wendling uses a high step to move up on the Comet Boulder in Rocktown, Georgia.

the high foothold and thus taking some of the weight off your arms. The high step can allow you to push yourself farther up the problem with the stored power in your bent leg, but it can also get you in trouble, especially on steeper terrain, by making your hips and butt stick out, thus pulling you off the rock. Playing around with high steps will help you to figure out when they are effective and when your feet are better left on lower holds.

Ideas for Bouldering Sessions

Don't know quite how to get started with your workouts or how to pace yourself? Here are some suggestions to help you get going.

Warming Up

When you arrive at the gym or your local area for a bouldering session, be sure to warm up adequately before the workout, starting the session with easy problems. Try to establish a circuit of familiar, easy problems with which you can begin every day at the boulders or in the gym. Try to pick about 10 problems of ascending difficulty that are relatively easy for you, and rotate a few in and out of your circuit now and again to alleviate any boredom. Starting each workout on familiar terrain will allow you to grasp how your body feels on a particular day and, thus, how hard you should push yourself for the remainder of your session. If warm-ups that are usually easy for you feel taxing, you know you're climbing tired, and you might want to reconsider your plans entirely, or else just have a really light and easy day on the rocks.

Remember that it's better to warm up too much than too little . . .

As you warm up and loosen up your muscles, if you're feeling good you can start to progress to problems that are a bit more difficult, listening to your body and taking your time before you try anything really challenging. Usually it takes me a good 30 to 45 minutes before my body feels adequately warmed up to demand full power, and I'm guessing that most boulderers require a similar amount of time before they feel fully powered up. Gradually you'll come to know just what it takes to get your muscles primed for performance. Remember that it's better to warm up too much than too little, even if you want to head straight for your project (a problem that challenges you and that you're making an effort to send).

After you're adequately warmed up, you can progress to attempting a problem or problems that challenge you. If there happens to be a problem at the outdoor area or in the gym that you think you could possibly onsight (successfully send on your first attempt) and you're feeling good, now is the time to try it. Scope the problem first, and then give it a shot. If you don't onsight it, it can always become either a quick send or a long-term project (a problem that takes multiple efforts—perhaps even days—to send), depending on how hard it is for you.

Working Projects with a Partner

If you're not interested in onsighting or there are no problems around that seem realistic for onsighting, one good way to get a workout is to select one to three problems to attempt during a given session, and then to work on them one at a time, preferably with a partner whose climbing ability is close to yours. Together you can pick the problem apart move by move, striving to eliminate extraneous or wasteful motions. Sometimes it's a good idea to start in the middle of a route or problem and work backward—this way, you learn to succeed at the difficult section and then start adding the less difficult moves, one by one, until you're back to the start of the problem.

Once you have the moves worked out, you should strive to make your movements as efficient and precise as possible while giving the problem a genuine effort. If you are trying to send a problem seriously, give yourself a good five or ten minutes to recover between attempts, or you will probably begin to see diminishing returns quite rapidly. Don't be self-conscious about grunting or even yelling when you try hard moves. For some reason, this can really help focus and direct the body in powerful motions, and it also helps remind you to keep breathing. Also, be a supportive partner, giving or even yelling words of encouragement while others climb (unless they request that you don't). It's amazing how the power of your belief in someone else or likewise someone else's belief in you can propel a boulderer through difficult sections of a problem, effectively overriding the internal voices of doubt and distrust. If you do reach an impasse or begin to lose focus and psych, it's probably time to move on to the next problem, perhaps returning to this problem later or on another day.

The Diet

If you find yourself trying one move over and over again to no avail, you can try going on a "diet"—and no, I'm not talking about restricting your food intake. The diet is a simple yet effective way to teach your body the proper coordination and technique required to successfully execute a stopper move (a move that you cannot seem to execute after repeated efforts). When you come to the move in question, ask a partner to stand behind you and give you a slight lift or push, usually around your shoulder blades or lower back. Often you'll discover that the tiniest bit of help, or "weight-off," makes a move much, much easier. Ultimately this usually means that the move is not too hard for you, unless, of course, your partner literally has to hold you on the wall. I've learned to do some of the hardest moves I've ever pulled off by having a partner give me repeated diets until I learned the proper body position to perform the moves on my own.

Focusing on Techniques

Another great way to stay focused and motivated throughout a workout is to select one or two of the preceding techniques and seek problems that demand their
usage. As I said earlier, getting a partner to play this game with you can make it
into a fun kind of mutually beneficial competition as you push one another to
find as many ways as possible to employ the new technique. This can still be effective if done toward the end of a workout or session in which you've pushed
yourself—you can even warm down practicing a specific technique (though
warming down with dynos probably wouldn't be a good idea).

Creating Problems with a Group of Boulderers

A favorite way of training for many boulderers involves gathering a group of those
who climb at similar levels to meet up at the gym on a regular basis to boulder together. After warming up, each person creates a boulder problem using the holds
already up on the walls. Then the group runs through each new problem one
by one until someone sends it or everyone gets tired of trying it. This is a terrific way to work on your weaknesses, especially if you boulder with people of different heights and with specific strengths different from yours, since people tend
to make up problems that highlight their own talents. You will be forced out of
your comfort zone—if you like slopers (handholds that are smooth and rounded,
devoid of bumps, edges, or other positive features, forcing all climbers to open
hand them), maybe your buddy will like crimpers (small edges that climbers use
as handholds that lend themselves to the crimp grip), or perhaps you're five foot
six and your friend is only five foot one. You'll also enjoy the camaraderie and
synergy that accounts for a big part of bouldering's popularity.

Add-On

A variation of this game is to play the game commonly known as add-on, in which
a group of two or more boulderers makes up a problem together, with members
taking turns adding moves (usually two to five apiece), thus creating one problem
for all to work on sending together once it is deemed finished.

Mini-Goals

Consider, too, approaching each bouldering session with mini-goals—flexible
goals detailing what you'd like to achieve during this particular climbing time.
You can always adjust them if you're not "feeling the love" or pump them up if

you're on fire, but it's great to head out to the rocks or the gym with a focused intent; you will almost always have a more effective session this way. Choose a problem you'd like to send or a particular move or technique you'd like to master. If you've been bouldering for a while, you can choose to work on an area that you've noticed is harder for you—maybe you're not as good on overhangs as you are on vertical terrain, or maybe you love big slopers but despise pockets. Too often boulderers fall into the trap of training only what they're good at, because it's more fun to succeed. Nonetheless, to become a well-rounded boulderer and to continue to improve consistently, you'll want to learn how to effectively climb on all types and angles of terrain, so train and boulder accordingly, setting goals to improve your weaknesses as well as to push your grade level.

Length of Workouts and Warming Down

While elite climbers arguably may be able to sustain a worthwhile intensity in a bouldering workout for up to five hours (with ample breaks, of course), you should not aim to start at this level, especially if bouldering is completely new to you. Learn to listen to your body, and when your performance starts to decline, start your warm-down. Don't be surprised if you're done with your workout after only an hour or so at first. At this point you should warm down on some of the same problems that you warmed up on. Follow this with some stretching—flexibility plays a huge and often overlooked role in both bouldering ability and injury prevention. Try to eat something that has a decent balance between protein and carbohydrates, such as one of the many energy bars on the market today, within 30 minutes of finishing your workout, since your muscles will be primed for recovery during that period.

Goal Setting: A Key to Staying Motivated

You wouldn't take on a new project at work without setting some clearly defined goals, so why should bouldering be any different? It's much harder to train and strive to achieve something when you don't have any specific targets in mind, any deadlines or dates or goals for your mind to hold on to while you push yourself in new directions. Considering this truth, once you've learned the lingo and started to achieve some bouldering successes, you might want to establish some goals for yourself to keep your interest and enthusiasm fresh.

Goals should be difficult but feasible, as psychological research has demonstrated that having about a 50 percent chance of success at an activity inspires people to give a challenge their best and most focused effort. If an activity is too easy, people lose interest; if it's too hard, they give up. If you've sent 10 V0s, another V0 may not be all that interesting as a goal or project, while sending a V6 would in all likelihood be entirely unrealistic and ridiculous to attempt. Use your common sense to figure out goals that will work for you. Following are some guidelines to help you on your way.

Establishing specific short-, medium-, and long-term goals should enable you to maintain higher levels of motivation on a day-to-day as well as a long-term basis than you would otherwise. For a novice, a short-term goal may be to send a V1 if you've already done a few V0s, while a medium-term goal may be to complete a V3 in a year, and a long-term goal could be to boulder V5 in a couple of years. Right now, bouldering V5 is probably a fairly unrealistic goal for you, but with focus and dedication, you should be able to accomplish this goal within two years, and maybe much sooner, depending on the natural abilities and talents you've brought to bouldering. But your short-term focus for now should be on sending a V1—a much more plausible expectation. You probably can't send every V1 out there, but you may have a 50 percent success potential, if not now, then soon, once you've made bouldering a regular activity in your life.

Try not to fall into the trap of coddling yourself once you attain a certain level of ability . . .

Always remember that these goals are not set in stone but should serve simply as guidelines to keep you enthused about bouldering and always striving for greater levels of expertise, strength, fitness, and agility—important components of any exercise or fitness program. Long-term goals serve as inspiring dreams for bouldering achievements, and you should cultivate the inner belief that they are ultimately attainable and model your short- and medium-term goals toward the eventual achievement of your long-term ones.

Remember that you will never achieve your goals if you don't make a concerted effort to work for them. This may seem obvious, but many boulderers—and people in general—reach a certain point of expertise or position of comfort and then allow themselves the luxury of lingering in one place, stagnating instead of exploring new directions and ideas. They become fearful of failure and pushing out of the comfort zone, ultimately stifling their creativity and lifelong learning. Try not to fall into the trap of coddling yourself once you attain a certain level of ability—mix it up, keep it interesting, and keep establishing new and challenging objectives that will keep you on your toes. View each "failure" as a part of the learning process, as a step bringing you closer to accomplishing your goals, realizing that you probably learn more from not succeeding than you do from continuous success. You will never break into new levels in bouldering—and life—without taking some measured risks, and usually when you're breaking into a new level in bouldering, success will come only after many attempts—or "failures," as our culture is so fond of labeling them.

Deciphering a Typical Bouldering Guidebook

Whether you buy the comprehensive guidebook for a bouldering area or download a guide from the Internet, you may experience some initial confusion when attempting to interpret the information contained within. You may also experience some difficulty in finding the boulders detailed or in figuring out the specific problems, but be patient and remember that the book is simply a guide to the particular games other boulderers have made up. If you can find some boulders to play on (that are within an area where bouldering is permitted, of course), ultimately it shouldn't matter too much whether or not you're doing the established problems, so long as you're having fun and challenging yourself.

No standard method exists for compiling boulder problems, so you will find much variation from guidebook to guidebook as to how the information is put together—just as you will find that the V0s in one area may be significantly more or less difficult than the V0s in another area, or even that great variation in difficulty occurs between problems with the same rating in the same area. Again, this is why grades shouldn't be the number one factor in your bouldering experience—having a good time and testing yourself should.

On the next page, I've included a photo of the Rubber Blanket in Sinks Canyon, Wyoming, with lines drawn on it showing some of its problems; this method is often used to detail specific sets, or lines, of holds that other folks have used to ascend a particular boulder. Probably about half the time guidebooks use a line drawing to show these details in lieu of an actual photograph, but the concept is the same. The photo or drawing will usually be accompanied by text entries describing each individual problem in greater detail. Each problem shown will usually have its name listed, perhaps the name of its first ascensionist (though this is not as common in bouldering as it is in route-climbing guides), a grade, whether or not it is a sit-down start (sds), and sometimes the potential for injury, indicated by a symbol such as an ambulance or a skull and crossbones (all of the landings at the Rubber Blanket are good). Guidebook authors also often choose to use a star system to indicate problems that they find particularly stellar for the area. Usually the book will include a table explaining each symbol used as well as the star system (I've used the three-star system below: one star signifies a good problem, two stars

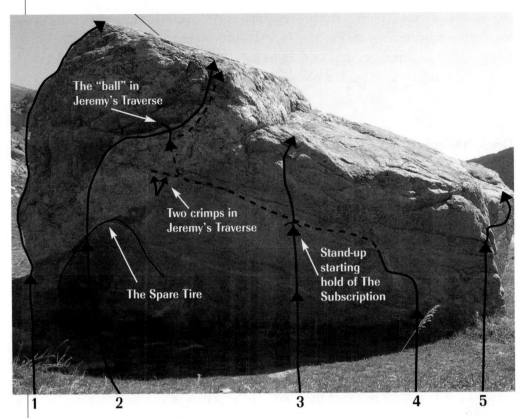

The "ball" in
Jeremy's Traverse

Two crimps in
Jeremy's Traverse

The Spare Tire

Stand-up
starting
hold of The
Subscription

1   2   3   4   5

Topo of The Rubber Blanket, Sinks Canyon, Wyoming

is a great problem, and three stars means it shouldn't be missed), so be sure to read the front matter to fully understand each particular guide. (For the sake of novices, I've defined certain terms within the problem descriptions.)

1. **Shelly's Arête (V5, sds).** * Start sitting down on tiny crimps left of the arête (the corner of the boulder) and climb up the arête.
2. **The Spare Tire (V0).** ** Climb the biggest holds on the left side of the boulder, starting with the "spare tire" and angling up and right.
3. **The Subscription (V4 or with sds, V6).** * Start on the sloping rail (just what it sounds like, a rail-like feature protruding from the rock's surface) in the middle of the face. Head straight up to a couple of crimps and then top out. For sds, start with both hands on the sharp, small diagonal rail below the other starting holds.
4. **Jeremy's Traverse (V7, sds).** *** A contrived classic. Begin sitting down near the right end of the boulder with both hands on a large rail. Pull off the ground and head left, moving through the starting holds of The Subscription, then onto an obvious jug (extremely or relatively large handhold). Match (put

both hands on the same handhold) and fire (go for the next hold quickly, probably dynamically unless you're really strong) for the ball, or grab a small crimp to the left and then throw (go dynamically) for the bigger holds. Top out. All holds above the dotted line drawn on the topo are off (not considered part of this problem).

5. **Menstruating Bitches (V2).** ** Starting on the right corner or even a little farther to the left, traverse around the corner to the right, continuing to traverse along the lip to the middle of the face until it becomes logical to top out (climb onto the top of the boulder).

Second Steps—Plateau-Busting Hints

When you first start bouldering, you're likely to notice improvements in your ability on a weekly, if not daily, basis. If you stick with it, however, you'll probably notice that gradually your improvements are not nearly so marked or consistent—and maybe they'll even come to a screeching halt. What happened?

What happened is a phenomenon that almost every boulderer experiences at some point. You have ascended your natural dramatic learning curve and made your way onto your first dreaded personal plateau—that place where you can continue to boulder and boulder and boulder just as you have been, yet you'll see little or no increase in ability. Though you are unlikely to ever again experience quite the same dramatic leaps and bounds forward that you did when you first began to boulder, there are steps you can take now to break through to the next level and jumpstart your learning curve again instead of stagnating on your plateau or, even worse, giving up on bouldering entirely. The following five suggestions may help you start that upward movement once again.

1. **Hire a climbing coach or trainer.** Whether you hire a coach to guide you for several months or for a one-time session, you should not discount the value of having a second set of eyes focused entirely on your climbing. Although partners can be great sources of information and feedback, ultimately most people are far more focused on their own climbing performance than on analyzing the strengths and weaknesses of those around them. Hiring an experienced coach or trainer to observe you and work with you can give you a much more realistic evaluation of your strengths and weaknesses than you can give yourself. Maybe you think your problem is lack of strength, but in reality, you're not employing the strength you already possess in the most efficient way. A coach can point out such weaknesses and can help devise a plan to

assist you in working on them, as well as help you formulate a more effective training program and establish realistic goals, among other benefits. The cost for a one-hour session usually runs from $30 to $60.

2. **Try to discern the areas of weakness in your bouldering** that hold you back, and then focus some or the majority of your workouts on those areas. This is one of the main reasons that people stop improving in bouldering—they simply become addicted to success and therefore select problems (both indoors and out) that showcase what they're already good at, while neglecting their weaker components. So if you hate slopers, learn to love 'em, and if you despise slabs, seek them out. You will experience far greater levels of improvement far more rapidly by consistently addressing the areas where you are weaker.

> *. . . if you hate slopers, learn to love 'em, and if you despise slabs, seek them out.*

3. **Mix it up.** Perhaps you've become too specialized at one specific area or on the type of rock or angles on which you spend most of your time. If there is another gym in town or there are other bouldering areas nearby, try to visit these places and add them to your circuit. Or you can plan a bouldering trip to an out-of-state area. Familiarity can breed boredom and stagnation, whereas new terrain can fan the flames and give you something different to work toward.

4. **Diversify.** Take a rock climbing lesson. Not only will you learn about the safety aspects of roped climbing, but also you may find that you actually like it as much, or maybe (gasp!) even more, than bouldering. Roped climbing has a different cadence and feel to it (think of long traverses and you'll start to get the idea), and you might find it a welcome change of pace. Spending some time on longer routes will likely yield some benefits in bouldering performance, too, allowing you greater endurance that could help you hang on for an extra move or two when you go back to the little rocks.

5. **Take a break.** As contradictory as this suggestion may sound, it can actually help to take some time off from your standard schedule, whether you rest for four days instead of two or for two full weeks. Bouldering is strenuous and demanding, and your body needs time to recover and recuperate. During times of rest, your muscles may actually assimilate the new moves you've been practicing. Enhance your rest by visualizing bouldering sequences that are hard for you. It's been shown that athletes who visualize a technique regularly can actually achieve as good or possibly even better results than athletes who physically practice a motion repeatedly, so use that amazing brain power to your advantage.

Beyond the Walls: Stretching, Boards, Weight Training, and Aerobic Exercise

Along with bouldering, rest, more bouldering, more rest, and more bouldering, you may wish to explore some additional options to enhance your bouldering performance and overall fitness level.

Stretching

In my opinion, stretching should be an integral part of every boulderer's training program, though I'd say at least 75 percent of the boulderers I know do not stretch regularly. I believe that a simple stretching routine, taking only 10 to 15 minutes, provides numerous benefits for bouldering performance, not to mention overall wellness. First, stretching can help improve your range of motion, making reaches less reachy, high steps less high, and drop knees less injury provoking, among other benefits. Second, I have read the results of scientific studies stating that people who stretched their muscles after lifting weights experienced significant gains in strength over their counterparts who did not stretch. If you're bouldering, you're lifting weights—your own body weight, of course—so it seems logical to assume that stretching following a bouldering session should result in increased strength gains similar to those experienced by the post-weight-lifting stretchers. Third, stretching, as we all know, can help loosen up tight muscles and reduce soreness following a strenuous workout. If you can't get motivated to stretch on your own, consider signing up for yoga or Pilates, which are also beneficial in increasing core strength and flexibility.

. . . stretching should be an integral part of every boulderer's training program . . .

Boards

You'll probably notice when you go to a climbing gym that it has one or more boards designed for climbing training purposes, such as a campus board, fingerboard, or system board. A campus board is an overhanging board (a board hung at an angle that is greater than vertical, like the inside of a tent or a triangle; it usually overhangs about 30 degrees from the bottom to the top) with uniformly sized (usually) wooden rungs spaced at regular intervals that begin at about the 5- or $5^1/_2$-foot level and go up to perhaps 10 feet. A campus board can have several sets of rungs, with each column of rungs uniformly sized but of different widths than the rungs of its neighboring columns. Boulderers use the campus board to train for power and timing for dynamic movements, using their upper bodies and arms to ascend and descend the rungs in control without using their feet. Think of climbing up the underside of a ladder without using your feet and you'll start to get the picture. I strongly recommend that beginners stay away from the campus board—it's a great way to injure tendons, rotator cuffs, and so forth if you don't yet have adequate muscle and supportive tissue development to campus (ascend the board using only your hands, with no help from your feet) in control. Once you have been bouldering for a year or two you could consider adding campusing to your workouts, but I'd encourage you to first consult with an experienced trainer who can help you assess whether or not campusing is a worthwhile component to add to your training program.

In addition to the campus board, most gyms have at least one fingerboard. The fingerboard—a single, somewhat large, often injection-molded piece of plastic featuring a variety of climbing grips—is usually hung at about the same height as you would hang a pull-up bar, and it can be used for the same purpose—to do pull-ups on climbing holds—as well as for developing particular climbing strengths, such as lock-offs (holding on to a hold with one arm bent and tensed, then being able to let go with the other hand and reach for the next hold statically, without dynamic movement), open-hand grip strength, and finger and hand endurance. Again, you'll probably find using the fingerboard totally unnecessary and potentially injurious as you start out as a boulderer, unless you want to use the biggest holds to do some pull-ups (though being able to do a hundred pull-ups does not translate into being a great climber). As with the campus board, I'd suggest that you wait awhile before you explore the options of how supplemental fingerboard workouts could help your bouldering performance. Then read up on them and consult with an experienced trainer before you embark on any fingerboard regimen.

. . . being able to do a hundred pull-ups does not translate into being a great climber.

Finally, the system board is another board your local gym might have. This board is a uniformly angled, flat, overhanging climbing surface with a variety of holds bolted onto it, possibly with large, identical square holds that each feature a number of different grips. Usually there will be several sets of the same types of holds lined up in columns, allowing people to design exercises that work specific grips, such as pinches, crimps, open-hands, slopers, and the like, as well as specific techniques, such as high steps, drop knees, backsteps, and so forth. The system board is likely to be the most useful tool of all the boards for the total beginner, because unlike the campus board or fingerboard, it allows you to practice particular movements or work on holding on to particular holds but still have your feet on the wall the whole time. For help figuring out good workouts on the system board, ask another climber who is using it or consult with an experienced trainer. Don't be scared to

Don't be scared to use your own imagination to come up with some workouts on your own . . .

use your own imagination to come up with some workouts on your own, though. If you're having trouble on slopers, for example, maybe try to do some up-and-down laps on slopey holds on the system board as a secondary warm-up or cool-down.

Weight Training

You might think that adding a serious weight-lifting component to your bouldering regimen will reap serious benefits, but as a beginner, it is not likely to yield the results you might expect. Bouldering is a movement-specific activity that recruits all sorts of muscles in all sorts of combinations, whereas weight-lifting tends to isolate specific muscles, often larger muscles, not forcing the smaller, supportive muscles to work in the same way they would when you boulder. I've actually seen bodybuilder types repeatedly deal with injuries that seemingly arise from the fact that they have extremely strong big muscles, but their smaller, supportive muscles and tissues are not as strong, meaning that when they execute hard pulls, the smaller muscles can't handle the load. This is not to demonize weight training or to deem it useless; rather, I believe that you will experience greater success initially if you focus your workout time on bouldering rather than supplementing it with weight training.

That said, once you've been bouldering for a while, you should consider hiring a trainer who can help you learn some opposing-muscle weight-training exercises, as well as some supplementary weight-training exercises to help improve your overall strength. Since climbing movements almost always require pulling, many climbers and boulderers develop a hunchback physique as their pulling muscles far surpass the size and strength of their pushing and raising muscles. Muscle imbalances like this not only look downright weird but can also lead to injuries. To avoid cultivating a Quasimodo-like build, then, you'll want to consider incorporating into your training some opposing-muscle exercises that open up your pectoral area and help you develop and retain overall flexibility and balance. This means not only weights, but possibly some push-ups and dips as well as stretches. A professional trainer can help you assess your individual goals and desires and design a weight- or resistance-training program tailored to your specific needs.

Aerobic Exercise

Along with weight training or exercises for opposing muscles, if you can, you should think about adding some sort of regular aerobic activity to the mix. Bouldering tends to be more anaerobic than aerobic, involving short bursts of maximal effort. While this is undoubtedly a good overall body workout, your lungs, heart, and overall fitness level will benefit from additional aerobic exercise. While regular aerobic exercise probably won't have any direct or noticeable correlation to improved bouldering performance, nonetheless, if you want to keep your body healthy and fit, you should probably go for a brisk walk, ride a bike, jog, swim, or engage in some similar activity two or three times a week for at least half an hour each time. You don't need to be maniacal about aerobic exercise if your main focus is bouldering—just choose something that seems fun and engage in it at a moderate level. I find that running a few times a week seems to help me loosen up and to reduce some post-climbing or bouldering-related muscle soreness, too.

Making the Most of Rest Days

If you fall in love with bouldering, as so many people have, you'll soon find that one of the most difficult disciplines to master involves resting enough and learning to respect the messages your body sends. Adequate rest is crucial, and its value should not be overlooked as a key component of every training program. Many elite climbers and boulderers subscribe to the two days on, one day off, two days on, two days off training plan for a reason, since this schedule maximizes climbing time while allowing for ample rest as well. A key to this cycle is the two-day-off rest period, a critical time during which the body can recuperate and heal from the wear and tear of bouldering.

Adequate rest is crucial, and its value should not be overlooked as a key component of every training program.

Bouldering makes your body work harder than you might think, with all of the subtle stresses it can place on areas that other forms of exercise usually don't tax, particularly your fingers. Without ample rest, you will be courting injury. What's taking two days off in the face of taking two months off due to overtraining and overuse injuries? As a novice, you might find that you need even more than two days off sometimes; if you fear that you cannot judge this adequately yourself, consult with a personal trainer or bouldering coach to help you learn to assess when enough is enough.

If you've made plans to boulder on a given day but you're still sore, you should probably forgo that plan and opt for one or more of my top three favorite rest-day activities—massage, hot tub, and visualization. In fact, you can easily incorporate all three of these activities into one ultrarelaxing day off from the rocks. While you're lying on the massage table, breathe deeply and picture your muscles relaxing and letting go of all the tension, aches, and pains. Or if that sounds boring, in your head run through the movements and motions of a problem that challenges you, picturing precisely how you will execute each move and how it will feel to pull over the top. Likewise, you can do the same sort of visualizing while you simmer for 10 minutes in a hot tub, massaging your forearms and fingers to encourage blood flow to these areas, which are likely congested and taut. Just remember that rest days should be days of total rest—a day in which you don't boulder but run instead *doesn't* count as a day off. After your massage, hot tub, and visualization, sink into the couch with a great book (bouldering-related or otherwise) or grab the remote control and savor the couch-potato sensation— you've earned it!

chapter 3

NOITHWEST

T HE NORTHWESTERN UNITED STATES—or more specifically, the Pacific
Northwest or Old Oregon country (as defined by the Library of Congress)—includes the states of Idaho, Oregon, Montana, Washington, and
Wyoming. Despite development and urban growth, these states still retain
some of that distinctive frontier flavor from their collective past. Vast tracts
of largely untrammeled public lands encompass millions of acres throughout
the Northwest and undoubtedly contain numerous climbing, bouldering,
and other recreational opportunities yet to be discovered or perhaps never
to be discovered. For the explorer and the adventurous at heart, then, Old
Oregon country offers plenty of undiscovered or relatively unknown bouldering areas to visit, as well as the opportunity to escape the crowded scene
and at times ego-permeated atmosphere that can prevail at more well-traveled bouldering areas. If you like to just get out there and explore, with little
concern about having an audience or climbing a problem of a certain grade,
you may find your heart's desire somewhere in the Pacific Northwest.

While Montana, Washington, and Oregon all have worthy bouldering
destinations that have received varying degrees of publicity, I've chosen
to include here just three Northwest destinations—two in my home state
of Wyoming and one in neighboring Idaho. In future editions of this book
I hope to include bouldering hot-spots in the three other states. If you visit
Wyoming's Sinks Canyon, you'll find bouldering on both high-quality

Leslie Paul bouldering in Cody, Wyoming.

granite and questionable sandstone—but if you're willing to explore, you might find a few gems here and there on the sandstone boulders, as I have during my many explorations of the canyon's slopes. If you want to boulder on sandstone without dealing with holds breaking, lots of cleaning, and bad landings, though, your best bet in the Northwest that I know of is Cody, Wyoming, past home of Buffalo Bill and present home to a small but enthusiastic crew of avid boulderers who are constantly finding and developing new problems on the mountainsides just outside of town. And if you're into checking out something completely different, the basalt bouldering of Dierkes Lake, Idaho, is unlike any other bouldering I've yet to experience, with a great mix of extremely overhanging hueco-filled roofs and vertical, crimpy, pocketed faces on bomber (extremely high-quality) rock.

Tarris Webber dynoing on the MC Boulder, Sinks Canyon, Wyoming.

Sinks Canyon—Lander, Wyoming

Most rock climbers who have heard of Lander, Wyoming, associate this small town of just under 7,000 residents with the "Legendary Wild Iris," a lofty sweep of short, steep, windswept white dolomite that sits high upon South Pass about a half hour away, made famous by Wyoming's home-grown climbing figures of note, Todd Skinner and Paul Piana. Occasionally, you'll run into other climbers who rave about a lesser-known, roped, route-climbing area in the Lander vicinity—that of Sinks Canyon, a remarkable destination in and of itself that lies a mere 6 miles south of Lander. Sinks Canyon has incredible natural features that have nothing to do with climbing, such as a river that plunges underground, weaving its way through a labyrinth of underground tunnels only to reemerge a quarter mile down the canyon in a placid, bubbling pool (known as the

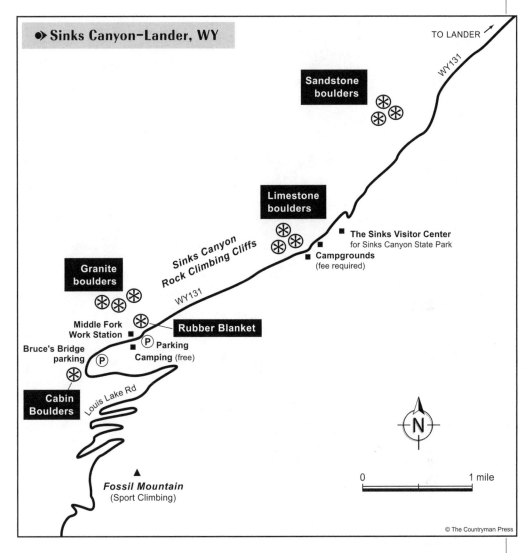

Sinks Canyon–Lander, WY

TO LANDER

WY131

Sandstone boulders

Limestone boulders

The Sinks Visitor Center
for Sinks Canyon State Park

Campgrounds
(fee required)

Sinks Canyon
Rock Climbing Cliffs

Granite boulders

WY131

Middle Fork
Work Station

Rubber Blanket

Parking

Bruce's Bridge parking

Camping (free)

Cabin Boulders

Louis Lake Rd

N

Fossil Mountain
(Sport Climbing)

0   1 mile

© The Countryman Press

Rise) that is home to enormous trout (no, you can't fish for them). Sinks Canyon is also known for its own brand of stellar dolomite roped route climbing, which rivals that of Wild Iris—particularly the lengthy pocket-filled endurance-oriented routes found in imposing Killer Cave.

Even those rock climbers who know about Killer Cave are unlikely to have heard of or explored the bouldering opportunities available in this natural playground. Don't be lured by the dolomite boulders littering the sides of the trails on the way to the route climbing—in my opinion, bouldering on dolomite usually equals pure junk, due to the inherent sharpness of the rock. But if you want to forgo tying in and clipping bolts for a day or two, set your sights lower or higher in the canyon and let your inner adventurer come alive as you poke around in the sandstone or head up higher for the high-quality granite.

Tarris Webber at the Rubber Blanket, Sinks Canyon, Wyoming.

Profiled here in detail you will find a single boulder that rivals any other individual boulder as a singular destination, capable of providing an entire afternoon's entertainment or a regular circuit with problems ranging from V0 to V9. The Rubber Blanket (though it has had other designations in the past) sits all by its lonesome adjacent to the Shoshone National Forest Middle Fork Work Station high up in the canyon. This boulder features a short approach, flat landings, and at least 15 established problems, with many more eliminates—all on one stone. If you run out of things to try or get bored making up games, just head on up the hill directly above the Rubber Blanket and check out the other granite boulders. Or you can drive up to Bruce's Bridge and poke around in the Cabin Boulders (see map).

The Lowdown

◈▶GETTING THERE

Driving directions: Access Lander via US 287 from the northwest or the southeast (US 287 is Main Street in Lander) or via WY 789 from the northeast, turning right onto US 287/Main Street in Lander. From the Lander Bar (126 Main Street), drive west on Main Street (US 287) for .3 mile. Turn left onto Fifth Street (WY 131). After .6 mile, turn right onto Fremont Street (still WY 131). Continue on WY 131 for roughly 6 miles to reach the canyon.

To find the Rubber Blanket boulder, set your odometer at the Sinks Canyon State Park sign and drive 3.3 miles until you see the Shoshone National Forest Middle Fork Work Station on your right. The Rubber Blanket is the large, squarish boulder about 100 yards down canyon from the work station. Hang a U-turn and park on the opposite (north) side of the road.

Nearest major airports: The Riverton Regional Airport (307-856-1307; www.fly riverton.com; 4800 Airport Road, Riverton) is about 30 miles from the canyon, but you'll probably pay a hefty price to fly there. Alternatively, consider flying into Denver International Airport (303-342-2000; www.flydenver.com; 8500 Peña Boulevard, Denver, CO) and renting a car. It's about a 375-mile drive to Lander, but the price difference might be worthwhile (most locals tend to fly in and out of Denver). Or consider flying into Salt Lake City International Airport (801-575-2400 or 800-595-2442; www.slcairport.com; 776 North Terminal Drive, Salt Lake City, UT), which is about a 300-mile drive from Lander.

Public transportation: The Wind River Transportation Authority (307-856-7118 or 800-439-7118; www.wrtabuslines.com) offers limited public transportation to Lander from Riverton Regional Airport as well as from Salt Lake City International Airport. You must call in advance to make reservations. There is no public transportation available to Sinks Canyon.

◈▶CLIMBING CONCERNS

Cost: Free.

Hours: Open 24 hours a day.

Land manager: The lower canyon is managed by Sinks Canyon State Park (307-332-3077; http://wyoparks.state.wy.us/sinks1.htm; 3079 Sinks Canyon Road, Lander, WY, 82520). The upper canyon lies within the Washakie Ranger District of the Shoshone National Forest (307-332-5460; www.fs.fed.us/ r2/shoshone/districts/washakie.htm; 333 East Main Street, Lander, WY, 82523).

Finding the boulders: Once you're in the canyon, you will see sandstone, limestone, and granite boulders, most of which have been climbed on at some point. The Rubber Blanket is easily accessed from the parking place described above—just walk across the grass to get there.

Type of rock: The Rubber Blanket is granite, but Sinks Canyon also has an abundance of sandstone, limestone, and granite boulders that vary in quality, height, and number of problems.

Five good problems: Five fun problems on the Rubber Blanket are The Spare Tire (V0), Menstruating Bitches (V2), The Subscription (V4), Shelly's Arête (V5), and Jeremy's Traverse (V7).

Range of grades: V0–V9, with the potential for even harder eliminates, depending on how much you want to contrive (make up rules about which holds you're allowed to use).

Prime season: Believe it or not, the Rubber Blanket and many of Sinks Canyon's additional boulders—and routes—are climbable year-round. The Rubber Blanket in particular makes a great destination on sunny winter days. On many occasions during my winter spent in Lander, the temperature in town would be below freezing all day, yet we'd be climbing in tank tops and cotton pants in blasting sunshine at the Rubber Blanket—after wading through knee-deep snow to arrive at the melted-out landing area at the base of this sun-warmed boulder. Nonetheless, you're best off visiting in fall or spring to guarantee suitable climbing temperatures. Summers can be hot, but you can find plenty of shady boulders here as well.

Dogs: Allowed, but must be leashed in the state park and in developed recreation sites of the national forest.

Special notes: Sinks Canyon, like much of Wyoming, is pretty unregulated. Help keep it that way by maintaining a low profile, picking up your trash, and leaving the boulders as you find them. Keep in mind that the development and popularity of the smaller rocks around Lander has waxed and waned through the years, with the result that some boulders have numerous names, grades, and variants of the same or similar problems.

Guidebooks to area problems: There is no comprehensive guide available to all the bouldering in Sinks Canyon. If you're planning a trip to the area, you should pick up a copy of *Lander Rock*, by Greg Collins and Vance White (2003). It includes maps and grades for some of the bouldering in Sinks Canyon as well as detailed information on sport climbing at Sinks, Wild Iris, and other areas around Lander. You might get lucky and find a copy of *Sinks Canyon Bouldering*, by Steve Bechtel, or another such guide put together by a local, at Wild Iris Mountain Sports in Lander (see *Other resources*).

Online resources: Slim at best. You'll find a few entries on RockClimbing.com (www.rockclimbing.com), as well as photos of a problem or two on a few other personal sites if you look for them. For sport routes, Dr. Topo (www.drtopo.com) offers free online guides to both Sinks Canyon and Wild Iris that are available for downloading.

Other resources: If you've never climbed before and you want to hire a guide, try Jackson Hole Mountain Guides and Climbing School (800-239-7642; www.jhmg.com; P.O. Box 7477, 165 North Glenwood Street, Jackson, WY) or Exum Mountain

Guides (307-733-2297; www .exumguides.com; Box 56, Moose, WY). For gear or supplies, try Wild Iris Mountain Sports (888-284-5968 or 307-332-4541; www.wildiris climbing.com; 333 West Main Street, Lander, WY).

The National Outdoor Leadership School (NOLS; 800-710-NOLS; www.nols.edu; 284 Lincoln Street), one of the nation's top educators in the arena of outdoors and wilderness skills, is based in Lander.

Lander hosts the annual International Climbers' Festival (www.climbersfestival.org) on the Thursday through Sunday after the Fourth of July. This informal festival usually draws quite a crowd and features climbing-related clinics, slide shows, movies, roped rock climbing, and more, all for a nominal entry fee.

Local climbing gyms: No public climbing gym, but at the time of this writing local climbers had pitched in to make the formerly public Gravity Club a seasonal, members-only co-op, with a

A few hidden gems await those willing to explore the sandstone in Sinks Canyon (Matt Wendling climbing).

$6 per day fee for guests, who are allowed in only with a member. For the most current information, your best bet is to check with the folks at Wild Iris Mountain Sports.

Nearby bouldering and climbing areas of note: If you want to sport climb, just hike up to the dolomite crags above the boulders in Sinks Canyon or drive on up to Wild Iris. Wyoming contains vast quantities of climbable rock in pockets throughout the state, including sandstone bouldering in Cody (see pages 70–76) and granite bouldering in Vedawoo, as well as traditional climbing opportunities at Devils Tower, Vedawoo, and the Tetons, among other locales.

Alan Pirie, Sinks Canyon, Wyoming. PHOTO BY MATT WENDLING

◆◆OTHER IMPORTANT STUFF

Camping: Free for up to three nights at City Park (see *Water* for detailed information). There is also free camping in the Shoshone National Forest for up to 16 days at a time—one area is located just across the road from the Rubber Blanket in an undeveloped camping area (that sees heavy use nonetheless) with an outhouse. Please do your part to keep this area clean. If you would like amenities like clean latrines and running water (no hookups), Sinks Canyon State Park has two pay campgrounds that cost $8 per night for nonresidents.

Nearby phone: There was a pay phone located at the parking area by Bruce's Bridge, less than a mile up-canyon beyond the Rubber Blanket, but it had been run over by a vehicle and was out of commission at the time of publication. If it has not been replaced, your best bet is to head back to Lander, where there are ample pay phones. Cell phone service in Sinks Canyon is sporadic at best.

Showers: Shower (and hot tub or swim, too) for $2 a person at the Lander Community Swimming Pool (307-332-2272; www.landerwyoming.org/default.htm, click on "Parks and Recreation;" 450 South Ninth Street). Coming back from the canyon, after about 6 miles hang a left onto Ninth Street and follow for .5 mile as it curves back toward Main Street; the swimming pool will be on your right.

Water: Fill up at City Park (307-332-4647; www.landerwyoming.org/default.htm, click on "Parks and Recreation"; 405 Fremont Street). From the Lander Bar on Main Street, go .2 mile to Fourth Street and turn left. After .6 mile turn right onto Fremont Street. The park will be on your left. Alternatively, you can fill your water at one of the two pay campgrounds located in Sinks Canyon State Park that you drive by on the way to the Rubber Blanket, as they do not charge a day-use fee.

In case of emergency: Dial 911 for all emergencies. The Sinks Canyon State Park Visitor Center (1 mile up-canyon from the park sign) is open 9 AM–6 PM Memorial Day weekend through Labor Day. The center does not have a public telephone, but it does have a phone line.

Drive to Lander Valley Medical Center (307-335-6365; 1320 Bishop Randall Drive). From the state park headquarters near the mouth of the canyon, drive 4.7 miles toward Lander on WY 131, keeping an eye out for Mortimore Lane on your right. Turn onto Mortimore Lane. After .7 mile, turn left onto Hillcrest Drive, which becomes Custer Street after .8 mile. After .2 mile, turn right onto Buena Vista Drive. Go .1 mile and then turn left onto Bishop Randall Drive. The hospital is less than .1 mile on Bishop Randall Drive.

Nearby Internet hookup: The Lander Library (307-332-5194; www.fremontcounty libraries.org/lander.htm; 451 North Second Street), offers Internet access. From the state park headquarters near the mouth of the canyon, drive 6.6 miles into Lander on WY 131/Fremont Street. Turn left onto Third Street. After three short blocks, turn right onto Cascade Street. Turn left onto Second Street and proceed several blocks, crossing Main Street, to reach the library (across from the courthouse) just after passing Amoretti Street.

Restaurants: Tony's Pizza Shack (307-332-3900; 637 Main Street), has the best pizza in town. Tony's is anything but a shack, with an awesome roof deck. Even vegetarians will find something suitable. Made-to-order pizzas, strombolis, sandwiches, and specialty salads. Inexpensive. Open Monday through Saturday 10–10 (closes at 11 in summer season); Sunday 4–10. From the state park headquarters in Sinks Canyon, drive back toward town on WY 131/Fremont Street for about 6 miles. Turn left onto Ninth Street and go .7 mile to Main Street. Turn right onto Main Street and proceed .2 mile to Tony's—you can't miss the cheerful checkered neon sign on your right.

Not in the mood for Italian? Then head down Main Street to the Gannett Grill (307-332-8228; www.landerbar.com/grillmain.php; 126 Main Street); or the Cowfish (307-332-7009; www.landerbar.com/cowfishmain.php; 128 Main Street); and finish with a drink and a game of pool or some live music at the Lander Bar (307-332-7009; www.landerbar.com; also at 126 Main Street). This triple treat (all under the same ownership) serves up the finest microbrews around, courtesy of the on-premise, award-winning Snake River Brewpub, attached to the Cowfish. For a fine meal on the town, the Cowfish will meet your needs with its trendy, upscale menu featuring marinated flank steak, grilled sea bass, and even some vegetarian options. Expensive. If you're not in the mood for fancy, you can settle for a simpler feast from the Gannett, known for its large salads and bodacious burgers, as well as pizza and appetizers. Inexpensive. From the state park headquarters in Sinks Canyon, drive back toward town on WY 131/Fremont Street for about 6 miles. Turn left onto Fifth Street and go .6 mile. Turn right onto Main Street and go .3 mile to the restaurants. Gannett Grill open daily 11–9 (winter) or 11–10 (summer); Cowfish open seven days 5–10; Sunday 9 AM–2 PM; Cowfish Pub open Monday through Saturday 4–midnight; Sunday 4–10 (bar menu available until 10 nightly).

For coffee and fresh baked goods in the morning, try the Wildflour Bakery & Espresso (307-332-9728; 545 Main Street); there is a drive-through coffee hut outside in the parking lot as well. Inexpensive. Another cool venue is the Global Café (307-332-7900 or 866-312-7900; www.landerglobalcafe.com; 360 Main Street), a smoke- and alcohol-free establishment where you'll find coffee, baked goods, home-cooked meals, comfy couches, a game room, and local or traveling performers practically every night of the week—just call or stop by and ask who's on stage and what's for dinner. Inexpensive.

Cody, Wyoming

Have you heard of Cody, Wyoming, the "Home of Buffalo Bill" and the "Gateway to Yellowstone Park"? If so, this small city in northwestern Wyoming probably conjures up images of the Wild West as it once was, and with good reason, as the town's name—and the town itself, really—originated with the fellow who came to embody the Old West in all its ruggedness, Colonel William F. "Buffalo Bill" Cody himself. Founded in 1895, in part through Buffalo Bill's efforts, Cody still

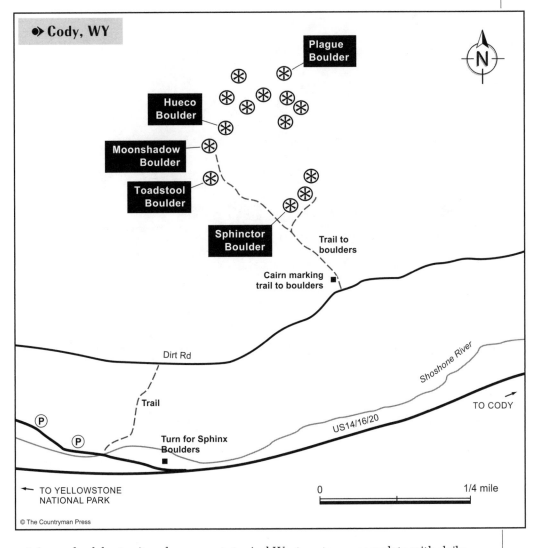

retains and celebrates its role as a prototypical Western town, complete with daily rodeos and gun battle reenactments during tourist season. These take place on the street in front of the Irma Hotel, opened in 1902 and named by Buffalo Bill for his youngest daughter. Trappings of Colonel Cody's legacy can be seen throughout the Cody area, from the Buffalo Bill Dam and Reservoir, which he helped secure the backing to construct, to the establishment of the Shoshone National Forest.

You might be asking what all this has to do with bouldering in Cody. The answer is nothing, really; it's just interesting that this quintessential Western town, named for a Western icon who embraced the qualities of self-reliance, individuality, respect, integrity, and exploration, happens to sit adjacent to some of the finest sandstone bouldering in the state. Littering the slopes of Cedar Mountain and Rattlesnake Mountain, which together form Shoshone Canyon, you will see

Matt Wendling bouldering in Cody, Wyoming.

tumbles and jumbles of boulders—some of which sport pure choss (breakable, fractured rock), and others of which lay claim to steep sandstone crimpfests or are testing slabs that would be considered classics even in better-known sandstone areas with more consistently dependable rock quality. When you head for the boulders outside Cody, then, think of your experience as an Old West adventure and don't be afraid to establish a new problem or explore another gully—but please, please don't follow in the footsteps of the individual who forever marred some of the boulders with his drill bit. If you can't climb it, leave it be, and let future explorers try their hands at what the wind, water, and weather spawned of their own accord.

The Lowdown

◆▶GETTING THERE

Driving directions: Approach Cody via US 14, US 16, US 20, or WY 120. To get to the Sphinx Boulders, one of the area's main attractions, drive west on US 14/16/20, Cody's main drag, out of town past the Wal-Mart (toward Yellowstone) into Shoshone Canyon. After passing the turnoff for Spirit Mountain Road on the left 1.8 miles after the Wal-Mart, start to look for a distinctive field of boulders on your right, nestled in a shallow gully. Shortly after you see this and less than 1 mile past Spirit Mountain Road, you will make a right turn onto a narrow road (the only right turn in the canyon) toward the Hayden Arch Bridge, less than .1 mile off the highway. Park all the way off the road on either side of the bridge. The trail to the boulders leaves from the northeast corner of the bridge.

Nearest major airports: Yellowstone Regional Airport (307-587-5096; www.flyyra .com/index.htm; 3001 Duggleby Drive, P.O. Box 2748, Cody), will land you close to the boulders. Alternatively, it may be less expensive to fly in to the City of Billings Logan International Airport (406-238-3420; www.flybillings.com; Aviation and Transit Department, 1901 Terminal Circle, Room 216, Billings, MT); about 100 miles from Cody.

Public transportation: None.

◆▶CLIMBING CONCERNS

Cost: Free.

Hours: Anytime.

Land manager: Depending on where you go, the boulders lie in lands managed by either the Wyoming Area Office of the Great Plains Region of the Bureau of Reclamation (307-261-5671; www.usbr.gov/gp/area_office_wyao.cfm; P.O. Box 163, Mills, WY, 82644) or the Cody Field Office of the Bureau of Land Management (307-578-5900; www.wy.blm.gov/cyfo/index.htm; 1002 Blackburn, P.O. Box 518, Cody, WY, 82414).

Finding the boulders: From the parking area for the Sphinx, find the obvious trail leading up the hillside from the northeast corner of the far side of the Hayden Arch Bridge. Follow this trail until you reach a dirt road. Take a right, and walk slightly downhill (east) along this road for a short distance, keeping your eyes peeled for another well-traveled trail heading up and to the left, marked by a cairn in a gully (you will pass several gullies before reaching the trail). Follow this trail up the hill; you should be able to see the boulders. If you'd like to explore Cody's other boulders, stop in at the Beta Coffee House (see *Other resources*) for the beta.

Type of rock: Sandstone.

Five good problems: Fun problems in the Sphinx Boulders include the Sphinctor Problem (V0, Sphinctor Boulder), The Terrible Twos (V3, Hueco Boulder),

Moonshadow Left (V3, Moonshadow Boulder), Mini Cave Center (V6, Toadstool), and The Plague (V10, Plague Boulder).

Range of grades: V0 to V10, with potential for harder problems as well.

Prime season: Spring and fall are the best times to visit. Winter days can be brutally cold and windy or else perfectly crisp and sunny, making for terrific friction. Summers can be blisteringly hot, though shade can be found if you know where to look.

Dogs: Dogs are allowed.

Special notes: Like much of Wyoming, the bouldering outside of Cody is basically unregulated. Help keep it this way by maintaining a low profile, parking completely off the road, and picking up all of your trash.

Guidebooks to area problems: Local bouldering enthusiasts Mike Snyder (co-owner of the Beta Coffee House) and Jeremy Rowan are compiling a guidebook of the area. Stop in at the Beta to find out when the book is coming out, or check at the local gear shops listed below.

Online resources: Slim. Look to RockClimbing.com (www.rockclimbing.com) for photos and some beta. A mini slide show, courtesy of Mike Snyder, can be found at New England Bouldering (www.newenglandbouldering.com/slideshows/cody/photo1.html).

Other resources: The best resource in town is undoubtedly the Beta Coffee House (307-587-7707; 1132 Twelfth Street), owned by prolific local boulderers Mike and Meg Snyder, who are happy to share information about their local haunts with you. If you need gear, your first stop should be at the Sierra Trading Post (307-578-5802; www.sierratradingpost.com; 1402 Eighth Street), where you will find bargains on all sorts of outdoor supplies. If they don't have what you need, stop in at Sunlight Sports (888-889-2463 or 307-587-9517; www.sunlightsports.com; 1251 Sheridan Avenue); or Foote's Mountaineering (307-527-9937; 1304 Sheridan Avenue). If you've never climbed or bouldered before and you'd like to hire a guide, try Jackson Hole Mountain Guides and Climbing School (800-239-7642; www .jhmg.com; P.O. Box 7477, 165 North Glenwood Street, Jackson, WY); or Exum Mountain Guides (307-733-2297; www.exumguides.com; Box 56, Moose, WY).

Local climbing gyms: None.

Nearby bouldering and climbing areas of note: Shoshone Canyon also has a small, dolomite sport-climbing area known as the Bridge Bands, as well as some additional sport climbing. Wyoming contains vast quantities of climbable rock of all varieties in pockets throughout the state, including sandstone, limestone, and granite bouldering in Sinks Canyon (see pages 62–70) and granite bouldering in Vedawoo, as well as traditional climbing opportunities at Devils Tower, Vedawoo, and the Tetons, among other locales.

In the climbing world, Cody is best known as an ice-climbing destination. Cody hosts the annual Waterfall Ice Roundup for ice climbers in February or March every year. Visit www .codyice.com, www.south forkice.com, and www .coldfear.com for more information.

◆ OTHER IMPORTANT STUFF

Camping: Buffalo Bill State Park (307-587-9227; http://wyoparks.state.wy.us/buffalo1.htm; 47 Lakeside Road). From the Sphinx Boulders, go west on US 14/16/20 until you see the entrance to Buffalo Bill State Park—about 9 miles outside of Cody. Year-round camping is available at the North Shore Bay Campground, where you can stay for up to 14 days at a time for $12 per site per night or $60 annual pass (nonresident); Wyoming residents pay half of those fees. Call 1-877-996-7275 to purchase an annual pass. A few sites can be reserved; the rest are first-come, first-served.

Cody is packed with many additional campgrounds (and hotels and motels). If you're there in the late spring through early fall and you'd like to camp somewhere closer to or in town, you should make reservations in advance. A list of campgrounds, complete with contact information, is available through the Cody Country Chamber of Commerce (307-587-2777; www.cody

Reid Leslie bouldering in Cody, Wyoming.

chamber.org/visitcody/lodging.htm; 836 Sheridan Avenue, Cody, WY, 82414).

Nearby phone: Wal-Mart Supercenter Store (307-527-4673; www.walmart.com; 321 Yellowstone Avenue) has pay phones. From the Sphinx Boulders, simply head east toward Cody on US 14/16/20; the store is on your left on the west side of town.

Showers: The Paul Stock Aquatics and Recreational Center, known by locals as the "Cody Qwad Center" (307-587-0400; 1402 Heart Mountain Street). From the Sphinx Boulders, drive east on US 14/16/20 into Cody. Turn right onto

Thirteenth Street 1.9 miles after Wal-Mart, following it for .2 mile to the recreation center (it becomes Heart Mountain Street).

Water: Ask politely at one of the many gas stations in town, or buy some at Wal-Mart on your way to the boulders.

In case of emergency: Dial 911 for all emergencies.

Drive to West Park Hospital (307-578-2375; www.westparkhospital.org; 707 Sheridan Avenue). From the Sphinx Boulders, head east into town on US 14/16/20, following it past the Wal-Mart for 1.5 miles farther. Turn left onto Sheridan and go .1 mile to find the hospital. For minor ailments and injuries, you can stop even closer to the boulders at West Park Hospital's Urgent Care Clinic (307-587-7207; 702 Yellowstone Avenue), located across the street from Wal-Mart, open 7 days a week.

Nearby Internet hookup: The Cody Library (307-527-8820; www-wsl.state.wy.us/park/cody.html; 1057 Sheridan Avenue). From the Sphinx Boulders, head back into town on US 14/16/20. The library is 1.7 miles beyond the Wal-Mart.

Restaurants: Stop in any morning for a cup of coffee—or one of numerous specialty drinks—and a homemade muffin or cinnamon bun at the Beta Coffee House (307-587-7707; 1132 Twelfth Street), and be sure to mention that you're in town to boulder if you want the real beta. Inexpensive. Open Monday through Friday 6:30–6; Saturday and Sunday 7–4. From the Sphinx Boulders, head east on US 14/16/20 back into town and take a right onto Twelfth Street; the coffee shop is less than .1 mile down the road.

For a downright pure Western dining experience, head east toward Cody on US 14/16/20 for a short distance (.1 mile beyond Wal-Mart) to Cassie's Supper Club & Dance Hall (307-527-5500; www.cassies.com; 214 Yellowstone Avenue). Since 1922, Cassie's has been serving up meals and entertainment to locals and passers-through alike. Specializing in fine, cut-to-order steaks and prime ribs, with chicken and seafood options on the menu as well. Cassie's won't disappoint in the protein department. Expensive. Open Monday through Saturday 11–2 and 5–10; Sunday 5–10.

Another yummy dining destination awaits at Maxwell's Fine Food and Spirits (307-527-7749; 937 Sheridan Avenue), where you can drool in anticipation after choosing from a wide selection of pizzas and pastas as well as full entrées of seafood, prime rib, and steak. Moderate to expensive. Open Monday through Saturday 11–9.

Dierkes Lake—Twin Falls, Idaho

Armed with a borrowed copy of *Basalt Climbs of South-Central Idaho*, by Mark Weber (1995), my husband and I figured that we'd check out the sport climbing at Dierkes Lake on our way through Idaho before visiting his grandparents, who live in the area. Upon our arrival at the Dierkes Lake/Shoshone Falls area early one crisp, sunny, late October morning, our eyes were instantly drawn not to the tall, blocky, overhanging cliffs but rather to the vast quantity of squarish basalt boulders scattered about the lakeshore like chunks of pepper ground out of a giant mill in the sky.

"Hey," I said tentatively, knowing that both of us were generally predisposed to clip bolts and climb longer routes, "don't you think people must boulder here?"

"Yeah, I was just thinking that myself . . . ," Matt trailed off.

I gazed back at the cliff with the routes, and then I studied the boulders again. Man, they looked good—great, solid stone; mostly flat landings; visible pockets; tall, vertical problems; and cool, steep, honeycombed overhangs.

"What would you think of just bouldering today?" I asked, and our fate was sealed. We hefted our pads and set out into the field to explore.

And lo and behold! Before too long, locals began to show up, starting with local legend and prolific route- and problem-establisher Mike May (to whom I'm deeply indebted for his feedback and assistance in compiling this section). Mike was an amenable guide, taking us under his wing and giving us a tour of the best

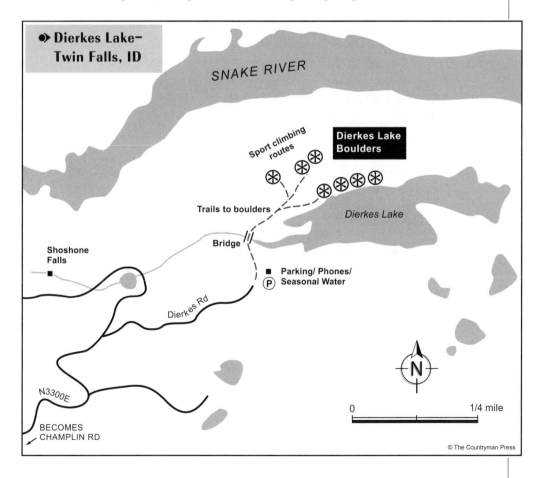

of the best problems. By midday we were bouldering in full force with a crew of strong, fun locals in the warm autumn sunshine, reveling in the fact that we had never even heard of Dierkes Lake bouldering, yet it was proving to be fantastic. In fact, we never did get around to trying out the sport routes—Mike gladly guided us around the boulders for our second day there, and then we had to mosey on our way, taking with us the memory of the best basalt bouldering I've yet to find. So if you're passing through southern Idaho and need a break, or if you just want to experience something a little bit different, add Dierkes Lake to your list of places worth stopping at for at least a couple days . . . it's a blast!

The Lowdown

➡️GETTING THERE

Driving directions: From I-84 East or West, take exit 173 toward Twin Falls. Head south on US 93 (Blue Lakes Boulevard North) for 4.7 miles. Turn left onto Falls Avenue East and proceed roughly 3 miles. Turn left onto Champlin Road and proceed about 2 miles, winding downhill (the road becomes North 3300 East) to the Dierkes Lake and Shoshone Falls area, staying straight on Dierkes Road to reach the parking area for Dierkes Lake.

Nearest major airports: Twin Falls has a regional airport, the Joslin Field–Magic Valley Regional Airport (800-453-9417 or 208-734-6232; www.tfid.org/airport; 492 Airport Loop). Salt Lake City International Airport (801-575-2400 or 800-595-2442; www.slcairport.com; 776 North Terminal Drive), is about 220 miles south in Utah.

Public transportation: There is no public transportation to the boulders at Dierkes Lake.

➡️CLIMBING CONCERNS

Cost: The entrance fee is $3 per car per day, or $25 for an annual permit. Fee is charged April 1 through October 1.

Hours: Open from 7 AM–9 PM daily.

Land manager: Owned and managed by the City of Twin Falls (208-736-2265; www.tfid.org/park_rec; Parks and Recreation Department, 136 Maxwell Avenue, Twin Falls, ID 83301).

Finding the boulders: You will have no problem finding the boulders on your arrival at Dierkes Lake; they are very eye-catching! From the parking area, you will easily find the trail that will take you across a bridge on the west side of the lake and into the boulders—where the trail splits into a Y, either path will take you to a plethora of boulders.

Type of rock: Basalt.

Five good problems: With no comprehensive guidebook to the area available at this time, recommending specific problems would be useless—especially since Dierkes is an ideal locale to explore and adventure. Every problem I attempted or climbed proved worthwhile, from the vertical, pocketed or crimpy faces to the fantastic, juggy overhangs. Let your imagination soar and have a blast!

Range of grades: More than 100 established problems ranging from V0 to V8 or harder, with the potential for much more development in the area, including adding difficult sit-down starts to many established stand-up-start problems.

Prime season: Best in spring and fall, with summers generally quite hot and winters extremely cold, though you could find a few good days here and there.

Dogs: Allowed, but they must be leashed at all times. You are responsible for picking up after your pet.

Special notes: There are no access issues at Dierkes Lake at this time. Please help keep it that way.

Guidebooks to area problems: No bouldering guides were available for Dierkes at press time, though one may be included in the next edition of *Basalt Climbs of South-Central Idaho*, by Mark Weber, or may be published separately. The previous edition of Weber's book (1995), which includes the sport climbing at Dierkes Lake, is still available through Chessler Books (800-654-8502; www.chesslerbooks.com).

Online resources: Go the Dierkes Lake section of Boise Climbs (www.boise climbs.com/twinballs_area.htm) for helpful beta about the area. Boise Climbs has more general information and resources about climbing in and around Boise. RockClimbing.com (www.rockclimbing.com) has a section on the sport climbing of Dierkes Lake with some references to the bouldering as well.

Other resources: If you've never climbed before and you want to hire a guide, try Sawtooth Mountain Guides (208-774-3324; www.sawtoothguides.com; P.O. Box 18, Stanley, ID) or Exum Mountain Guides (307-733-2297; www.exum guides.com; Box 56, Moose, WY).

If you need bouldering supplies, stop in at Riverat Whitewater Toyz (208-735-8697; www.rock-n-riverats.com; 138 Second Avenue South). From the intersection of Falls Avenue East and Champlin Road, proceed 2 miles south on Champlin Road. Turn right onto US 30 and go about 3.5 miles, turning right at 2.9 miles and then turning left after less than .1 mile to stay on US 30. Turn left onto Shoshone Street North and go .1 mile. Turn left onto Second Avenue South and go less than .1 mile to find the store.

For camping supplies, there's always Wal-Mart (208-324-4333; www.walmart .com; 2680 South Lincoln, Jerome). From the intersection of Falls Avenue East and Champlin Road, proceed 2.9 miles west on Falls Avenue East. Turn right onto Blue Lakes Boulevard/US 93 and go 4.7 miles. Merge onto I-84 West and go 4.7 miles. Take exit 168, and turn right onto ID 79. Go .4 mile to find the store.

Local climbing gyms: At the time of publication, Twin Falls had no public gym, though one is in the planning stages.

Nearby bouldering and climbing areas of note: In addition to the adjacent sport climbing at Dierkes Lake and numerous other local destinations in the vicinity of Twin Falls, Idaho has ample opportunities for all types of climbing enthusiasts. These include the world-famous traditional and sport climbing of City of Rocks National Reserve, near the Utah border in the center of the state; basalt sport climbing of Massacre Rocks State Park, 10 miles west of American Falls off I-86; and alpine climbing in the Sawtooth Mountain Range northeast of Boise, among numerous other opportunities.

➡OTHER IMPORTANT STUFF

Camping: You cannot camp at Dierkes Lake. You can camp for free with no amenities for up to 14 days on the public land located on the other side of the Perrina Memorial Bridge off US 93. From the intersection of Falls Avenue East and Champlin Road, go west on Falls Avenue East for 2.9 miles. Turn right onto Blue Lakes Boulevard/US 93 North, and keep your eyes open for Golf Course Road on the right after crossing the bridge (if you end up back at I-84, you've gone too far). Turn right (east) onto Golf Course Road. Be sure to drive a good distance down the road before selecting a site, as this is also a local favorite place for target practice and other such fun—and the camping tends to be very exposed.

If you want more amenities, from March 20 through October 31 you can camp at the Twin Falls/Jerome KOA (800-562-4169; www.koakampgrounds.com/where/id/12109.htm; 5431 US Highway 93, Jerome). Tent sites cost $18–$27 per night and include showers. From the intersection of Falls Avenue East and Champlin Road, go west on Falls Avenue East for 2.9 miles. Turn right onto Blue Lakes Boulevard/US 93 North and proceed 6.2 miles to the campground.

Nearby phone: There is a pay phone located at the Dierkes Lake/Shoshone Falls area.

Showers: In addition to the KOA (see *Camping*), you can stop by or call the YMCA/Twin Falls City Pool (208-734-2336; 756 Locust Street North) for public swimming hours. From the intersection of Falls Avenue East and Champlin Road, go west on Falls Avenue East for 2.7 miles. Turn left onto Locust Street North and go .1 mile to find the pool.

Water: Available at the Dierkes Lake/Shoshone Falls area June through August, when the snack bar is open. Otherwise, fill up before you visit, or stop and ask politely at a local gas station.

In case of emergency: Dial 911 for all emergencies.

Drive to Magic Valley Regional Medical Center (208-737-2000; 650 Addison Avenue West). From the intersection of Falls Avenue East and Champlin Road, go west on Falls Avenue East for 2.9 miles. Turn left onto Blue Lakes Boulevard/US 93 and go .9 mile. Turn right onto Addison Avenue/US 93 and go 1.6 miles to the hospital.

Nearby Internet hookup: Twin Falls Public Library (208-733-2964; www.twinfalls publiclibrary.org; 201 Fourth Avenue East). From the intersection of Falls Avenue

East and Champlin Road, proceed 2 miles south on Champlin Road. Turn right onto US 30 and go about 3.5 miles. Turn right at 2.9 miles and then turn left after less than .1 mile to stay on US 30. Turn right onto Second Street East and go less than .1 mile to find the library on the corner of Second Street East and Fourth Avenue East.

Restaurants: You'll find all sorts of national chain restaurants in Twin Falls, from fast food to not-so-fast sit-down establishments serving familiar favorites.

For those rainy rest days better spent lolling around with a cup of coffee and a good book, where better to go than a Barnes & Noble Booksellers (208-733-5554; www.barnesandnoble.com; 1239 A Pole Line Road East)? That's where I found myself on just such a day in Twin Falls, munching on a freshly baked pastry and washing it down with sips of strong coffee. Inexpensive. Open Monday through Saturday 9 AM–10 PM; Sunday 10–7. From the intersection of Falls Avenue East and Champlin Road, drive 2.9 miles west on Falls Avenue East. Turn right onto Blue Lakes Boulevard/US 93 and go .9 mile. Turn right onto Pole Line Road and go .1 mile to find the café and store.

For something a little different, head for A Taste of Thai (208-735-8333; www.therestaurantdirectory.com/Idaho/TwinFalls-r.htm; 837 Pole Line Road), where you can enjoy savory and sweet delights at this family-owned, family-operated establishment. A mix-and-match entrée selection includes plenty of options for vegetarians. Inexpensive–moderate. Open Monday through Thursday 11–9; Friday 11–10; Saturday 12–10; and Sunday 10–8. From the intersection of Falls Avenue East and Champlin Road, drive 2.9 miles west on Falls Avenue East. Turn right onto Blue Lakes Boulevard/US 93 and go .9 mile. Turn left onto Pole Line Road and go less than .1 mile to the restaurant.

chapter 4

CALIFORNIA

WHEN YOU THINK OF CALIFORNIA, you might think of beaches, bleached blondes, and boogie boards. Or perhaps the most populated state in this country calls to mind urban settings dense with humanity, where buildings rise instead of mountains and a permanent, drab, gray layer of concrete covers most surfaces more thickly than the exuberantly hued grasses and wildflowers that carpet natural landscapes in the springtime.

Then again, perhaps you already know the truth—that despite modern California's plenitude of beach bunnies and Hollywood glitterati, vast expanses of the third-largest state in the nation retain the remote, often idyllic, natural splendor that once drew wildlife lovers like Sierra Club founder John Muir and renowned photographer Ansel Adams to explore and document the startling and visually consuming magnificence of its mountains, valleys, rivers, and cliffs in the 19th and 20th centuries.

These are the types of locales that you will find documented here— from the thickly wooded sandstone playground of Castle Rock State Park, to the stunning mountainous backdrop and lunarlike bouldering of the Buttermilks, to the instantly recognizable desert landscape of Joshua Tree National Park, covered with its distinctive, rounded rock formations. Each of these California bouldering destinations preserves a strong sense of its past isolation and innate wonder despite the almost constant presence of

An unknown boulderer at the Buttermilks.

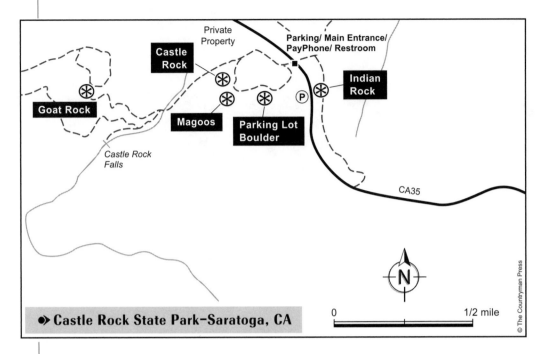

Castle Rock
Goat Rock
Private Property
Parking/ Main Entrance/ PayPhone/ Restroom
Indian Rock
Magoos
Parking Lot Boulder
Castle Rock Falls
CA35
N
0   1/2 mile
© The Countryman Press

➤ Castle Rock State Park—Saratoga, CA

numerous other boulderers, climbers, and explorers. These places allow for a simple and easy escape from the hustle and bustle of urban existence that continues unabated not too far away, or for a much-needed burst of warmth (if you're lucky) for those who travel to these parts from colder climes in the late fall to early spring.

Castle Rock State Park—Saratoga

You can almost picture Robin Hood and his Merry Men galloping around the corner of one of the wonderfully featured boulders clustered under the canopy of the thick, leafy woods of Castle Rock State Park. In late November Castle Rock looks like Wyoming or New England in late summer, with the trees lush and green and towering, blocking nearly any sunshine from reaching the floor of the forest. Tightly packed, mostly short sandstone boulders form natural jungle gyms that attract children wearing play clothes and tennis shoes as well as adult boulderers attired in the hippest climbing gear and familiar with the ins and outs of the sport. I felt silly when I visited for having a crash pad, chalk bag, and climbing shoes when five-year-olds were scrambling around me on the very same boulders, supervised by parents who were probably about my age. What a wonderful reminder that the game we play is just that—a game—in which we figure out the hardest, often most contrived, ways to climb up little rocks.

In any event, Castle Rock's boulders challenge visitors—both children and adults—with true slopers, sans any sort of cheater bumps or ripples for those not accustomed to open-handed holds. Sometimes you'll feel as though you're just sticking your open palm on a chalked surface that is not a hold by any definition I know of, except for the fact that someone else put their chalk-covered hand in that same place on the rock. Footholds tend to be either huge or nonexistent, but luckily, when your foot slides off of that nothing you've pasted it on and your hands slip down the smooth plane of the "holds" you're trying to pull on, more likely than not you'll come down on a perfectly flat landing surface, and probably you won't fall that far, since most of the boulders are not too tall. If you're a total beginner, you'll have a great time learning on these boulders, and if you're more experienced, you'll find yourself reveling in their distinctively different feel, from the amazing, rippling, wavy features to the perfect, nonabrasive texture of this sandstone.

The Lowdown

◆ GETTING THERE

Driving directions: From Saratoga, take CA 9/Saratoga Avenue 7.9 miles west to CA 35. Turn left onto CA 35 and proceed 2.5 miles to the park entrance on the right (west) side of the road. Avoid approaching the park from the northwest on CA 35/Skyline Boulevard. Though many mapping programs suggest this route, it involves a winding, one-lane road that can be quite frightening. Driving this route will not hasten your arrival.

Nearest major airport: The Norman Y. Mineta San José International Airport (408-277-4SKY; www.sjc.org; 1732 North First Street #600, San Jose) is less than 25 miles from Castle Rock State Park.

Public transportation: None.

◆ CLIMBING CONCERNS

Cost: If you park in the official parking lot, Castle Rock costs $5 a day. There is plenty of free parking on the sides of Skyline Boulevard around the park's entrance as well.

Hours: The hours are 6 AM–sunset, and they are enforced.

Land manager: California State Parks (408-867-2952; www.parks.ca.gov/default.asp?page_id=538; 15000 Skyline Boulevard, Los Gatos, CA 95033).

Finding the boulders: From the main parking area, you can approach the boulders via a path that leads straight up to the Parking Lot Boulder and then to Castle Rock and the Magoos, or else you can take the trail leading left, which will loop you around to Castle Rock proper and the Magoos (they are across the trail from one another). Both approaches are short.

Matt Wendling bouldering at Castle Rock State Park.

Type of rock: Sandstone.

Five good problems: There are a number of excellent V0-ish problems on the first Magoo boulder located just off the trail—this boulder also has the Cave Traverse (V4), as well as a V7 and a V10 on it. Down the hill you'll find Slap (V5) and the Hueco Wall (V5)—both impressive slopey problems. Across the trail at Castle Rock, you should check out the Beak Traverse (V3) and Butterfly Mantle (V5).

Range of grades: An abundance of mellow to moderately graded problems with great landings suitable for beginning to intermediate boulderers, as well as a handful of challenging double-digit beauties.

Prime season: With the mild coastal climate, climbing is possible year-round; spring and fall are the best times to go.

Dogs: Prohibited.

Special notes: Please avoid climbing at this area after it rains. If the boulders get wet at all, the holds break quite easily. Since it is imperative to have good friction here (you will see what I mean), climbing on the rocks when they are wet would probably not be rewarding anyway—so look but don't touch if the weather doesn't cooperate, and don't ruin the problems for other folks.

Guidebooks to area problems: *Bouldering Guide to the Castle Rock Area*, by Bruce Morris (MorComm, 2002); available online at www.rei.com.

Online resources: You can download *A Little Bouldering Guide of Castle Rock* for free from Dr. Topo (www.drtopo.com). For information about where to purchase the guidebook locally or just more info on the Castle Rock area, visit http://our world.compuserve.com/homepages/b_morris/press.htm. You'll find information on climbing, weather, and road conditions at Total Climbing Online (www.total climbingonline.com). The Southern California Mountaineers Association (www.rockclimbing.org) provides basic rock climbing instruction in addition to hosting numerous trips throughout the year. A list of helpful links—topos, slide shows, photos, and more—is available at www.stanford.edu/~clint/ba/icastle .htm. For more general information about climbing and bouldering in California, go to the Web sites of the Bay Area Climbers (www.bayareaclimbers .com) and CaliforniaBouldering.com (www.californiabouldering.com). In addition to the official Web site (see *Land manager*), a good general resource is the Santa Cruz State Parks page on Castle Rock (www.santacruzstateparks.org/ parks/castlerock/index.php).

Other resources: If you need rock climbing instruction in this area, you can contact Vertical Adventures Rock Climbing School (800-514-8785 or 949-854-6250; www.vertical-adventures.com) or Uprising Adventure Guides (888-254-6266 or 760-320-6630; www.uprising.com). For bouldering gear, stop by REI-Saratoga (408-871-8765; www.rei.com; 400 El Paseo de Saratoga, San Jose), where there is also an indoor climbing wall. The Bay Area has a number of additional REIs; just log on to the Web site to find the one closest to you.

Local climbing gyms: In addition to the indoor climbing wall at REI, Los Gatos has an outdoor climbing facility, Arête Rock Climbing Park (14700 Oka Road), about 15 miles from Castle Rock State Park. Less than 30 miles away you'll find indoor climbing at Pacific Edge Climbing Gym (831-454-9254; www.pacificedgeclimbinggym.com; 104 Bronson Street #12, Santa Cruz). You can find information about other area gyms at www.bayareaclimbers.com.

Nearby bouldering and climbing areas of note: Castle Rock State Park has top rope and lead climbs, as do several other areas along Skyline Boulevard. Also in the San Francisco Bay Area, you can climb and boulder at Mount Diablo

State Park, about 60 miles north of Castle Rock State Park. For more ideas, see www.bayareaclimbers.com.

●▶OTHER IMPORTANT STUFF

Camping: Camping in Castle Rock State Park is available only for backpackers who hike in to primitive sites—not a realistic option for boulderers. The Saratoga Springs Campground (408-867-9999; http://mail.saratoga-springs.com; 22801 Big Basin Way [CA 9]) is the best option close to the park. Though it is pricey by dirtbag climber standards, costing $25 a night to set up a tent (or $150 a week), you do get to partake of amenities such as hot showers, water, laundry, a video arcade, and a swimming pool. Make reservations. From the park, head back toward Saratoga via CA 35 and CA 9. The campground is 5.5 miles from the intersection of CA 35 and CA 9.

Matt Wendling bouldering at Castle Rock State Park.

Nearby phone: There is a pay phone at the main parking lot.

Showers: Saratoga Springs Campground (see *Camping*).

Water: Saratoga Springs Campground (see *Camping*).

In case of emergency: Dial 911 for all emergencies.

To reach the Community Hospital of Los Gatos (408-378-6131; 815 Pollard Road), head back to Sara-toga the same way you approached Castle Rock State Park. Continue through Saratoga on CA 9 until you reach CA 85. Turn right and proceed 2.4 miles to the Winchester Boulevard exit. After .2 mile, turn left onto Winchester Boulevard. Go .3 mile and turn left onto Knowles Drive. After .4 mile turn right onto Pollard Road, where you will see the hospital.

Nearby Internet hookup: You drove by it on your way to the park—stop in at the Saratoga Library (408-867-6126; www.santaclaracountylib.org/saratoga; 13650 Saratoga Avenue [CA 9]).

Restaurants: For an absolutely delectable and extravagant meal on the town, make reservations or try your luck at Viaggio (408-741-5300; www.viaggiorestaurant.com; 14550 Big Basin Way [CA 9], Saratoga). A wide selection of Mediterranean food includes more than 20 entrées (a cheaper option is to order some of the daily tapas specials). Expensive. Open Tuesday through Saturday 11:30–2 and 5–10; Sunday 11–2:30 and 5–9. From the parking lot at Castle Rock, turn left onto CA 35 and proceed 2.5 miles to CA 9. Turn right, and continue 7.1 miles to the restaurant.

In the morning, grab a cup of coffee—or rich hot chocolate—and a freshly baked pastry or muffin from the Prolific Oven (408-378-9880; www.prolific-oven .com; 18832 Cox Avenue, Saratoga). You can also get some cookies for snacks later in the day. Inexpensive. Open Monday through Friday 7:30 AM–9 PM; Saturday and Sunday 8 AM–9 PM. From the parking lot at Castle Rock, turn left onto CA 35 and proceed 2.5 miles to CA 9. Turn right, and continue 10.5 miles on CA 9/Saratoga Avenue. Turn right onto Cox; the Prolific Oven is less than .1 mile away on Cox.

The Buttermilks (Peabody Boulders)—Bishop

The dramatic, often snowcapped mountains of the Sierra Nevada range form a postcard backdrop for this well-known bouldering destination situated just outside of the charming, somewhat isolated city of Bishop, population 3,600. Between the small-town atmosphere and the free, undeveloped camping opportunities close to the bouldering, you might find yourself wondering

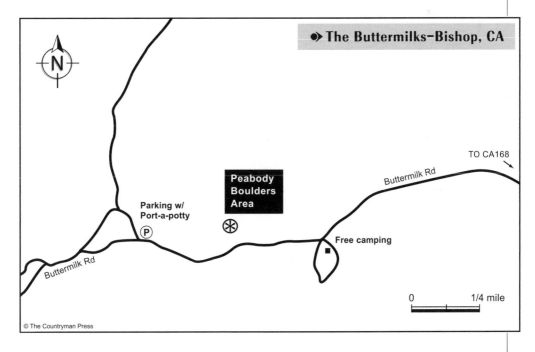

whether you're still in California. Upon wandering through the mystical moon-scape of the Buttermilks' impressive granite boulders, which vary in size from reasonable to bowel-shaking highballs that might be bolted routes in a different area, most visitors will already be taken in by the mystique of this one-of-a-kind setting before their hands even touch the rock.

While the bouldering area retains a sense of remoteness, you will likely not experience any sort of isolation from other climber types while at the Peabody Boulders area of the Buttermilks, especially during the peak seasons when the masses arrive from points near and far. The phenomenally high-quality granite boulder problems of the Buttermilks, coupled with the nearby areas of the Happy and Sad Boulders and the Druid Stones, have put Bishop on the map as a top bouldering area. Bishop has become a popular winter destination in lieu of Hueco Tanks State Historical Site since the establishment of the PURP (see the Hueco Tanks section, beginning on page 156, for details), particularly for those folks who prefer to experience a world-class bouldering area without the constant scrutiny, regulations, and hassles. That said, future access to all of the Bishop areas is al-ready a concern due to the burgeoning amount of traffic. In fact, access could be-come restricted—or worse—in the near future, particularly if boulderers do not respect the environment or maintain good relationships with officials.

The Lowdown

◆ GETTING THERE

Driving directions: From US 395 in Bishop (the main drag), go east on West Line Street, taking a left when it forks to follow CA 168. After a total of 7 miles, look for Buttermilk Road on your right. Buttermilk Road is mostly dirt, but it is decent enough that even folks in RVs drive it. Proceed 3.5 miles and you will see cars parked on the sides of the road and the boulders on your right. There is a main parking lot on the right after a hill where you will find a porta-potty. Please be sure to park off the road.

Nearest major airports: There are no major airports near Bishop. The closest major airport is 200 miles north—the Reno/Tahoe International Airport (775-328-6870; www.renoairport.com; 2001 East Plumb Lane, Reno, NV).

Public transportation: From the Reno/Tahoe International Airport, you can take an Inyo Mono Transit Crest Bus (800-922-1930 or 760-872-1901; www .countyofinyo.org/transit/transit.htm) to downtown Bishop for $28. Reserva-tions are highly recommended, and the bus service does not operate every day of the week, so be sure to call for a current schedule. Once you arrive in Bishop, you only have about 10 miles to go to reach the boulders—if you've made it this far, you can certainly figure out a way to get there, right?

◆CLIMBING CONCERNS

Cost: The Buttermilks are free of charge.

Hours: You can boulder at the Buttermilks any time.

Land manager: Inyo National Forest (760-873-2400; www.fs.fed.us/r5/inyo; 351 Pacu Lane, Suite 200, Bishop, CA 93514).

Finding the boulders: The Peabody Boulders are scattered about just north of Buttermilk Road and east of the parking area with the porta-potty. Trails lead to the developed boulders; please use the established trails.

Type of rock: Granite.

Five good problems: As is the case with all world-class bouldering areas, suggesting only five problems for even this small portion of the Buttermilks seems almost criminal, so I'm choosing to suggest a few of my favorite boulders instead. I chose not to map individual boulders at the Buttermilks on the included map, due to the high concentration of boulders and their obvious nature. (They are easily found by asking nearly anyone you encounter, or via Dr. Topo's guide, should you not have a comprehensive guidebook.) Great warm-ups from V0 to V3 abound at the Tut Boulder, including some gnarly slabby test pieces with weird knobby protrusions. The Iron Man Traverse (V4) is eternally popular due to the uniqueness of the feature—a continuous positive rail spanning an entire face of a boulder. By far my favorite boulder to date at the Peabody area has to be the Drifter, an immense monolith featuring hard movements up the difficult lower face of the boulder coupled with fun and easy but highball top outs that involve climbing an extremely pleasurable 20- or 30-foot expanse of VB/V0- or so to the summit—exhilarating and superb.

Range of grades: Everything from easier than V0 to open projects with a decent concentration of problems in each grade range for all levels of boulderers.

Prime season: The best time to visit is from late fall to early spring. Around the holidays—Thanksgiving, Christmas, and New Year's—you will likely wait in line to try any decent problem. To reduce impact and crowding, plan your trip at a different time than most school holidays, if possible.

Dogs: Allowed, but must be on a leash no more than 6 feet in length. Please clean up after your pet.

Special notes: Please stay on the well-traveled trails and roads and avoid trampling the vegetation. Be considerate when you dispose of solid waste—i.e., use the porta-potty, or if you cannot, don't go anywhere near the boulders or near any running water, and bury it when you're done. Pick up your trash and take it with you when you leave. Cooperate with the rangers if you camp on Forest Service land—they will issue you a free fire permit (or you need to obtain one from the office in town) even if you wish to use a propane stove. They may run your license plate, too, but don't be offended. They are simply doing their job, and it is your duty to be cooperative and polite, for the sake of everyone else who boulders here.

Guidebooks to area problems: If you're planning to spend any time in Bishop at all, your best bet is probably to go big and buy *The Bishop Bouldering Survival*

Kit, 2nd edition, by Mick Ryan (Rockfax, 2003). This guide contains not only the Peabody area boulders but also most of the other major destination bouldering areas around Bishop, as well as other helpful information about the area. Rockfax (www.rockfax.com; see *Online resources*) has a number of additional "MiniGUIDES" and resources available, and you can order the guidebook on-line directly from the site.

Online resources: By far the most helpful and prolific online resource for this area is Rockfax (www.rockfax.com). Here you will find ample background information about the Buttermilks (www.rockfax.com/bishop/buttermilks.html) as well as numerous helpful "MiniGUIDES"—many of which are free to download, such as the *Staying in Bishop MiniGUIDE*.

Dr. Topo (www.drtopo.com) also has a decent free guide to the area for downloading. For more general information, check out CaliforniaBouldering.com (www.californiabouldering.com). Another great resource with lots of useful links is Gordie's Ramblings in the High Sierra (www.mgordonphotography.com/sierra/sierra.htm).

Other resources: When you're in town, stop by Wilson's Eastside Sports (760-873-7520; www.eastsidesports.com; 224 North Main Street), for all of your climbing equipment needs—they even rent out crash pads. If you need a climbing guide, contact the Sierra Mountain Center, LLC (760-873-8526; www.sierramountaincenter.com; 174 West Line Street) or Sierra Mountaineering International (760-872-4929; www.sierramountaineering.com; 236 North Main Street).

Local climbing gyms: None at this time.

Nearby bouldering and climbing areas of note: The Bishop area has a plethora of bouldering and climbing areas of note, in addition to being in relatively close proximity (roughly 100 miles) to the world-renowned big walls and boulders of Yosemite National Park. Around Bishop, check out the Happy and Sad Boulders and the Druid Stones for more bouldering. Owens River Gorge has great sport climbing, especially in the more moderate grades. The eastern Sierras also offer ample opportunity for mountaineering, traditional alpine climbing, and ice climbing.

◆ OTHER IMPORTANT STUFF

Camping: If you're planning to boulder only at the Buttermilks and you're not wild about crowds and scenes, you can camp pretty much anywhere along the road that takes you out to the Buttermilks, so long as you drive on the side roads that are already established. You are allowed to stay for free for up to 28 days in any 6-month period, but you need a free fire permit to use your propane stove, so be sure to stop by the offices in town or inquire with a ranger in the likely event that you see one.

Another popular camping option is "the Pit," located on Bureau of Land Management (BLM) land on the same turnoff as Pleasant Valley Campground (see *Water*). The Pit is the major climber hangout and the center of the Bishop

Alli, Cave Route, Buttermilks, California. Photo by Matt Wendling

bouldering scene. A donation of $1 per night is asked to help maintain the porta-potty and keep the place clean. Instead of proceeding 1 mile from US 395 to Pleasant Valley Campground after turning right onto Pleasant Valley Road, keep your eyes open for a dirt road leading left up a hill and marked by a small brown sign indicating camping. Follow this road to the Pit.

Nearby phone: There are no phones at the boulders. Bishop has a number of pay phones.

Showers: Try Brown's Town Campground (760-873-8522; www.thesierraweb.com/recreation/browns/browns.html), 1 mile south of Bishop on US 395. The facility also has an old-fashioned ice cream fountain and camping supplies.

Water: Available at the Pleasant Valley Campground, should you choose to stay there ($10/night). Take US 395 7 miles north of Bishop. Turn right onto Pleasant Valley Road and proceed 1 mile to the campground. Alternatively, you can ask politely at one of several gas stations in town.

In case of emergency: Dial 911 for all emergencies.

Drive to the Northern Inyo Hospital (760-873-5811; www.nih.org; 150 Pioneer Lane). From the boulders, drive back toward town on CA 168 and West Line Street for a total of 6.4 miles. Turn left on Pioneer Lane to find the hospital, which is .6 mile from Main Street.

Nearby Internet hookup: Bishop Branch Library (760-873-5115; www.qnet.com/~library/library.html; 210 Academy Avenue). From West Line Street and North Main Street in Bishop, head west on West Line for less than .1 mile. Turn right onto North Warren Street and proceed .1 mile to Academy Avenue, where you will find the library on the corner. Internet service is also available at Kava Coffeehouse (see *Restaurants*).

Restaurants: No stop in Bishop would be complete without a treat from Erick Schat's Bakkerÿ (888-224-7647; www.schatsbakery.com; 763 North Main Street). In addition to the famous Original Sheepherder Bread, Schat's bakes up a variety of other breads, energy bars, rolls, pastries, cookies, and even beef jerky. Inexpensive. Open Monday through Friday 8–4.

If you dig good coffee and a funky coffeehouse setting, stop in for a cup of joe at Kava Coffeehouse (760-872-1010; www.kavacoffeehouse.com; 206 North Main Street). You'll also find some fine food—including quiche, bagel sandwiches, and granola—fun games, and Internet stations to while away the time while you take a break from climbing. Inexpensive. Call for current hours.

For dinner, one option is to fill up at the Imperial Gourmet Chinese Restaurant (760-872-1144; www.395.com/imperialgourmet; 785 North Main Street), where you can choose from routine Chinese fare like kung pao beef and shrimp fried rice to more exotic dishes like minced squab with lettuce and spicy salty and pepper squid. Imperial Gourmet has plenty of vegetarian options. Inexpensive to moderate. Open Sunday through Thursday 11–10; Friday and Saturday 11–10:30.

Joshua Tree National Park

You'll know you've found the right place when the landscape outside your car window appears as though the sky opened up and rained down granite rocks of varying sizes across the desert, from giant multipitch domes to hundreds upon hundreds of boulders. The vast quantity of Joshua trees might clue you in, too. If you're not impressed already, then prepare for sensory overload when you stop to stretch your legs or set up camp. From the moment you open your door in Joshua Tree National Park and take a deep breath, you'll inhale that mysteriously indescribable yet unmistakable scent of the park's desert—a spicy mélange made up of the dust rising from the gravelly ground cover; the desert fauna clutching the ground resolutely with their tough, woody roots; the air so arid it is almost peppery when it enters your nostrils; and the coarse, textured rock, metallic in odor, rendered alive with the visions and echoes of history, both geological and human.

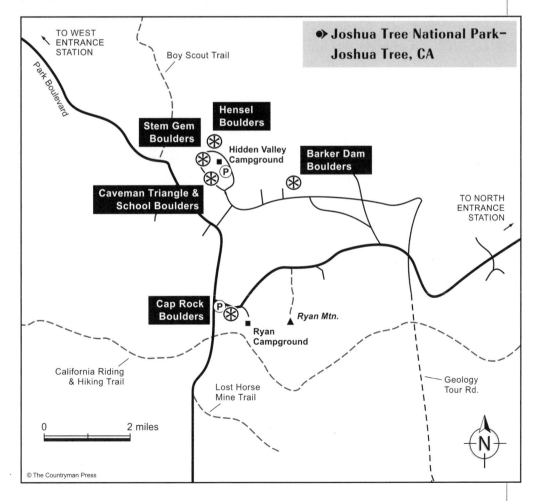

One of this country's premier rock climbing destinations of today, Joshua Tree also possesses tremendous historical significance for the overall rock climbing community in the United States. The park's vastness and scope should not be underestimated. It contains more than 5,000 established rock climbs, some of which date back to the mid-20th century and claim notable climbing figures such as Royal Robbins and Tom Frost as their first ascensionists.

The boulders, then, were never the main focus at Joshua Tree, and this remains true to this day, with the majority of vertically inclined visitors appearing to have more interest in J Tree's incredible traditional climbing opportunities (along with a few bolted routes here and there). Nonetheless, the sheer quantity and undeniable quality of the bouldering, the easy access to much of it, and the gorgeous setting make J Tree a great place to drop your crash pad and stay awhile. If you choose to camp in Hidden Valley Campground, you will immediately be surrounded by some of the most popular and long-established bouldering in the park, with many problems ascending the boulders around the campsites and many more within an easy 5- to 10-minute walking distance. When I visited, the scene was mellow and friendly, with few folks present who had any sort of "serious" interest in bouldering, making for fun and noncompetitive sessions on the rocks.

The Lowdown

➡ GETTING THERE

Driving directions: Take CA 62 from the east or west to the village of Joshua Tree. Look for signs indicating the entrance to the park (Park Boulevard), and follow the road to Hidden Valley Campground—a great place to start your introduction to J Tree's bouldering.

Nearest major airports: Palm Springs International Airport (760-318-3800; www.palmspringsairport.com; 3400 East Tahquitz Canyon Way, Palm Springs), about 40 miles from the town of Joshua Tree.

Public transportation: There is no public transportation that will take you into the park.

➡ CLIMBING CONCERNS

Cost: $10 per vehicle for a 7-day permit or $25 per vehicle for an annual permit.

Hours: The park is always open.

Land manager: The National Park Service (760-367-5500; www.nps.gov/jotr; 74485 National Park Drive, Twentynine Palms, CA 92277).

Finding the boulders: Hidden Valley Campground has an abundance of obvious boulders surrounding the paved loop. You'll find the classic Stem Gem near campsite 18, along with more problems, including The Pusher and The Totem. Also around the campground are the Caveman Boulder, Triangle Boulder, School Boulder (all on the left/west as you enter the campground loop), and Hensel Boulder (by campsite 12), among others. Across the main road from Hidden Valley, you can find more boulders. Cap Rock and Ryan Campground, farther down the road, also have a plethora of obvious boulders, as does Barker Dam.

Type of rock: Granite, mostly of an abrasive sort that can potentially destroy skin quickly.

Five good problems: Test your mettle on The Pusher (V0+, Hidden Valley), The Totem (V2, Hidden Valley), Stem Gem (V3, Hidden Valley), Soar Eagle (V6, Cap Rock), and Bald Eagle (V7/8, Cap Rock).

Range of grades: An abundance of problems in the V0 range and below, though beginners will likely find many of the V0-ish problems quite challenging—J Tree has few "gimmees." There are ample problems in the mid-range and upper levels, but there is great potential for more. People interested in establishing new problems should find plenty of them awaiting first ascents with a little bit of exploration.

Prime season: Joshua Tree is a great winter destination, with late fall and early spring being good times to plan a visit as well. Remember that it's the desert, though—nights can be wickedly cold, and a bone-chilling wind can pick up on some otherwise warm days, too.

Dogs: It's best not to bring your pup. Dogs are not allowed on trails or more than 100 feet from legally open roads and campgrounds. They must be on a leash not more than 6 feet in length at all times and may not be left unattended in a vehicle or tied to an object.

Special notes: If you want to try a boulder problem that is in an occupied campsite, please ask the folks camping there for permission before chucking down your pad and starting your session.

Coyotes are always of concern to park staff, and you are likely to see coyotes in the campground. Please do not feed them, as this can ultimately lead to their demise if they become too acclimated to people. Also be particularly wary if you do have your dog with you.

Stay on trails and do not damage vegetation. Be careful where you place your pad.

Guidebooks to area problems: The latest and greatest bouldering guidebook—almost 300 pages long and detailing more than 1,000 problems—is *A Complete Bouldering Guide to Joshua Tree National Park*, by Robert Miramonte (2003), available for purchase at www.fixeusa.com.

Online resources: To get you started, download a free guide from those great guys at Dr. Topo (www.drtopo.com). Friends of Joshua Tree (760-366-9699; www.friendsofjosh.org; P.O. Box 739, Joshua Tree), is a nonprofit organization dedicated to preserving access to Joshua Tree National Park for climbers, and their Web site is an extremely helpful resource for planning a visit. For details about all aspects of climbing in Joshua Tree, visit Climbing Joshua Tree (www.climbingjtree.com). A surfeit of sites exists with non-climbing-specific details on Joshua Tree National Park as well, such as www.joshua.tree.national -park.com.

Other resources: Joshua Tree Outfitters (888-366-1848; www.joshuatreeout fitters.com; 61707 CA 62, Joshua Tree) not only will outfit you with camping and climbing gear (rentals, too), but also will do your grocery shopping if you wish—you can even call ahead and have your kibbles ready and waiting when you arrive. Across the street from Coyote Corner (see *Showers*) is Nomad Ventures (760-366-4684; www.nomadventures.com), another climbing outfitter. Also across the street from Coyote Corner you will find Park Center (760-366-3448; http://joshuatreeparkcenter.com) a great place to stop for information about the park, maps, and gifts and to view artwork by local artists, as well as to grab a bite to eat—or a boxed lunch to go—at the Park Rock Café (760-366-3622; www.parkrockcafe.com). Inexpensive.

If you want to hire a guide—even to learn about bouldering—contact the Joshua Tree Rock Climbing School (800-890-4745 or 760-366-4745; www.joshuatreerockclimbing.com) or Vertical Adventures Rock Climbing School (800-514-8785 or 949-854-6250; www.vertical-adventures.com). Women who would like to be taught about rock climbing by another woman can check out their options at WomenClimb.com (800-94-CLIMB; www.womenclimb.com).

For more general information about bouldering in California, check out CaliforniaBouldering.com (www.californiabouldering.com).

Local climbing gyms: About 40 miles away in Palm Springs, you can pull down on plastic at Uprising Outdoor Adventure Center (888-254-6266 or 760-320-6630; www.uprising.com/Pages/Center_Home.html; 1500 South Gene Autry Trail, Palm Springs).

Nearby bouldering and climbing areas of note: The classic route-climbing areas of Tahquitz and Suicide Rocks are about 70 miles from Joshua Tree.

❖OTHER IMPORTANT STUFF

Camping: Until February 2004 camping in most Joshua Tree National Park campgrounds was free, but now a fee of $5 per campsite per night applies to the formerly free campgrounds, including Hidden Valley Campground, Ryan Campground, and Jumbo Rock Campground. There is a 14-day camping limit in the park.

Probably the best alternative to camping in the park is to try the Joshua Tree Climbers' Ranch (www.womenclimb.com/climbers_ranch/index.htm), "for climbers by climbers," a privately owned, 18-acre bivouac spot with water and porta-potties less than 15 minutes from Hidden Valley Campground. To get there, turn left off Park Boulevard when leaving the park in Joshua Tree and proceed .1 mile to Sunset Road. Turn left onto Sunset and start driving up the hill. When you stop seeing houses on your right, watch for a small, 12-foot road about 400 feet past the last house on your right—you need to drive over the curb to access this road at present (near the corner of Sunset and Alta Loma). The current policy for camping states, "Take what you need; give what you can." The rules for the Climbers' Ranch are few and easy to follow—mostly you just need to be low-key and respectful of others. Exit the ranch via Hillview Road.

Nearby phone: Coyote Corner (see *Showers*) has a pay phone. The Oasis Visitor Center in Twentynine Palms has a pay phone. The Black Rock Nature Center has an emergency telephone. The village of Joshua Tree has a number of additional pay phones available as well.

Showers: Coin-operated showers are available at Coyote Corner (760-366-9683, www.joshuatreecoyotecorner.com; 6535 Park Boulevard, Joshua Tree), an eclectic gift/camping/climbing-supplies shop located at the intersection of Park Boulevard and CA 62—the park entrance of choice if you camp at Hidden Valley Campground or the Joshua Tree Climbers' Ranch.

Water: You can fill your water for free at Coyote Corner—but it's nice to drop some money into the donation jar inside the store to show your appreciation for this service.

In case of emergency: Dial 911 for all emergencies.

To reach the Hi-Desert Medical Center (760-366-6126; 6601 White Feather Road, Joshua Tree), head for the intersection of Park Boulevard and CA 62. Take a right onto CA 62 and drive 2.1 miles. Take a right onto White Feather Road and proceed .1 mile to the hospital.

Nearby Internet hookup: The Joshua Tree Branch of the San Bernardino County Library (760-366-8615; www.sbcounty.gov/library/branch/main.htm; 6465 Park Boulevard), is conveniently located across the street from Coyote Corner (see *Showers*).

Restaurants: Close to the park entrance and Climbers' Ranch is the Crossroads Café & Tavern (760-366-5414; www.crossroadscafeandtavern.com; 61715 CA 62), where you can find moderately priced salads, sandwiches, and soups—healthy and great food—plus beverages (coffee, beer, and wine) and often live music. Inexpensive. Open Sunday through Tuesday and Thursday 7 AM–8 PM; Friday and Saturday 7 AM–9 PM; closed Wednesday. To get there, turn left onto CA 62 off Park Boulevard when leaving the park in Joshua Tree and proceed .3 mile to the restaurant.

Another great hang is The Beatnik Café (760-366-2090; www.jtbeat.com; 61597 CA 62). Settle in with a cup of coffee or a stein of beer and some ice cream or other food and listen to music, watch an independent film, get on the Internet, drum, or sing some karaoke, depending on the day's scheduled event or your mood. Inexpensive. Open Sunday through Thursday 7 AM–midnight; Friday and Saturday 7 AM–2 AM. Entertainment begins at 8 nightly. To get there, turn left onto CA 62 off Park Boulevard when leaving the park in Joshua Tree and proceed .5 mile to the café.

See also Park Rock Café, listed in *Other resources*.

chapter 5

UTAH AND COLORADO

FROM UTAH'S CANYONS AND VISTAS of red-hued sandstone stretching as far as the eye can see to Colorado's soaring snowcapped peaks, you can't beat these two neighboring states for breathtaking scenery, temperate weather, and proximate climbing destinations of all genres. And while everyone has probably heard of Rocky Mountain National Park and Zion National Park, both states feature numerous less-frequented public lands with marvelous natural treasures to be discovered—both for the pure enjoyment of nature left mostly to its own devices as well as for climbing and bouldering opportunities. In fact, with the preponderance of bouldering destinations available for all seasons, relatively close to one another, and on numerous types of stone in these two states, it wouldn't be too much of a stretch to label Utah and Colorado together as the country's bouldering heartland. Then again, the climbing bounty could be a result of the large number of boulderers and climbers who have chosen to call these states home, leading to more exploration and development of new areas than has yet to happen in other locales.

Utah and Colorado possess such a vast quantity of worthy bouldering areas that selecting a scant five to include in this book proved quite difficult—I could easily write up 25 worthwhile bouldering destinations in

Matt Wendling bouldering at the Secret Garden,
Little Cottonwood Canyon, Utah.

these states alone. So I had to choose bouldering areas based simply on my personal predilection for them, meaning that many high-quality areas are not included in this work, for which I am truly sorry. Nonetheless, you should find plenty of fun stuff to get you started. Utah is home to three of my current favorite bouldering spots in the country—isolated, powerful quartzite challenges in the desert at Ibex; fantastic and compelling sandstone pockets, edges, and slopers in Joe's Valley; and last but not least, technical granite test pieces in Little Cottonwood Canyon, which is easily accessed from Salt Lake City. For Colorado, you'll find information about the easily accessible, winter-friendly, and historically significant bouldering of Flagstaff Mountain, near the hip city of Boulder, nestled in the shadow of the Flatirons, as well as the lesser known and unique bouldering of Castlewood Canyon State Park, south of Denver—a great place for city dwellers to head for after-work sessions when light and weather permit.

Ibex—Delta, Utah

Cracked plates of mud stretch out across the parched, dry lake bed at the Ibex bouldering area almost as far as the eye can see, a faint, blurred mirror, perhaps, of the plated skin of dinosaurs who may have roamed this arid, windswept sandscape (located roughly 50 miles west of Delta, Utah) back when it was a lush, limpid lake teeming with fauna and flora. Basking in the hot sun one early March morning, I could almost picture the enormous ancient beings dipping their long necks low to the water to scoop up mouthfuls of nutrient-rich seaweed, chomping and crunching on the bright green, dripping bundles of sustenance as they plodded along slowly through the vast expanse of water some afternoon millions of years in the past . . .

But today's Ibex sports a beauty of a different sort, being one of the most isolated and desiccated bouldering areas to be found, a sun-beaten, dehydrated landscape of vast emptiness that sees a scant few inches of precipitation annually. A sensation of having entered a place where time ceases to pass, or at least begins to melt into a meaningless construct, brings to mind the flaccid timepieces depicted in Dali's *The Persistence of Memory* as you escape the rhythms of civilization and find yourself gazing off into the great barrenness surrounding the boulders. This powerful sense of emptiness dwarfs not only you and your friends, but also the boulders and the cliffs behind them, despite their impressive heights. All you need to do if you start to take your bouldering performance here too seriously is to step back and take a look around to remember how little any of it

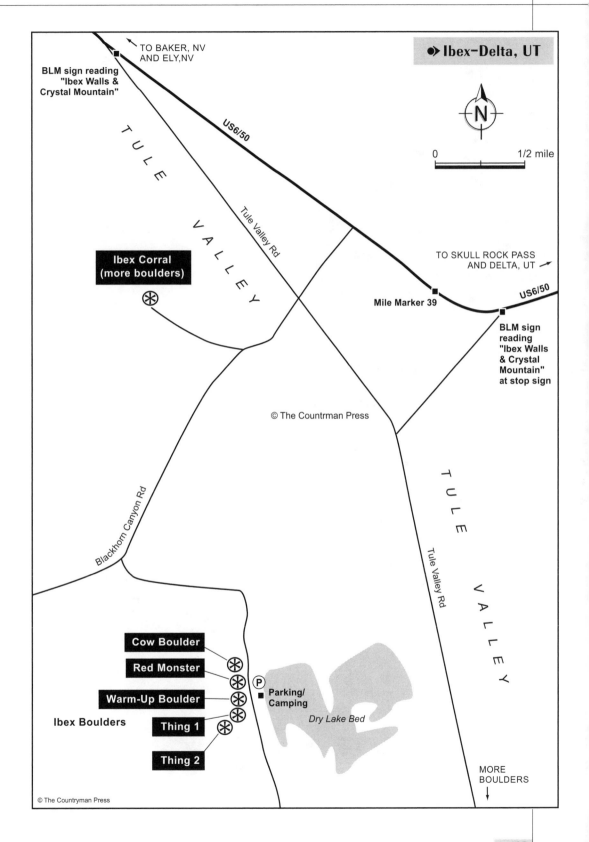

Ibex-Delta, UT

TO BAKER, NV
AND ELY, NV

BLM sign reading
"Ibex Walls &
Crystal Mountain"

US6/50

T U L E

V A L L E Y

Tule Valley Rd

N

0   1/2 mile

TO SKULL ROCK PASS
AND DELTA, UT

**Ibex Corral
(more boulders)**

Mile Marker 39

US6/50

BLM sign
reading
"Ibex Walls
& Crystal
Mountain"
at stop sign

© The Countrman Press

Blackhorn Canyon Rd

T U L E

V A L L E Y

Tule Valley Rd

Cow Boulder

Red Monster

P

**Parking/
Camping**

Warm-Up Boulder

Ibex Boulders

Dry Lake Bed

Thing 1

Thing 2

MORE
BOULDERS

BJ Tilden bouldering in Ibex, Utah.

matters in the face of this natural masterpiece that exists virtually unchanged by human intrusions (of course, this could change if boulderers and other users disrespect this gorgeous and unique environment).

A backdrop featuring towering cliffs of quartzite makes the main boulders of Ibex appear, at first glance, much smaller than their actual heights. For the most part they are quite tall, and the majority of the problems could be classified as highball or at least close to it. The hard stone abounds in crisp crimps, pinches, and slopers, with a pocket tossed in here and there. Sidepulling (pulling on holds that afford the most efficient and sensible usage when pulled at from a sideways angle rather than straight down or at another angle) and squeezing are mandatory on many classics, as is solid body tension to stay on the often small, slick, and solitary footholds. Powerful, dynamic moves nonetheless require some finesse for successful execution—a certain comprehension of exactly when to drop a foot off or exactly how to shift your body weight to make a pinch usable so that you can move your foot up to the next lone foothold. Expect a total body workout when you visit Ibex—you will feel sore from the tips of your fingers (that rock gets abrasive) through your core and right down to your toes . . . but it's worth it for the quality and concentration of classic problems as well as the distinctive setting.

The Lowdown

◈▶GETTING THERE

Driving directions: For best results, refer to a detailed atlas of Utah. From Salt Lake City, take I-15 South for about 80 miles (depending on your starting point). Take exit 225 and turn right onto UT 132. Follow UT 132 for 34.2 miles. Turn left onto US 6 and proceed 17.6 miles to Delta. When you reach Delta, US 6 will join US 50. At this junction, set your odometer and continue to follow US 6/50 for another 50 miles. After 50 miles, watch the mile markers —you will be making a left turn off US 6/50 onto a dirt road just before or just after mile marker 39. The shortest way to reach the main boulders at Ibex is from the turnoff just before mile marker 39, but at my last visit in March 2004, the BLM sign marking this entrance had been knocked down, making it next to impossible to see if you arrive at night, and difficult enough by daylight (the sign was propped up at the base of the stop sign on this road's entrance to US 6/50). If you miss this turnoff, don't sweat it—just take a left onto the dirt road 53.1 miles from the intersection of US 6 and US 50, indicated by a BLM sign for Ibex Wells and Crystal Mountain, which you will see on the right side of the road just after mile marker 39 (and after passing another BLM sign on the right for Blind Canyon, where you can also turn—see the map for more details). Turn left and proceed about 3.5 miles along this dirt road, which will curve to your left and head toward the obvious band of cliffs (also next to impossible to see at nighttime). The main bouldering area can be found just below the cliffs. Please don't just drive randomly through the desert or dry lake bed; try to stick to established tracks to minimize your impact.

From the south, drive north on I-15 to exit 174. Turn left onto UT 64 and go 2 miles. Turn left onto US 50, turning left again at 23.5 miles to stay on US 50. From the junction of US 6 and US 50 about 4 miles later, follow the directions above.

From the west, take US 6/50 west from Ely, Nevada, for almost 100 miles. After about 90 miles, after you pass mile marker 38, start looking for the BLM signs on your left. You can readily see the first BLM sign for Ibex Wells and Crystal Mountain before mile marker 39 on the left side of the road. If you wish, turn right and follow this road 3.5 miles to the bouldering and camping just under the obvious cliffs. If you miss this turn, keep your eyes out for the other entrance. After passing the entrance to Blind Canyon, also indicated by a BLM sign, look for a stop sign at an entrance road onto US 6/50 and the fallen BLM sign propped up against it on your right just after mile marker 39. Turn right, drive for 2.1 miles, and turn right again to head across the dry lake bed roughly 1 mile toward the cliffs to find the boulders.

Nearest major airports: Salt Lake City International Airport (801-575-2400 or 800-595-2442; www.slcairport.com; 776 North Terminal Drive) is about 180 miles from Ibex.

Public transportation: None.

> CLIMBING CONCERNS

Cost: Free.

Hours: Always open.

Land manager: Utah Bureau of Land Management, Fillmore Field Office (435-743-3100; www.ut.blm.gov/fillmore_fo; 35 East 500 North, Fillmore, UT 84631).

Finding the boulders: The main boulders at Ibex—Red Monster, Cow, Warm-Up, Thing 1, and Thing 2—are located beneath the cliffs adjacent to the camping.

Type of rock: Quartzite.

Five good problems: For those looking for V0–V3 problems, look no further than the Cow Boulder, which has a quality array in this range. Four other good problems include Mr. Sit and Spin (V3, Warm-Up Boulder), Ju (V6/7, Red Monster), White Arête (V7, Thing 1), and Meat and Potatoes (V8, Thing 2).

Range of grades: Though Ibex has gained a reputation as a better destination for those who can boulder at least V5 consistently, it does have a decent assortment of quality problems in the V0–V3 range, particularly on the Cow and Warm-Up Boulders. Those able to climb V6 to V10 will find a plenitude of highly concentrated problems on Red Monster, Thing 1, and Thing 2. The potential for more and harder problems exists as well.

Prime season: Ibex is best experienced in spring or fall. Winters can have nice, sunny days but also can have horrendous winds that make it next to impossible to climb. Summer temperatures will scorch you off the rocks.

Dogs: Allowed.

Special notes: The terrain at Ibex is fragile and unique, and therefore it is highly recommended that you refrain from having campfires—see Leave No Trace, www.lnt.org, for details on the negative impacts of campfires in the backcountry. Please do your part to help alleviate the increasingly negative impact of boulderers' pooping at Ibex by packing out your toilet paper and pooping responsibly. Go well away from the boulders or any trafficked area, dig a hole at least 6 inches deep, and then bury and disguise your business when done.

You are on your own at Ibex—it is the middle of the proverbial nowhere—so bring all of your supplies with you, including plenty of fuel in your car and plenty of food and water. You are 40–50 miles from any services. Pack out all of your trash.

Guidebooks to area problems: The 374-page *Bouldering Guide to Utah*, by Mike Beck, Jeff Baldwin, and Marc Russo (Springhill Press, 2003), includes more than 5,000 problems in 22 areas. The 216-page *Utah Bouldering*, by Chris Grijalva, Noah Bigwood, and Dave Pegg (Wolverine Publishing, 2003), includes Little Cottonwood, Joe's Valley, Ibex, Big Bend, and Ogden.

Online resources: The listing for Ibex on RockClimbing.com (www.rockclimbing.com) has some general information and a dozen photos. For more general information about bouldering and climbing in Utah, try ClimbingSaltLake.com (www.climbingsaltlake.com). UtahClimbers.com (www.utahclimbers.com) is a public forum for Utah climbers. The Salt Lake Climbers Alliance (www.salt lake climbers.org) has useful information about access, other pertinent area issues, climbing, and environmental responsibility. If you look hard enough, you'll find a few personal Web sites out there with photos and trip reports from Ibex as well.

Other resources: If you've never rock climbed or bouldered before and you want to hire a guide, try Moab Desert Adventures (877-ROK-MOAB or 435-260-2404; www.moabdesertadventures.com; 801 East Oak Street, Moab, UT) or Exum Utah Mountain Adventures (801-550-3986; www.exum.ofutah.com; c/o Black Diamond Center, 2070 East 3900 South #B, Salt Lake City).

The Wasatch Mountain Club (801-463-9842; www.xmission.com/~wmc; 1390 South 1100 East, Suite 103, Salt Lake City) offers members the opportunity to commune with and participate in organized activities with others interested in outdoor pursuits like rock climbing.

If you need to pick up camping supplies, stop in at the Delta Sports Center (800-413-3432 or 435-864-3432; www.deltasports.com; 299 North Highway 6). From the intersection of US 6 and South 500 East Street on the west side of Delta, go east on US 6 for 2 miles to find the store.

Local climbing gyms: About 140 miles away in Provo, you'll find indoor climbing at The Quarry (801-418-0266; www.thequarry.net; 2494 North University Parkway).

Nearby bouldering and climbing areas of note: Utah has gained quite a reputation as a world-class bouldering destination, with good reason. Along with many more boulders in and around the Ibex area, Little Cottonwood Canyon (see pages 118–126) and Joe's Valley (see pages 110–118), are among the state's numerous additional bouldering hot spots. You'll also find limestone sport climbing at American Fork and Logan Canyon, traditional climbing at Indian Creek and Big Cottonwood Canyon, and big wall climbing in Zion National Park, among many, many other noteworthy climbing areas in Utah.

◆▶OTHER IMPORTANT STUFF

Camping: Primitive camping with no amenities is free adjacent to the boulders. Please park and camp in the dry lake bed on the east side of the dirt road that runs north–south beside the boulders.

Nearby phone: Delta has numerous pay phones, including one at Hart's Food and Gas (435-864-4671; 76 US 6). From the intersection of US 6 and South 500 East Street on the west side of Delta, go east on US 6 for 1.2 miles to find the phone. Cell phones get sporadic service at best at the boulders in Ibex. You can also find pay phones to the west in Baker, Nevada (see *Restaurants*).

Showers: Shower at the West Millard Swimming Pool (435-864-3133; 201 East 300 North, Delta). From the intersection of US 6 and South 500 East Street on the west side of Delta, go east on US 6 for 1.3 miles. Turn left onto North 200 East and proceed .3 mile to the swimming pool. You can also find showers to the west in Baker, Nevada (see *Restaurants*).

Water: No drinking water nearby. Your best bet is to bring what you need with you. If you need to fill up, ask politely at one of the many gas stations in Delta, or purchase water at one of them. You can also fill water to the west in Baker, Nevada (see *Restaurants*).

In case of emergency: Dial 911 for all emergencies.

Drive to Delta Community Medical Center (435-864-5591; 126 South White Sage Avenue). From the intersection of US 6 and South 500 East Street on the west side of Delta, proceed 1.9 miles east on US 6/50, staying on US 50 when it splits from US 6. Turn right onto South White Sage Avenue and proceed .1 mile to the medical center.

Nearby Internet hookup: Delta City Library (435-864-4945; www.deltautah .com/pages/library.htm; 76 North 200 West). From the intersection of US 6 and South 500 East Street on the west side of Delta, proceed .9 mile east on US 6. Turn left onto North 200 West and proceed less than .1 mile to the library. Note that the library is open only in the afternoon and not on Sundays or holidays (I wouldn't want you to drive all that way for nothing).

Restaurants: About 50 miles away from Ibex, Delta has many options in the fast-food and semi–fast-food departments, which you will see for yourself if you drive down the town's Main Street (US 6), some of which are open even on Sundays.

For that protein fix—and a whole lot more—dine at the Loft Steak House (435-864-4790; www.theloftsteakhouse.com; 411 East Main Street, Delta). Choose from prime rib, chicken, or halibut steak, among other entrées, all of which come with a bunch of sides. Moderate to expensive. Open Wednesday through Saturday

Mike Snyder bouldering in Ibex, Utah.

5–10. From the intersection of US 6 and South 500 East Street on the west side of Delta, go 1.6 miles to find the restaurant on US 50 just after it splits from US 6.

If you want to have some food and fun 'round the clock, head west on US 6/50 for about 40 miles to Baker, Nevada, where among other restaurants and amenities you will find the Border Inn (775-234-7300; www.greatbasinpark .com/borderinn.htm), conveniently located on US 6/50 just after the Utah-Nevada border. Inexpensive. Not only do they have a restaurant featuring reasonably priced American fare open from 6 AM–10 PM daily (except for Christmas), but they also offer camping, a motel, groceries, cocktails and beer, snacks, an ATM, slot machines, a pool table, a service station, and more.

Joe's Valley—Orangeville, Utah

If you like sandstone for bouldering for the same reasons that I place it in a category above all other types of rock for bouldering, you will likely lose your heart to Joe's Valley, located about 30 miles southwest of Price, Utah. Brilliantly hued red, tan, and black boulders varying in size from one- or two-move wonders to limb-trembling highballs lie clustered in little gardens (helping to keep crowds minimal) all around the area collectively known as Joe's Valley. These boulder gardens can be found in three main areas: **New Joe's,** the **right fork of Cottonwood Canyon,** and the **left fork of Cottonwood Canyon.** Pockets, positive crimps, and even some slopers pepper the boulders' flanks, which range in angles from true technical slabs to ab-clenching overhangs. Though some complain of skin soreness, for me the rock at Joe's is less abrasive than the sandstone I've bouldered on

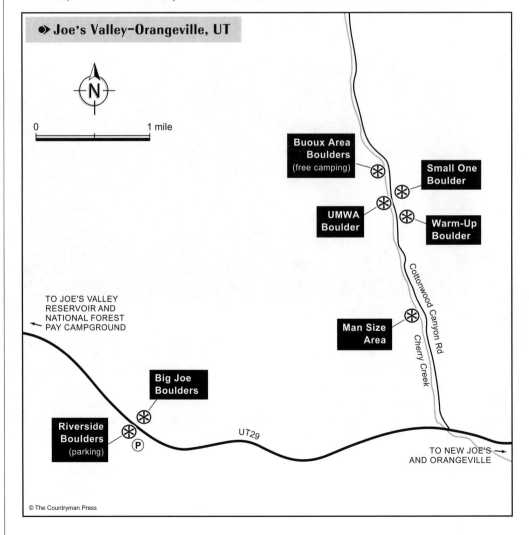

BJ Tilden ascends The Rail, a Joe's Valley classic.

Leslie Paul on Phoney Baloney in Area 51, Joe's Valley, Utah.

elsewhere. With an abundance of fairly evenly distributed problems ranging from V0 to V13 or harder, plenty of undiscovered or unclimbed boulders, a low level of sandiness on holds and top outs, and relatively secure and unfettered access, Joe's Valley should be on every boulderer's list of desirable destinations.

Beyond the bouldering, if you enjoy the surreal landscapes for which Utah is known, you'll find the area around Joe's to be beautiful in its own desolate and windswept way. Towering chosspiles (piles of loose, fractured, and/or dirty or sandy rock) of sandstone line the canyons that hold the boulders (hmmm, I wonder where all of those boulders came from?), and desert vegetation and wildlife abounds—as well as hunters, so watch your back when it's hunting season. All in all to me Joe's Valley represents a bouldering destination that has it all—free camping, free bouldering, a plenitude of problems at all levels, incredible natural surroundings, and no major access issues. Please help keep it that way by maintaining a low profile, obeying all posted speed limits, avoiding trespassing at closed areas, dealing politely with locals, and picking up after yourself. We wouldn't want Joe's to turn into another Hueco Tanks.

The Lowdown

➨ GETTING THERE

Driving directions: From US 6 north or south, take UT 10 south in Price. Proceed 27.4 miles. Make a slight right onto UT 29. After about 4 miles, you will reach Orangeville. Drive through Orangeville past the Food Ranch (your place for one-stop shopping!) to a T intersection. Take a right, and follow this road (still UT 29) as it bends left. The **New Joe's** areas (Area 51 and such) are found by turning right onto UT 57, a little more than 3 miles beyond the Food Ranch. A bit more than 3.2 miles later, just before mile marker 10, turn right onto a dirt road that will bump and jostle you as you drive up, curving left to the parking area, near an active oil well; don't park near it.

To reach the areas in the **right fork of Cottonwood Canyon,** continue to drive on UT 29 another 3 miles or so toward the reservoir until the road splits—you will see a sign for Cottonwood Canyon Road on the right. Turn here for the right-fork areas (many are visible right off the road).

Additional areas are located in the **left fork** as well—to reach Riverside, one of my favorite left-fork areas, drive up the left fork (following the sign for Joe's Valley Reservoir) and look for parking on the left after 3 miles. The Riverside area is down the hill from here; the Big Joe area is across the street and up the hill.

Nearest major airports: Salt Lake City International Airport (801-575-2400 or 800-595-2442; www.slcairport.com; 776 North Terminal Drive) is about 150 miles from Joe's Valley.

Public transportation: None.

➨ CLIMBING CONCERNS

Cost: Free.

Hours: You can boulder whenever you feel like it, but you cannot stay overnight at the Area 51 parking area.

Land manager: Much of the bouldering in Joe's Valley lies within the Manti-La Sal National Forest (435-637-2817; www.fs.fed.us/r4/mantilasal; 599 West Price River Drive, Price, UT 84501). Some of the bouldering lies on private land, so be sure to obey all signs (i.e., no camping, no fires, and no trespassing). When in doubt, stay out!

Finding the boulders: For **Area 51,** after parking, head down the wide path/road on the opposite side of the parking lot from where you entered, keeping your eyes open for a cairn on the right a short distance down the road, marking a path leading uphill. This is the path to Area 51.

For the **right-fork areas,** after you turn right onto Cottonwood Canyon Road, look for some of the more obvious boulders (Warm-Up, UMWA, Small One) right off the road; make sure to park your car completely off the road. To find Man Size—one of the better areas that lies a short hike off the road—1 mile after the turnoff from UT 29, park in the pullout on the left with the trees that resemble bonsai. Look for an obvious trail leading away from this pullout up the hill; this will take you to Man Size. Directions to the Buoux area can be found in *Camping*. Joe's has many more worthy areas as well, so don't be scared to poke around as long as you stay on public land.

Type of rock: Sandstone.

Five good problems: The Rail (V1/2, Riverside), Super Sloper (V3, Area 51), Walrus (V5, UMWA), SPAM (V7, Area 51), and Resident Evil (V10, Area 51) are just a few of the unique challenges you will find yourself faced with at Joe's.

Range of grades: From V0 to V13 with the potential for harder lines and more filling in.

Prime season: Joe's is best visited in early spring and late fall but has the potential for decent days in winter. Summers generally are too hot for serious sending, though shade can be found. Rain and even snow can put a damper on your trip in fall and spring; I've experienced both a number of times in these seasons.

Dogs: Allowed.

Special notes: One area in the right fork called Imperial Stout is closed, as it is on private property and the owner wishes to keep boulderers out. Please respect this closure, which is clearly marked with NO TRESPASSING signs. The Innumerables area, across the creek along UT 29, is also closed at this time.

Expect almost every business and service nearby to be closed on Sunday, with the exception of the Food Ranch.

Guidebooks to area problems: There are now two well-researched, comprehensive guidebooks to bouldering areas around Utah—the 374-page *Bouldering Guide to Utah*, by Mike Beck, Jeff Baldwin, and Marc Russo (Springhill Press, 2003), which includes more than 5,000 problems in 22 areas, and the 216-page *Utah Bouldering*, by Chris Grijalva, Noah Bigwood, and Dave Pegg (Wolverine Publishing, 2003), which includes Little Cottonwood, Joe's Valley, Ibex, Big Bend, and Ogden.

Online resources: You can download a free and decent guide from Dr. Topo (www.drtopo.com). Thedeadpoint.com has a Joe's Valley guide as well (www.thedeadpoint.com/guides/joes.html). For more general information about bouldering and climbing in Utah, try ClimbingSaltLake.com (www.climbingsalt lake.com). The listing for Joe's on RockClimbing.com (www.rockclimbing.com)

has more than 30 photos as well as some helpful beta. UtahClimbers.com (www.utahclimbers.com) is a public forum for Utah climbers. The Salt Lake Climbers Alliance (www.saltlakeclimbers.org) has useful information about access, other pertinent area issues, climbing, and environmental responsibility.

Other resources: If you've never rock climbed or bouldered before and you want to hire a guide, try Moab Desert Adventures (877-ROK-MOAB or 435-260-2404; www.moabdesertadventures.com; 801 East Oak Street, Moab, UT); or Exum Utah Mountain Adventures (801-550-3986; www.exum.ofutah.com; c/o Black Diamond Center, 2070 East 3900 South #B, Salt Lake City).

The Wasatch Mountain Club (801-463-9842; www.xmission.com/~wmc; 1390 South 1100 East, Suite 103, Salt Lake City) offers members the opportunity to commune with and participate in organized activities with others interested in outdoor pursuits like rock climbing.

For camping supplies and other bouldering-relevant stuff (last time I came through they had copies of *Bouldering Guide to Utah* for sale), stop at the Food Ranch (435-748-2725; 315 East 300 North; it's on UT 29, Orangeville)—you passed it on your way to the bouldering. You can also try Price at Pinnacle Sports (435-613-7529; 730 West Price River Drive). To satisfy all of your needs for climbing supplies, go to Provo's Mountainworks (801-371-0223; 2494 North University Parkway), about 100 miles away.

Local climbing gyms: About 100 miles away in Provo, you'll find indoor climbing at The Quarry (801-418-0266; www.thequarry.net; 2494 North University Parkway).

Nearby bouldering and climbing areas of note: Utah has gained quite a reputation as a world-class bouldering

Many attempt but few succeed—BJ Tilden tries his luck on one of Joe Valley's most striking lines, Black Lung.

Dave Thompson, Feels Like Grit, Joe's Valley, Utah. PHOTO BY MATT WENDLING

destination, with good reason. Little Cottonwood Canyon (see pages 118–126) and Ibex (see pages 102–109) are among the state's numerous additional bouldering hot spots. You'll also find limestone sport climbing at American Fork and Logan Canyon, traditional climbing at Indian Creek and Big Cottonwood Canyon, and big wall climbing in Zion National Park, among many, many other noteworthy climbing areas in Utah.

➤OTHER IMPORTANT STUFF

Camping: See *Showers* for two nearby pay campgrounds that also have water and showers. Primitive, free camping is available near the bouldering in the right fork of Cottonwood Canyon. One area where you can set up camp is the Buoux area, located on the left side of the road 2.4 miles after the fork. Watch out for a rather steep drop-off when you pull off the road into the pullout. The National Forest has seasonal pay campgrounds with limited facilities (no showers) in the vicinity as well; for contact information, see *Land manager*.

Nearby phone: The Food Ranch (see *Other resources*) has a pay phone.

Showers: Head for Huntington State Park (435-687-2491; www.stateparks.utah .gov/visiting/visiting.htm; P.O. Box 1343, Huntington), located about 8 miles north of Orangeville on UT 10. For $5 you can shower and enjoy the park for the day ($14 will pay for overnight camping). You can also head to Millsite State Park (same fees and contact info as above). Drive south on UT 10 for 7.5 miles to Ferron and then drive 4 miles west on Ferron Canyon Road.

Water: The Food Ranch has always allowed me to fill my water there, as I usually purchase other items when I stop there and always ask politely.

In case of emergency: Dial 911 for all emergencies.

Head for Castleview Hospital (435-637-4800; 300 North Hospital Drive, Price). Drive north on UT 10 from Orangeville for 26.7 miles. Merge onto US 6 West toward Helper. Proceed 1.9 miles and then make a U-turn at 760 North Street onto US 6 East. After .2 mile, take exit 240 toward Price. Go .4 mile and then make a sharp right onto West 100 North (Westwood Boulevard). Go .1 mile. Turn right onto Hospital Drive. Proceed .1 mile to the hospital.

Nearby Internet hookup: Orangeville Branch Library (435-748-2726; http://lib.emerycounty.com/library/orangeville/orangeville.html; 125 South Main Street). As you enter Orangeville on UT 29 coming from the boulders, drive past the T intersection where you turned right on your way to the boulders and continue on Main Street .3 mile to reach the library.

Restaurants: The closest place to grab a bite to eat is the Food Ranch (435-748-2725; 315 East 300 North [UT 29]), where you'll find not only grocery items but also deli food from the Castle Valley Pizzeria and Deli, baked goods, and lots of other goodies. Inexpensive. Monday through Saturday 6 AM–9 PM; Sunday 7 AM–8 PM.

For something above and beyond pizza, subs, or the like (which you'll find on Main Street in Orangeville and in neighboring towns), schedule a meal on the town for your rest day and head north to Price, where there are a number of restaurants to choose from, featuring Chinese, Greek, and Italian fare.

For Chinese food, try China City (435-637-8211; 350 East Main Street, Price). The house specialty is cashew chicken, but China City has much else to choose from. Inexpensive. Open daily 11 AM–10 PM. From Orangeville, return to US 10 and drive 27.5 miles north. Turn right onto Main Street and go .3 mile to find the restaurant.

If you're on the road early or late, or you simply want down-home American cooking, from breakfast served all day to burgers and steaks, stop at locally owned JB's of Price (435-637-1840; www.koal.net/Coupons%20by%20 Computer/jbsrest.shtml; 715 East Main Street), where you're not likely to spend more than $10 on your food at any time of the day unless you try pretty hard. Inexpensive. Open 6:30 AM–midnight daily. From Orangeville, return to US 10 and drive 27.5 miles north. Turn right onto Main Street and go .6 mile to find the restaurant.

Little Cottonwood Canyon—Salt Lake City, Utah

Tucked just minutes away from the fast-paced urban beat of Salt Lake City, the boulders and cliffs of Little Cottonwood Canyon enjoy a long history as a rock climbers' and boulderers' playground, for good reason. Though quarrying for granite for building purposes has altered some of the rocks (evidenced by some of the problems having holds formed by tools rather than natural processes), most of Little Cottonwood's vast quantity of boulders remain in their natural states, offering technically challenging slabs and vertical problems as well as steep and demanding powerful lines, all on mostly perfect granite. Broken up into little, or even large, gardens of boulders mostly set back in the trees lining both sides of the canyon, Little Cottonwood has an appeal that stems not merely from its easy accessibility, short approaches, and huge amounts of bouldering, but also from the quality problems available at all grade levels and the lovely natural setting that remains quite pristine in spite of its close proximity to the city.

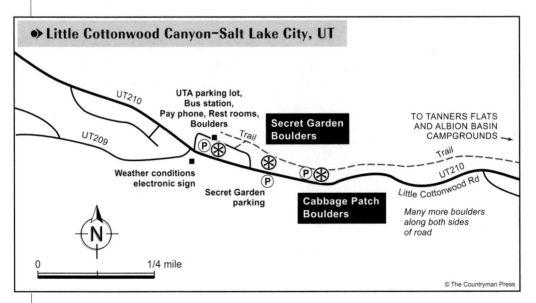

Of course, the explosive growth in popularity has called greater attention to bouldering's impact around the country, with particular scrutiny at areas like Little Cottonwood Canyon, which sees a ton of traffic due to its location and easy access. Boulderers visiting the canyon must take it upon themselves to be positive ambassadors for the rest of the community, to preserve and ensure future access. While I've stated before some basic ethics and guidelines that boulderers should adopt, I feel the need to state several of them again here, in the interest of making sure that you are aware and alert to some key areas of concern. Please obey speed limits and drive carefully—it is easy to miss turnouts and parking areas in Little Cottonwood, and they can fill up quickly. Don't cram another car into a full parking area; park elsewhere and walk that extra .1 mile. Watch for traffic when on foot and cross roads safely. Leave your dog at home—it cannot even be in your car (see *Dogs* and *Special notes* for details and more caveats about Little Cottonwood). Be aware that the Church of Jesus Christ of Latter-day Saints (or the Mormon Church) owns and manages some of the land upon which popular boulders lie; at present, these are open, but should you encounter NO TRESPASSING signs, you *must* respect them. I'm sorry to fill up the introduction with rules, but it is crucial that we work together on these issues to keep Little Cottonwood Canyon on the map as a bouldering destination.

The Lowdown

➡GETTING THERE

Driving directions: From I-80 east or west of Salt Lake City, take the Belt Route, I-215, south at exit 130. Follow the Belt Route 5.4 miles, and then take exit 6 (6200 South, Brighton and Solitude). Merge onto UT 190 East and follow it for almost 2 miles, then stay straight to join UT 210. After about 4 miles, you will see the weather and conditions sign at the entrance to Little Cottonwood Canyon. See *Finding the boulders* to start your adventure.

From I-15 north or south of Salt Lake City, take the Belt Route, I-215, east at exit 302. Follow the Belt Route 5.1 miles, and then take exit 6 (6200 South, Brighton and Solitude). Merge onto UT 190 East and follow it for almost 2 miles, then stay straight to join Wasatch Boulevard (UT 210). After about 4 miles, you will see the weather and conditions sign at the entrance to Little Cottonwood Canyon. See *Finding the boulders* to start your adventure.

Nearest major airports: Salt Lake City International Airport (801-575-2400 or 800-595-2442; www.slcairport.com; 776 North Terminal Drive), is about 25 miles from Little Cottonwood Canyon.

Public transportation: You can get relatively close to—or sometimes right to—the bouldering in Little Cottonwood Canyon by taking a Utah Transit Authority (UTA; 888-RIDE-UTA; www.utabus.com or www.rideuta.com) bus. November through

April you can ride via routes 96, 97, and 98 all the way to the Park & Ride at the base of Little Cottonwood on a UTA ski bus. The rest of the year, you'll find it's more of a walk from the closest stop (route 21), especially if you're carrying a crash pad.

●▶CLIMBING CONCERNS

Cost: Free.

Hours: 6 AM–10 PM (you risk a ticket if you leave your car parked along the road outside of these hours).

Land manager: The Salt Lake Ranger District of the Wasatch-Cache National Forest (801-733-2660; www.fs.fed.us/r4/wcnf/unit/slrd/index.shtml; 6944

Matt Wendling bouldering at the Secret Garden, Little Cottonwood.

South 3000 East, Salt Lake City, UT) manages much of the land in Little Cottonwood Canyon. The Church of Jesus Christ of Latter-day Saints (LDS Church; 801-240-1000; www.lds.org; 50 East North Temple Street, Salt Lake City, UT 84150), owns and manages some of the land as well.

Finding the boulders: Upon entering Little Cottonwood Canyon, you will see a sign displaying the current temperature and weather conditions. Across the street from that sign is a large parking lot (the bus stop) where you can park to access the boulders around the lot. You can also easily walk up the road to the Secret Garden boulder from this lot or else drive bit more than .1 mile up the canyon to a small pullout on the right. Park here and walk across the road to the obvious boulders. The Secret Garden has numerous great V0s as well as good mid-range problems and some challenging test pieces.

I also really like the Cabbage Patch, a little bit farther up the road (about .3 mile from the sign). Park in one of two pullouts on the left, and walk about 10 feet to the visible boulder. You can follow trails behind this boulder to find more fun stuff.

Little Cottonwood has many, many additional boulder gardens worth visiting, so if you run out of things to play on or want more beta, grab one of the guidebooks or hook up with a local.

Type of rock: Granite.

Five good problems: Good problems in the areas described above—along with an incredible amount of mostly unnamed V0s at both places worth doing—include Fat Albert Gang (V2, Cabbage Patch), Christopher Reeve (V2 or V6, Cabbage Patch), Twisted (V4, Secret Garden), The Dean Problem (V6/7, Cabbage Patch), and Copperhead (V10, Secret Garden).

Range of grades: A little something for everyone, from technical, moderate slabs with good landings to overhanging, double-digit power fests.

Prime season: Depending on your comfort zone, the prime seasons are either autumn and spring (if you're me) or winter (if you don't mind chancing cloudy, 45-degree or colder days and the potential for snow). Some folks feel that the friction so necessary for success on many of Little Cottonwood's problems is far superior in winter, and maybe it is, but I just can't take the snow or the chill!

Dogs: Not allowed—not even in your car. (See *Special notes* for details).

Special notes: A good place to check before your visit for the latest access concerns and issues, as well as for local regulations and ethics, is the Salt Lake Climbers Alliance Web site (www.saltlakeclimbers.org). It is particularly important that you make yourself an aware and responsible user of this area, since access concerns are ongoing. The Access Fund (www.accessfund.org) also has an area-specific posting on Little Cottonwood Canyon.

Be aware that you cannot swim or bathe (or even wash dishes or food) in the water in Little Cottonwood Canyon for the same reason that your dog (and any other domestic animal) is not allowed in the canyon—it is a watershed area that supplies some of Salt Lake City's drinking water, so trying to keep the water contaminant-free is a high priority. You can get a ticket for bringing your dog and for getting in the water, so please don't do either of these things.

Don't litter. Don't chip the rock. Don't trample or cut vegetation. Don't poop anywhere near the boulders or near water (and bury your poop per Leave No Trace [www.lnt.org] guidelines if you can't make it to the restroom facilities located at the parking lot across from the current conditions sign at the entrance to the canyon). Leave your loud music (or any audible music) and cursing at home or in the car. I could go on and on . . . so again, check the Web sites above before you visit, and use your common sense.

Guidebooks to area problems: There are two comprehensive guidebooks to bouldering areas around Utah—the 374-page *Bouldering Guide to Utah*, by Mike Beck, Jeff Baldwin, and Marc Russo (Springhill Press, 2003), including more than 5,000 problems in 22 areas, and the 216-page *Utah Bouldering*, by Chris Grijalva, Noah Bigwood, and Dave Pegg (Wolverine Publishing, 2003), which includes Little Cottonwood Canyon, Joe's Valley, Ibex, Big Bend, and Ogden.

Online resources: For an awesome, free, online guide complete with color photos of the boulders with problems drawn on them, check out Thedead point.com (www.thedeadpoint.com/guides/little.html). For more general information about bouldering and climbing in Utah, try ClimbingSaltLake.com (www.climbingsaltlake.com). The listing for Little Cottonwood Canyon on Rock Climbing.com (www.rockclimbing.com) has some helpful beta about both bouldering and route climbing in the canyon as well as photos. UtahClimbers.com (www.utahclimbers.com) is a public forum for Utah climbers. The Salt Lake Climbers Alliance (www.saltlakeclimbers.org) has useful information about access, other pertinent area issues, climbing, and environmental responsibility.

Other resources: If you've never rock climbed or bouldered before and you want to hire a guide, try Moab Desert Adventures (877-ROK-MOAB or 435-260-2404; www.moabdesertadventures.com; 801 East Oak Street, Moab, UT) or Exum Utah Mountain Adventures (801-550-3986; www.exum.ofutah.com; c/o Black Diamond Center, 2070 East 3900 South #B, Salt Lake City).

The Wasatch Mountain Club (801-463-9842; www.xmission.com/~wmc; 1390 South 1100 East, Suite 103, Salt Lake City) offers members the opportunity to commune with and participate in organized activities with others interested in outdoor pursuits like rock climbing.

You can find gear and camping supplies (and climbing walls—call stores for open climbing times) at one of two nearby REIs (www.rei.com): REI-Salt Lake City (801-486-2100; 3285 East 3300 South) and REI-Sandy (801-501-0850; www.rei.com; 230 West 10600 South, Suite 1700); or at Galyan's (801-456-0200; www.galyans.com; 41 South Rio Grande, Salt Lake City), which also has a climbing wall. Numerous additional outdoor retailers can be found in the Salt Lake City area, such as Outdoor Gear and Equipment (801-463-0266 [fax]; www.outdoorgearandequipment.com; 2840 Commonwealth Avenue) and International Mountain Equipment (801-484-8073; www.imeutah.com; 3265 East 3300 South), a retail equipment store that also rents out rock climbing shoes.

Local climbing gyms: In addition to the indoor climbing walls located at the stores listed in *Other resources*, the Salt Lake City area has several facilities dedicated mainly to indoor climbing, including the Front Climbing & Yoga Club (801-466-7625; www.thefrontslc.com; 1450 South 400 West), and Rockcreation Sport Climbing Center (801-278-7473; www.rockreation.com/sl/home.htm; 2074 East 3900 South).

Nearby bouldering and climbing areas of note: Utah has gained quite a reputation as a world-class bouldering destination, with good reason. Joe's Valley (see pages 110–118) and Ibex (see pages 102–109), both included in this book, are among the state's numerous additional bouldering hot spots. You'll also find limestone sport climbing at American Fork and Logan Canyon, traditional climbing at Indian Creek and Big Cottonwood Canyon, and big wall climbing in Zion National Park, among many, many other noteworthy climbing areas in Utah.

➽ OTHER IMPORTANT STUFF

Camping: You cannot park your car overnight or camp along the canyon road—and you are likely to get ticketed if you do. Little Cottonwood Canyon has two seasonal, developed Forest Service campgrounds, neither of which permits dogs. Tanner's Flat, 4.15 miles up the canyon, is open from May through October and costs $16 a night. Albion Basin, 10.9 miles up the canyon, is open

Alli, Twisted, Little Cottonwood Canyon, Utah. PHOTO BY MATT WENDLING

from July through September and costs $12 a night. For information on exact opening and closing dates or to make reservations, contact the National Recreation Reservation Service (877-444-6777; www.reserveusa.com).

Salt Lake City has numerous additional campgrounds, including the Salt Lake City KOA (800-562-9510 or 801-355-1214; www.koa.com/where/ut/44143.htm; 1400 West North Temple, Salt Lake City), where you will pay from $22 to $27 a night for a tent site. The campground has hot showers, a pool, and a hot tub, among other amenities. It's best to make reservations in advance. From the intersection of UT 210 and UT 209 (the fork as you drive down the canyon), follow UT 210, the right (north) fork, for 3.8 miles, where it changes to UT 190. Continue on UT 190 for 1.6 miles and then merge onto I-215 North. Go north on I-215 for 6.4 miles; it becomes I-80 West. Stay on I-80 West for 3.6 miles. Merge onto I-15 North (the exit is on the left and is marked Reno/Salt Lake/2100 South/1300 South/900 South). Go 3.5 miles and then exit once again onto I-80 West at exit 311. After another 1.6 miles, take exit 118 and turn right onto South Redwood Road (UT 68). Go .2 mile and turn right onto West North Temple; you'll see the campground after .4 mile.

Nearby phone: There is a pay phone located in the parking lot at the base of the canyon.

Showers: The Cottonwood Heights Recreation Center (801-943-3190; www.cottonwoodheights.com; 7500 South 2700 East) has multiple swimming pools—and showers, of course—that can be used by nonmembers for $4.50 per person. You can also opt to use the track or other equipment at the center (fees vary). From the intersection of UT 210 and UT 209 (the fork as you drive down the canyon), take the right (north) fork, UT 210, and proceed 2.6 miles. Turn left onto South 3500 East and go .4 mile. Turn left onto Bengal Boulevard and go 1.1 miles. Turn right onto South 2700 East and go .3 mile to find the center.

Water: If you are camping at Tanner's Flat or Albion Basin in Little Cottonwood, you can get water there. Otherwise it's best to bring water with you. Ask politely or purchase some at one of Salt Lake's many gas stations and grocery stores.

In case of emergency: Dial 911 for all emergencies.

The Salt Lake City area has numerous medical facilities. One nearby option is Alta View Hospital (801-501-2600; 9660 South 1300 East, Sandy). From the intersection of UT 210 and UT 209 (the fork as you drive down the canyon), go west on UT 209, the left (south) fork, for 4.3 miles. Turn left onto South 1300 East and proceed .3 mile to the hospital.

Nearby Internet hookup: The Whitmore Library (801-944-7533; www.slco.lib.ut.us/whitmore.htm; 2197 East Fort Union Boulevard). From the intersection of UT 210 and UT 209 (the fork as you drive down the canyon), follow UT 210, the right (north) fork, for 3.8 miles. Turn left onto Fort Union Boulevard and follow it for 2 miles to reach the library.

Restaurants: Whatever you want to eat, Salt Lake City probably has a restaurant to accommodate your tastes, from fast food (including the nation's first KFC) to haute cuisines of all genres.

I often use visits to Salt Lake as an excuse to partake of the city's startlingly good sushi restaurants. One favorite of mine is Tsunami (801-467-5545; 2233 South Highland Drive), where you will find finely crafted versions of all the standards (California rolls, tuna, freshwater eel, and so forth), plus fantastic and yummy variations (try the caterpillar roll). Other entrées are available as well, including options for vegetarians. Expensive. Open Monday through Thursday 11:30–2 and 6–10; Friday 11:30–2 and 6–10:30; Saturday 6–10; and Sunday 6–9. From the intersection of UT 210 and UT 209 (the fork as you drive down the canyon), follow UT 210, the right (north) fork, for 3.8 miles, where it changes to UT 190. Continue on UT 190 for 1.6 miles and then merge onto I-215 North. Go north on I-215 for 6.4 miles; it becomes I-80 West. Stay on I-80 West for 1.5 miles. Take exit 126 toward Sugarhouse. Turn right onto South 1300 East (UT-181) and go .1 mile. Turn left onto Wilmington Avenue and go .2 mile. Turn left onto Highland Drive and go less than .1 mile to find the restaurant.

Alli, Shot Hole Arête, Little Cottonwood Canyon, Utah. Photo by Matt Wendling

Closer to the bouldering of Little Cottonwood, the Porcupine Pub & Grille (801-942-5555; www.porcupinepub.com; 3698 East 7000 South [Fort Union Boulevard]) features 24 draft beers, plenty of vegetarian options, a tempting dessert menu, and brunch on weekends served until 3 PM. Inexpensive to moderate. Open Monday through Friday 11–11; Saturday 9:30 AM–11 PM; and Sunday 9:30 AM–10 PM. From the intersection of UT 210 and UT 209 (the fork as you drive down the canyon), follow UT 210, the right (north) fork, for 3.8 miles. Turn left onto Fort Union Boulevard and proceed less than .1 mile to find the restaurant.

In the morning, you'll find a plethora of options for gourmet coffee all around the Salt Lake City area, but if you want to support a homegrown business, get your morning cup of brew at Beans and Brews (801-944-8807; www.beansandbrews.com; 2335 East 7000 South [Fort Union Boulevard]). They also serve tea and cocoa, as well as a variety of pastries and other goodies. Inexpensive. From the intersection of UT 210 and UT 209 (the fork as you drive down the canyon), follow UT 210, the right (north) fork, for 3.8 miles. Turn left onto Fort Union Boulevard and proceed 1.8 miles to find the coffee shop.

Flagstaff Mountain—Boulder, Colorado

During the five or so years that I lived in Boulder, Colorado, I developed a deep appreciation for the myriad challenges contained upon the reddish-hued boulders scattered down the flanks of Flagstaff Mountain. At least as much as any other bouldering area I've visited, Flagstaff tends to blend in its boulder problems a number of disciplines and techniques, necessitating not simply pure power or excellent technical abilities, but a honed combination of the two. Visitors to Flagstaff will find problems requiring them to perform adeptly timed deadpoints between tiny crystals or to traverse through a lengthy series of somewhat technical and pumpy moves only to finish with a delicate, powerful, and scary crux sequence, among other challenges. Some folks just hate this kind of climbing,

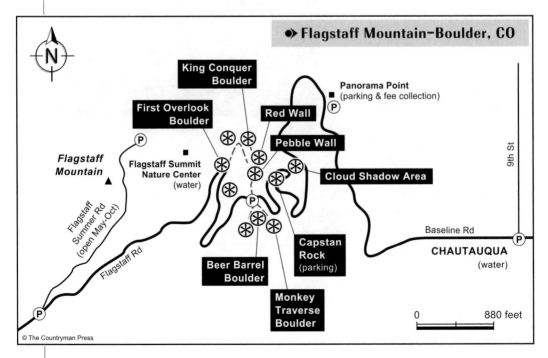

citing numerous reasons and excuses for their distaste, but I dig it—in fact, I think it's pretty cool that I've watched even "easy" problems at Flagstaff school some top-notch boulderers. On one outing where I was present, it took three boulderers who've all sent V10s multiple efforts to successfully climb a Flagstaff V2. Good stuff!

Though surely not the most popular Front Range bouldering destination these days, with the proximity of Horsetooth Reservoir, Carter Lake, Lumpy Ridge, Rocky Mountain National Park, Morrison, and the Flatirons, Flagstaff stood out in my mind as a place worthy of inclusion in this book. This is due not only to my personal affinity for the style of bouldering but also to its easy accessibility from the bustling activity of the trendy city of Boulder, a place filled with beautiful people who all appear to be involved in some sort of adventurous endeavor that helps them stay fit—if not rock climbing or bouldering, then mountain biking, trail running, skiing, snowboarding, or all of the above. If you're passing through, then, you might find yourself wowed or even intimidated by all of the SUVs topped with roof racks loaded with shiny outdoor toys, or by the incredible number of superfit, superhuman joggers, bikers, hikers, and walkers pounding the pavement or the trails. Don't be scared—you'll probably be able to find some space for yourself to at least take a turn climbing one of the many boulders on Flagstaff Mountain. And sometimes, you might even have the whole boulder to yourself!

The Lowdown

➡ GETTING THERE

Driving directions: From US 36 East or West, turn west onto Baseline Road. Follow Baseline west for about 1.5 miles, after which it curves to the right and becomes Flagstaff Road, which winds its way up Flagstaff Mountain. Stop at the information kiosk and fee station near Panorama Point on the east side of the road to pay your fee, or continue 1.2 miles farther to park on the left next to another fee collection station (additional parking is just ahead on the right). This parking area is a central place to leave your car, with easy walking access to the majority of the bouldering.

Nearest major airports: Denver International Airport (303-342-2000; www.flydenver.com; 8500 Peña Boulevard, Denver, CO), is about 45 miles from Flagstaff Mountain.

Public transportation: From the airport, you can ride to Boulder (via skyRide) and get pretty close to Flagstaff Mountain (via route 210 in Boulder) by taking a Denver Regional Transportation District (RTD) bus (800-366-7433 or 303-299-6000; www.rtd-denver.com; 1600 Blake Street, Denver).

Alli, Monkey Traverse, Flagstaff Mountain, Colorado. PHOTO BY MATT WENDLING

◆CLIMBING CONCERNS

Cost: Free for residents of Boulder County. For others, the cost is $3.00 per vehicle per day. Flagstaff Mountain has six well-marked self-service fee stations along the road; simply stop and follow the directions at the station to ensure that you do not receive a fine. Or you can purchase an annual pass for $15 in person or via mail from Open Space and Mountain Parks Administration (66 South Cherryvale Road, Boulder, CO 80303).

Hours: Open daily from 5 AM–midnight.

Land manager: City of Boulder Open Space and Mountain Parks Department (303-441-3440; www.ci.boulder.co.us/openspace; P.O. Box 791, Boulder, CO, 80306).

Finding the boulders: From the second parking area described above you can cross the road and follow the trail leading to the obvious boulders (Pebble Wall and, behind it, Red Wall), bypassing the switchbacks and continuing straight. Additional boulders, including the King Conquer Boulder, line the ridge up from these two boulders, with trails leading to them as well. Alternatively, you can follow the trail leaving from behind the fee collection station to find the Monkey Traverse, Beer Barrel, and numerous other boulders.

Type of rock: Fountain sandstone, a coarse, hard, and gritty rock.

Five good problems: My favorite problems include Southwest Corner (Beer Barrel, V0), Monkey Traverse (V4), Eric Varney Direct (Red Wall, V5), Face Out (King Conquer, V5), and Conquer Traverse (King Conquer, V7), among many other classics in the area.

Range of grades: More than 200 established problems ranging from V0 to V10, with the greatest concentration of problems in the V0–V4 range as well as a handful of ultraclassic test pieces in the V5 and up range.

Prime season: Flagstaff is best enjoyed on cool, crisp, sunny days, meaning that fall, winter, and spring can yield optimal temperatures, though winter days can be snowy and cold or simply too mucky around the bases of the boulders following a big snowmelt. For the most part, bouldering on Flagstaff in the summer tends to be grim, as the heat and small, sharp holds do not make for a fun combination.

Dogs: Allowed, but you must keep your dog leashed to a person (not a tree or other object) at all times unless it can meet the stringent voice- and sight-control requirements—see www3.ci.boulder.co.us/openspace/visitor/dogs.htm to see if your pooch can handle the rules. If you have doubts, put your dog on a leash, or face a hefty fine (up to $1,000) or jail time (up to 90 days) if a ranger observes you or your dog breaking the rules. You also must pick up after your dog or face the same potential penalties.

Special notes: Access at Flagstaff Mountain could become seriously threatened in the near future if boulderers do not respect the rules and regulations set forth for boulderers by the City of Boulder Open Space and Mountain Parks Department (OSMP). These include the following: Do not cut trees, move rocks, or otherwise alter the natural environment; do not litter, including not leaving climbing tape or wrappers behind (and pick up after others if necessary); remain on established trails; use care not to crush vegetation when you place your crash pad; if possible, use colored chalk that matches the rock or no chalk at all; and follow the principles of Boulder-based Leave No Trace (www.lnt.org). For detailed information, visit www3.ci.boulder.co.us/openspace/visitor/climbing/bouldering.htm.

Guidebooks to area problems: You have a choice when you visit Flagstaff, depending on your budget and whether you plan to visit other areas in Colorado as well. The most inexpensive option is to pick up a copy of *Rock & Ice: The Boulder Bouldering Map*, compiled by a number of Boulder-area climbers (Rock & Ice, 2001), which includes topos and information covering not only Flagstaff Mountain but also five other Boulder-area bouldering destinations.

If you'd prefer a guidebook to the bouldering in the area, for $18 you can pick up a copy of *Best of Boulder Bouldering*, by Bob Horan (Falcon Publishing, 2000).

Another option is to pick up a copy of *Colorado Bouldering*, by Phillip Benningfield (Sharp End Publishing, 1999), a 370-page tome with a plethora of Colorado bouldering destinations guaranteed to keep you busy for years. If that's still not enough, you can shell for the 269-page companion book, *Colorado Bouldering 2*, by Phillip Benningfield and Matt Samet (Sharp End Publishing, 2003).

Online resources: Your best bet is to visit ClimbingBoulder.com (www.climbing boulder.com), a site that has excellent, extensive information about bouldering on Flagstaff in addition to numerous other Boulder bouldering and climbing areas. FrontrRangeBouldering.com (www.frontrangebouldering.com) has lots of information on other bouldering areas around Boulder. Another up-and-coming Web resource is boulderCLIMBS (www.boulderclimbs.com/climbing), put together by accomplished Boulder climber and prolific guidebook author Richard Rossiter.

Other resources: Boulder has long been one of the country's rock climbing epicenters, as the vast amount of climbing-related resources in the town illustrates, starting with gear shops. Choose from Boulder's incarnation of REI, REI-Boulder (303-583-9977; www.rei.com; 1789 28th Street) or Eastern Mountain Sports (303-442-7566; www.ems.com; 2550 Arapahoe Avenue) or from independently owned stores like Neptune Mountaineering (303-499-8866; www.neptunemountaineering.com; 633 South Broadway, Suite A), which houses a cool assortment of historical climbing and skiing paraphernalia, and Mountain Sports (800-558-6770 or 303-442-8355; www.mospo.com or www.mountainsportsboulder.com; 2835 Pearl Street Suite B).

If you've never climbed before and you want to hire a guide or take a lesson, either contact one of the gyms listed below or choose from among a number of local guide services, including the Colorado Mountain School (888-267-7783 or 970-586-5758; www.cmschool.com; 341 Moraine Avenue, P.O. Box 1846, Estes Park; CO); Mountain Guides (303-258-0630; www.cmtnguides.com; 373 Bonanza Drive, Nederland); Alpine World Ascents (800-868-5429, 303-485-1511,

or 303-443-0212; www.alpine
worldascents.com; P.O. Box
1013, Boulder) or Expeditions
International (303-666-5523;
www.mtnguides.com; P.O. Box
17294, Boulder), among
others.

Local climbing gyms: You
have a selection of indoor
climbing gyms in Boulder, including the Boulder Rock
Club (303-447-2804; www
.boulderrock.com; 2829
Mapleton Avenue), The Spot
Bouldering Gym (303-379-
8806; www.thespotgym.com;
3240 Prairie Avenue), the
Colorado Athletic Training
School (CATS) Rock Climbing
(303-939-9699; www.cats
boulder.com/climbing.html;
2400 30th Street).

**Nearby bouldering and
climbing areas of note:**
Colorado's Front Range
possesses one of the highest
concentrations of quality
bouldering in the nation,
with an ample variety of rock
types, sizes, and styles of
bouldering to choose from.
Nearby bouldering areas of
note include the Flatirons,
Mount Sanitas, Horsetooth
Reservoir, Carter Lake, El-

Alli, Varney, Direct, Flagstaff Mountain, Colorado.
PHOTO BY MATT WENDLING

dorado Canyon, Morrison, and Castlewood Canyon (see pages 133–139), to
name just a few. Decent sport climbing can be found close by in Boulder
Canyon, Clear Creek Canyon, the Industrial Wall, and Table Mountain, among
others. Traditional climbers shouldn't miss out on Eldorado Canyon, with additional traditional opportunities available in Boulder Canyon, Rocky Mountain
National Park, and Lumpy Ridge. Colorado offers many more climbing destinations of all genres than those listed here as well.

►OTHER IMPORTANT STUFF

Camping: Camping in Boulder is a notoriously difficult prospect. Don't risk getting caught on Flagstaff Mountain after curfew (midnight), even if you're sleeping in your car, as curfew is strictly enforced. One nearby camping option is the Boulder Mountain Lodge (800-458-0882 or 303-444-0882; www.boulder guide.com/Lodge; 91 Fourmile Canyon), where you can pay $14 per night for a site that allows three people, one tent, and one vehicle ($5 per person extra for more than three). The weekly rate for a site is $80. Amenities include showers, hot tubs, and seasonal pools, with limited water and wastewater hookups as well as a public pay phone. No reservations. From the intersection of Baseline and Broadway, turn left (north) onto Broadway and proceed 1.4 miles. Turn left (west) onto Canyon Boulevard/CO 119 and go 2.8 miles. Make a slight right onto Fourmile Canyon Road; the campground is less than .1 mile further on the left.

Nearby phone: There is an outdoor pay phone at the Chautauqua Dining Hall (900 Baseline Road). To access it, drive down Flagstaff and back onto Baseline. Turn right into Chautauqua, and loop around to the dining hall, the large white structure set behind the grassy open area. Wild Oats Market, just past the intersection of Broadway and Baseline, has pay phones as well.

Showers: See *Local climbing gyms*, or stop by one of the City of Boulder's swimming pools or recreation centers, such as the North Boulder Recreation Center (303-413-7260; www3.ci.boulder.co.us/parks-recreation; 3170 Broadway). From the intersection of Baseline and Broadway, turn left (north) and drive 2.6 miles to the center. $5.60 gains you access to showers, as well as use of the pool, gymnasium, drop-in fitness, and weight room. Call for seasonal hours before you go.

Water: During summer months, you can fill your water at the pump cistern outside of the Flagstaff Summit Nature Center, 3.4 miles up Flagstaff Road from the base of the mountain. Turn right onto Flagstaff Summit Road and go .5 mile to find the center and the pump. Alternately, you can fill up and use the restroom from 10–4 daily at the Chautauqua Ranger Cottage. Turn left off Baseline at the sign for Chautauqua Park; the cottage is located at the south end of the parking area. If you ask nicely, most gas stations and stores in town are likely to let you fill your bottles, too—they're used to outdoorsy folks.

In case of emergency: Dial 911 for all emergencies.

Drive to Boulder Community Hospital (303-440-2273; North Broadway and Balsam). From the intersection of Baseline and Broadway, turn left (north) and drive 2.1 miles to reach the hospital.

Nearby Internet hookup: Boulder Public Library (303-441-3100; www.boulder .lib.co.us; 1000 Canyon Boulevard). From the intersection of Baseline and Broadway, turn left (north) onto Broadway and drive 1.2 miles. Turn left onto Marine Street. After less than .1 mile, turn right onto 11th Street. Proceed less than .1 mile to the parking lot at 11th Street and Arapahoe Avenue, right by the main entrance to the library.

Restaurants: Boulder has an abundance of distinguished dining establishments as well as feed-your-face eateries, making it hard to recommend a scant few. If you're in town for any period of time, a stroll down the Pearl Street Mall (just head north on Broadway to find Pearl Street) will tempt you with many dining options, as well as talented street entertainers and an abundance of specialty shops.

For fast and filling, try Noodles & Company (303-247-9978; www.noodles.com; 2850 Baseline Road), a Colorado-based chain that serves up piping hot bowls of noodles in all sorts of flavors and styles. Plenty of selections are available for vegetarians, including a salad menu. Inexpensive. Open Sunday through Wednesday 11–9; Thursday through Saturday 11–10. From the intersection of Baseline and Broadway, head east on Baseline .3 mile to find the restaurant.

One of *the* places to see and be seen around Boulder—as well as to enjoy a great, if a bit more pricey, meal—is the Med, or Mediterranean Restaurant (303-444-5335; www.themedboulder.com; 1002 Walnut Street). You can sit amongst the hip crowd either indoors or outside on the patio and sip a microbrew or a glass of wine while popping a variety of tapas (tasty little appetizers) into your mouth while you await the main event. Expensive. Open Sunday through Wednesday 11–10; Thursday through Saturday 11–11; lunch served until 3 PM daily. From the intersection of Baseline and Broadway, drive 1.4 miles north on Broadway. Turn left onto Canyon Boulevard/CO 119 and go less than .1 mile. Turn right onto 11th Street and start looking for a parking spot. After less than .1 mile on 11th, turn left onto Walnut; the restaurant is less than .1 mile on Walnut.

Boulder is home to an abundance of coffee shops of both the evil empire sort and the independent or local chain sort to hook you up in the morning with java and breakfast food. The closest stop on the way to Flagstaff Mountain is Peaberry Coffee (303-499-7337; www.peaberrycoffee.com; 2400 Baseline Road), located at the corner of Baseline and Broadway. Open Monday through Friday 6 AM–10 PM; Saturday 6:30 AM–10 PM; and Sunday 7 AM–10 PM.

Castlewood Canyon State Park—Franktown, Colorado

Not too far south of Denver lie the more than 2,000 acres that make up Castlewood Canyon State Park, a showpiece of preservation that encompasses the northern end of the distinctive Black Forest, or Palmer Divide, unique due to its peninsular geological form. Protruding east like a long, elevated finger (elevations in Castlewood Canyon State Park range from 6,000 to 6,200 feet) from the mountains of the Front Range, the ridgelike Black Forest splits the drainages of the Platte and Arkansas Rivers, separating two dissimilar ecosystems—the Front Range foothills and the plains grasslands. The resulting ecosystem—complete with Cherry Creek flowing through the canyon as a water source—has proven hospitable to a startlingly diverse array of flora and fauna. Visitors to Castlewood Canyon State Park

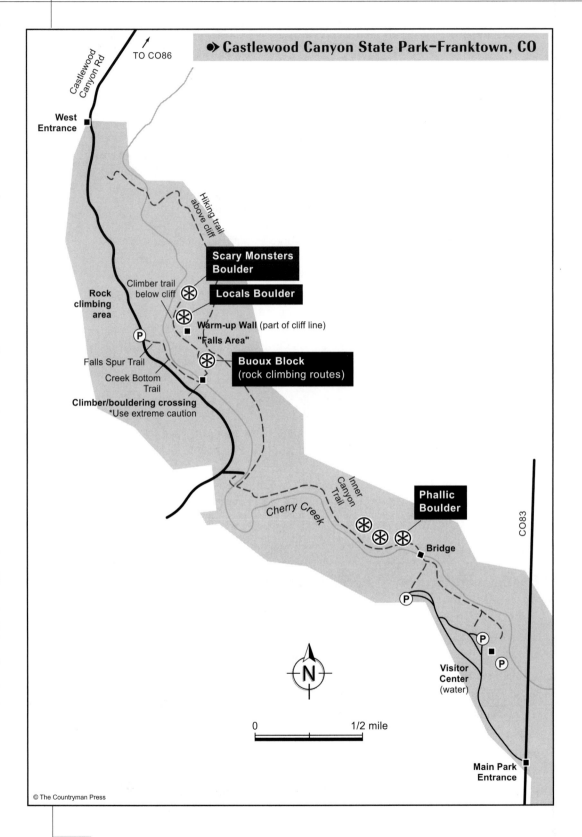

◆ **Castlewood Canyon State Park–Franktown, CO**

TO CO86

Castlewood Canyon Rd

West Entrance

Hiking trail above cliff

Scary Monsters Boulder

Climber trail below cliff

Locals Boulder

Rock climbing area

Warm-up Wall (part of cliff line)

"Falls Area"

Buoux Block (rock climbing routes)

Falls Spur Trail

Creek Bottom Trail

Climber/bouldering crossing
*Use extreme caution

Inner Canyon Trail

Cherry Creek

Phallic Boulder

CO83

Bridge

N

Visitor Center (water)

0   1/2 mile

Main Park Entrance

© The Countryman Press

will find plant life that includes ponderosa pines and Douglas firs along with wet-lands and short-grass prairie, as well as mule deer, coyotes, rattlesnakes, and more than 100 species of birds, among other fauna.

Because of its close proximity to Denver, Castlewood Canyon makes for an easy after-work escape into nature in the summer for those who live and work on the south side of the city or in its southern neighbor, Castle Rock. And though Castlewood Canyon may not have the best bouldering the Front Range has to offer, its location and inspiring environment—as well as the interesting nature of the rock itself—prompted its inclusion as a selected destination. Not only will you find yourself in a fantastic setting, but also you'll find yourself itching to pull and step on the knobs and pebbles (or the pockets they leave behind) of the Castle Rock conglomerate, an odd and distinctive rock made up of cobbles ce-mented into a hardened matrix of volcanic ash that has proven extremely resis-tant to erosion.

The Lowdown

➡GETTING THERE

Driving directions: From I-25 North or South, take exit 182 at Castle Rock. Turn east onto CO 86. Drive about 6 miles to Franktown. Turn south onto CO 83 (South Parker Road). Drive 5 miles south to the main park entrance. You can also access the park from CO 86 by turning right (south) onto Castlewood Canyon Road and following it 2.3 miles to the park's west entrance.

Nearest major airports: Denver International Airport (303-342-2000; www.fly denver.com; 8500 Peña Boulevard, Denver, CO), is about 40 miles from Castlewood Canyon State Park.

Public transportation: None.

➡CLIMBING CONCERNS

Cost: $5 per vehicle a day. Annual passes to all Colorado State Parks cost $55 per vehicle and can be purchased at Castlewood Canyon or online at http://parks .state.co.us/home/fees.asp.

Hours: 8 AM until sunset year-round.

Land manager: The land manager can be contacted at Castlewood Canyon State Park (303-688-5242; http://parks.state.co.us/default.asp?parkid= 76&action=park; 2989 South State Highway 83, Franktown, CO 80116).

Finding the boulders: Though figuring out where the sport climbs are is no sweat (just look to the canyon walls), finding some of the boulders in Castle-wood Canyon can be trying, even with a great map and guidebook, so bear with me (and look at the map of the park). Some of the easiest boulders to locate are accessible from the main entrance. Park at the westernmost parking area and walk north down the paved Inner Canyon Trail. Cross the bridge and turn left, and after a short walk you'll find the unmistakable Phallic Boulder, filled with easy, if somewhat frightening, highballs. Numerous additional boulders are located just alongside and off this trail a little farther west.

From the west entrance to the park you can access a number of classic areas, but the approach is rather grim, so be patient and use caution. Park in the last parking area on the left. Take the Falls Spur down to Creek Bottom Trail. After walking south a short way on Creek Bottom, you will see the falls on your left. Scramble down the hillside above the falls (look for marks of other climbers' passings), cross the creek, and scramble up a steep, eroded gully on the other side, using great caution. You will find a north–south trail as well as a trail heading straight up the hill toward the cliffs. Take the distinct trail up the hill to the cliffs, passing the Buoux Block (sport routes) on the way. When you reach the base of the cliffs, go north for roughly 150 yards to reach the Warm-Up Wall, a short section of cliff characterized by perfect flat landings. A faint network of trails or just your curiosity and explorative nature will enable you to find the boulders—Locals Boulder and Scary Monsters, in particular—located in the shrub oak down the hillside and west of the Warm-Up Wall. I promise that the frustration of being lost for a bit is worth your while, for these boulders house some of Castlewood's finest problems.

Type of rock: Conglomerate.

Five good problems: Unnamed V0 (Warm-Up Wall), Unnamed V1 (Warm-Up Wall), Unnamed V2 (Scary Monsters Boulder), Scary Monsters (V5), and Locals Only (V5, Locals Boulder) are all fine representations of Castlewood's breed of bouldering.

Range of grades: Established problems ranging from V0 up to at least V7/8, with the likely potential for more.

Prime season: Great for bouldering in any season of the year, since the boulders face all directions and have varying degrees of shade or sun, depending on the plant life surrounding them and their position in the canyon. Your best bets are probably spring and fall for perfect sending temperatures—especially fall.

Dogs: Dogs must be on a leash not more than 6 feet in length at all times.

Special notes: Hooray! This park actually acknowledges rock climbing and bouldering as two of its activities and attractions (though placing fixed hardware requires a special-use permit). Do your part in showing that climbers and boulderers are an environmentally conscious user group and clean up your trash, watch your language (families hike here), and pay the entry fee. Be aware that rattlesnakes dwell in Castlewood Canyon, and use caution, particularly if your pooch is with you. Campfires are prohibited, as is alcohol, except 3.2 beer.

Guidebooks to area problems: Pick up a copy of *Colorado Bouldering*, by Phillip Benningfield (Sharp End Publishing, 1999), a 370-page tome with a plethora of

Colorado bouldering areas—including Castlewood Canyon—guaranteed to keep you busy for years. There is also a 269-page companion book—with more areas as well as new problems in the areas covered in the first book—*Colorado Bouldering 2*, by Phillip Benningfield and Matt Samet (Sharp End Publishing, 2003).

Online resources: Castlewood Canyon State Park has a page dedicated to rock climbing (http://parks.state.co.us/default.asp?action=article&contentid=612& parkid=76), or go to the park's home page and click on "Things to Do," then choose "Rock Climbing." ClimbingBoulder.com (www.climbingboulder.com) has information about specific problems and areas to boulder in Castlewood Canyon, as well as sport climbing information. FrontRangeBouldering.com (www.front rangebouldering.com) has information on other bouldering areas nearby.

Other resources: If you need to stock up on gear, REI (www.rei.com) has four stores nearby, depending on what direction you're headed or coming from. These include REI-Englewood (303-858-1726; 9637 East County Line Road), about 15 miles away; REI-Lakewood (303-932-0600; 5375 South Wadsworth Boulevard), about 25 miles away; REI-Denver Flagship (303-756-3100; 1416 Platte Street), with a 45-foot indoor climbing wall, about 30 miles away; and REI-Colorado Springs (719-260-1455; 1376 East Woodmen Road), about 35 miles away.

If you have never climbed or bouldered before and you'd like to hire a guide or take a lesson, either contact one of the gyms listed below or the REIs listed above or choose from a number of local guiding services, including the Colorado Mountain School (888-267-7783 or 970-586-5758; www.cmschool.com; 341 Moraine Avenue, P.O. Box 1846, Estes Park), Colorado Mountain Guides (303-258-0630; www.cmtnguides.com; 373 Bonanza Drive, Nederland), Alpine World Ascents (800-868-5429, 303-485-1511, or 303-443-0212; www.alpine worldascents.com; P.O. Box 1013, Boulder), or Expeditions International (303-666-5523; www.mtnguides.com; P.O. Box 17294, Boulder); among others.

Nearby in Golden, you'll find the American Mountaineering Center, headquarters for the American Alpine Club (303-384-0110; www.americanalpine club.org; 710 10th Street, Suite 100), "a nonprofit organization dedicated to promoting climbing knowledge, conserving mountain environments, and serving the American climbing community," and the Colorado Mountain Club (303-279-3080, www.cmc.org; 710 10th Street), "the state's premier outdoor organization and one of the largest outdoor recreation, education, and conservation clubs in the country."

Local climbing gyms: About 15 miles away in Centennial, you'll find Rock'n & Jam'n 2 (303-254-6299; www.rocknandjamn.com; 7390 South Fraser Street), brand new in 2004. Denver has several other indoor climbing facilities, including Paradise Rock Gym (303-286-8168; www.paradiserock.com; 6260 North Washington Street Unit 5), and Thrillseekers (303-733-8810; www.thrill seekers.cc); 1912 South Broadway).

Nearby bouldering and climbing areas of note: Colorado's Front Range possesses one of the highest concentrations of quality bouldering in the nation, with an ample variety of rock types, sizes, and styles of bouldering from which to choose. Nearby bouldering areas of note include the Flatirons, Horsetooth Reservoir, Carter Lake, Eldorado Canyon, Morrison, and Flagstaff Mountain (see pages 126–133), to name just a few. Decent sport climbing can be found close by in Clear Creek Canyon, Devils Head, and Table Mountain, as well as south of Colorado Springs at Shelf Road. Traditional climbers shouldn't miss out on Eldorado Canyon, with more traditional opportunities available in Boulder Canyon, Rocky Mountain National Park, and Lumpy Ridge. Colorado offers many more climbing destinations of all genres.

❧OTHER IMPORTANT STUFF

Camping: Not allowed in the park. You can camp close to Castlewood Canyon in style at Lake of the Rockies Retreat, Camping & Cabin Resort (719-481-4227 or 800-429-4228; www.lakeoftherockies.com; 99 Mitchell Avenue, Monument), where you will find showers, Internet access, laundry facilities, a heated pool, hot tubs, and more. Open April 1 through October 31; expect to pay in the neighborhood of $20 per night for a tent site, depending on the dates. From the main entrance to the park, drive south on CO 83 for 18.4 miles. Turn right onto CO 105. After 5.2 miles, turn left onto Third Street. Proceed .4 mile, and then turn left onto Washington Street. After .1 mile, turn right onto Second Street. Go .1 mile, and then turn left onto Mitchell Avenue. Go .4 mile to find the campground.

Another nearby camping option is the Castle Rock Campground (303-681-3169 or 800-387-9396; www.castlerockcampground.com; 6527 South I-25, Castle Rock). Rates start at $19.50 a day for a tent site with two people and no hookups. From the main entrance of the park, drive north on CO 83 for 4.3 miles. Turn left onto CO 86. Go 6.5 miles. Make a slight right onto Fifth Street. After .3 mile, turn right onto Wilcox; it becomes Wolfensberger Road/ CR 46. Merge onto I-25 South. After 7.8 miles, take exit 174 toward Tomah Road. Turn right to access the campground.

Nearby phone: If it's an emergency, go to the park headquarters. Otherwise, you'll find ample pay phones north along CO 83 at the numerous gas stations and shopping centers lining the road in Franktown and Parker.

Showers: Go to the Parker Recreation Center (303-841-4500; www.parkeronline .org/recreation_information/recreation_center.asp; 17301 Lincoln Avenue, Parker), where $4 will gain you access not only to showers but also to an indoor pool with a waterslide and sauna, tons of workout equipment, and more. From the main entrance to Castlewood Canyon State Park, go north on CO 83 for 14.5 miles. Turn left onto Lincoln Avenue and go .8 mile to find the center.

Water: Available in the park.

In case of emergency: Dial 911 for all emergencies. The park headquarters has a telephone line.

Drive to Parker Adventist Hospital (303-269-4000; www.parkerhospital.org; 9395 Crown Crest Boulevard, Parker). From the main entrance of the park, drive north on CO 83 (South Parker Road) for 16.1 miles. Turn right into the newly developed Crown Point area (Crown Crest Boulevard)—the hospital is on the southeast corner of E-470 and South Parker Road.

Nearby Internet hookup: Parker Public Library (303-841-3503; http://douglas .lib.co.us; 10851 South Crossroads Drive, Parker) is easy to find. From the main entrance of Castlewood Canyon State Park, drive north on CO 83 (South Parker Road) for 13.2 miles. Turn left onto East Main Street. After less than .1 mile, turn right onto South Crossroads Drive and proceed less than .1 mile to the library.

Restaurants: If you're headed south, stop in on the way at Grumpy Gringo (303-660-9905; www.grumpygringo.com; 215 Wilcox Street, Castle Rock). Open daily at 11 AM, the restaurant serves up freshly prepared Mexican entrées including enchiladas, flautas, tacos, and even some "real gringo" items, along with six homemade sauces (including a vegetarian sauce). Inexpensive to moderate. From the main entrance of the park, go north on CO 83 for 4.3 miles. Turn left onto CO 86 and proceed 6.5 miles. Make a slight right onto Fifth Street. After .3 mile, turn left onto Wilcox. The restaurant is less than .1 mile on Wilcox.

If you're driving north toward Denver, stop for a bowl of tasty pasta at Noodles & Company (720-842-5330; www.noodles.com; 11153 South Parker Road, Parker), a Colorado-based chain that serves up a wonderful assortment of pasta dishes as well as salads, soups, and bread. Inexpensive. Open Sunday through Wednesday 11–9; Thursday through Saturday 11–10. From the main entrance of the park, drive north on CO 83 for 13.2 miles. Make a U-turn at East Main Street and go .3 mile south on South Parker Road to find the restaurant.

Need coffee? One option is Capri Coffee Break (303-841-6928; www.capri coffee.com; 13049 South Parker Road, Parker), next to King Soopers, where you'll find all sorts of coffee concoctions and smoothies. From the main entrance of the park, drive north on CO 83 for 15.4 miles. Make a U-turn at Crown Crest Boulevard and go .3 mile south on South Parker Road.

chapter 6

SOUTHWEST

I T'S WHERE OCTOPI-LIKE SAGUARO CACTI spread their twisted and warped arms, frozen in loopy gestures of defiance against the heat and aridity of their desert environs, and it's where towering, majestic ponderosa pines line the sides of roads, standing tall as the dominant trees in the thickly wooded forests that cover the landscape as far as the eye can see. It's also a region where Native Americans found bastions of security, constructing amazingly wrought places to live in equally breathtaking settings, such as the remarkably engineered structures set in caves high in the cliffs of Gila Cliff Dwellings National Monument in New Mexico. And it is an area where the wind batters the rocks, trees, and mountains, sculpting amazing features into cliff faces and smaller rocks alike. From the high-altitude city of Flagstaff, Arizona, to the border city of El Paso, Texas, the Southwest's fantastic diversity of cultures, climates, communities, and climbing areas should prove interesting and inspirational to the visiting boulderer.

Winter draws crowds of boulderers here—or, more specifically, to Hueco Tanks State Historical Site. There you will discover a full-blown bouldering scene, complete with visiting rock stars, spraylords aplenty, nightly gatherings around campfires to share beta, sends, and gossip, and, of course, internationally renowned bouldering of the highest quality. If such a scene doesn't appeal to you, don't worry—just head north into New Mexico and set up a solitary, misanthropic camp at the isolated City of

Scott Pettitt perches atop the amazingly featured Island Entrance Boulder
at Priest Draw, near Flagstaff, Arizona.

Rocks State Park, where you are unlikely to see another person, let alone a boulderer, due to its remote location and lack of established (or at least recorded) boulder problems, which keeps the number chasers in a bouldering galaxy far, far away. Stop, too, at Box Canyon, near Socorro, New Mexico, where you will probably encounter a group of enthusiastic locals who are working hard to develop the potential of this oft-overlooked area. And though you may immediately think "desert" when contemplating a visit to Arizona, think again if you want to check out the higher-elevation bouldering areas around Flagstaff, like Priest Draw.

Priest Draw—Flagstaff, Arizona

Located just outside Flagstaff, Priest Draw features its own distinctive brand of bouldering on impeccable limestone bands and boulders. Though vertical and gradually overhanging boulders and sections of the short cliff bands are available, the standout characteristic of this area is its abundance of horizontal or near-horizontal boulder problems on incredibly featured roofs of flawless limestone. Pockets and slopers cover the stone, which has to be some of the most solid limestone anywhere. Almost all of the rocks have some sort of cheater ridge or edge allowing for better purchase for the not-so-sloper inclined climbers.

In addition to perfect rock, the boulders at Priest Draw are set in a lovely area with ponderosa pines, are easily accessible, and offer bouldering options for anyone, from the most inexperienced novice to the world-class expert. Boulders like the Triangle Boulder and the Island Entrance Boulder will wow you on your first visit with their unbelievably featured surfaces—huge jugs, horns, and runnels make for tremendous warm-ups and beginner fun. The Island Entrance Boulder, in particular, seems like a naturally sculpted jungle gym. If you're an intermediate or advanced boulderer, you can't leave Priest Draw without sampling at least one of its horizontal roofs—some of them are actually quite "easy," at least in the world of bouldering.

The Lowdown

➨GETTING THERE

Driving directions: From Route 66 (the main drag) and Beaver Street in Flagstaff, continue on Route 66 West for .9 mile as it turns a corner, and then stay straight to get on South Milton Road and proceed for 1 mile. Turn right onto West Forest Meadows Road (AZ 89 Alternate). After .1 mile, make a left onto South Beulah Boulevard, following AZ 89 Alternate. Continue for .6 mile,

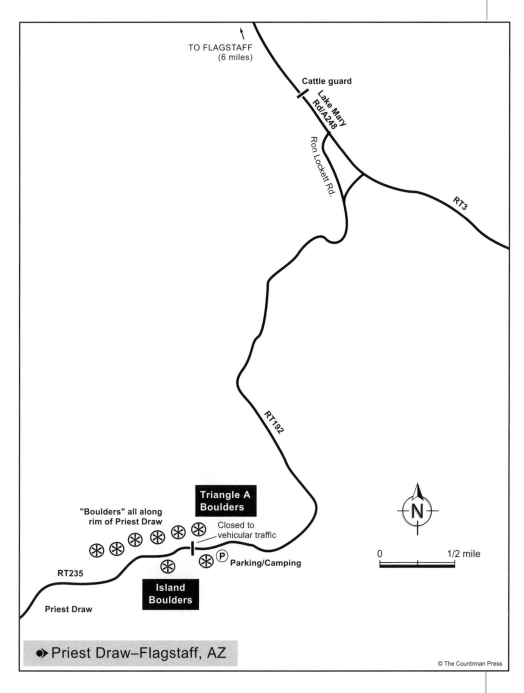

TO FLAGSTAFF
(6 miles)

Cattle guard

Lake Mary Rd/A248

Ron Lockett Rd.

RT3

RT192

Triangle A Boulders

"Boulders" all along rim of Priest Draw

Closed to vehicular traffic

N

0   1/2 mile

Island Boulders

RT235

P Parking/Camping

Priest Draw

● Priest Draw–Flagstaff, AZ

© The Countrman Press

and then turn left onto Lake Mary Road (AZ 487). Stay on Lake Mary Road for 6.5 miles, crossing over two cattle guards. Just .5 mile after the second cattle guard, turn right onto Ron Lockett Ranch Road. Proceed on this road for a total of 3 miles. The first .5 mile will pass private residences, and the remaining 2.5 miles is on a decent dirt road suitable for two-wheel-drive vehicles unless it's wet. Parking is located adjacent to a dirt fence (the road behind the fence,

Forest Service Road 235, used to provide an even closer drive-up to the boulders, but it has been closed to vehicular traffic).

Nearest major airports: Flagstaff Pulliam Airport (928- 556-1234; www.flagstaff .az.gov/index.asp?ID=184; 6200 South Pulliam Drive, Suite 204, Flagstaff), will bring you close to the boulders, but it might cost a bit more than flying to Sky Harbor International Airport (602-273-3300; http://phoenix.gov/aviation; 3400 E Sky Harbor Blvd, Suite 3300, Phoenix), 150 miles south in Phoenix.

Public transportation: None.

➤CLIMBING CONCERNS

Cost: Free.

Hours: Since camping is allowed along the dirt road that takes you to the boulders, you can boulder whenever you feel like it, but driving in and out late at night or early in the morning should be avoided, since people live along the access roads.

It's not all horizontal roofs! Boulderers play on Priest Draw's beginner-friendly Triangle Boulder.

Land manager: Coconino National Forest (928-527-3600; www.fs.fed.us/r3/coconino; 2323 E. Greenlaw Lane, Flagstaff, AZ 86004).

Finding the boulders: If you follow the directions in *Driving directions*, the boulders will be hard to miss. The first ones that come into sight on the right before the main parking area are the Triangle Boulder and its satellites. There are more boulders lining the hillside to the right of the closed road, as well as at the Island—an obvious outcropping of boulders on a small hill—on the left of the closed road. You can see many of these boulders from the parking area.

Type of rock: Limestone.

Five good problems: Since Priest Draw doesn't have a comprehensive guidebook, I've chosen not to select problems but, instead, to suggest a few boulders that should not be missed. For easier outings, try the Triangle Boulder and the obvious boulder at the entrance to the Island that you can see from the parking lot—it is wild. If you're seeking steep rock, challenge yourself on the famous Egyptian problem or its neighbors or test your horizontal skills on the shorter, less intimidating roof to the left of the Egyptian.

Range of grades: Priest Draw spans the range admirably, with the easiest of the easy suitable for the ultrabeginner to the stoutest of the stout guaranteed to challenge any strong man or woman.

Prime season: Due to the area's high elevation, winter days can bring inclement weather, so plan your visit a little earlier or later than the dead of winter if you want to ensure that you'll be able to sample the sick overhangs of Priest Draw in the sunshine. Climbable days exist year-round, but your best bet is to visit spring through fall. Summer can be hot, and winter can be quite cold.

Dogs: You can bring your pooch, but keep it under control—preferably on a leash—and clean up after it.

Special notes: In Priest Draw, please use your common sense—and please bury your feces and don't poop in the draw (hike up above the rim). Spraylords and number chasers should stay home or tone down their pursuit of fame when visiting Priest Draw, since locals prefer not to have a guidebook published detailing problems or grades. Just go and have a good time testing yourself and enjoy the freedom of "gradeless" ascents—you might actually like it!

Guidebooks to area problems: As of this writing, a comprehensive guidebook does not exist. You might be able to get your hands on a small informational brochure with topos at the climbing gym (see *Local climbing gyms*).

Online resources: You can download a simple, free guide to bouldering in Priest Draw from Dr. Topo (www.drtopo.com). For information on statewide bouldering areas, check out Arizona Bouldering (www.arizonabouldering.com). AZ Climbing (www.azclimbing.com) has more general statewide climbing information. You can find a helpful list of areas to climb and boulder near Flagstaff at Climbingsource.com (www.climbingsource.com/LocalBeta/Arizona/flagstaff.html).

Other resources: The Arizona Mountaineering Club (623-878-2485; www.azmountaineeringclub.org; 4340 E. Indian School Road, Ste. 21–164,

Phoenix, AZ 85018) offers beginner rock climbing lessons and organized outings. The Arizona Climbing and Adventure School (480-363-2390; www.climbingschool.com; P.O. Box 3094, Carefree, AZ 85377) offers climbing lessons for all levels.

Local climbing gyms: Vertical Relief Climbing Center (928-556-9909; www.verticalrelief.com; 205 South San Francisco Street) is located in the heart of Flagstaff.

Nearby bouldering and climbing areas of note: Flagstaff and its environs have much to offer both rock climbers and boulderers. A sampling of the nearby climbing areas includes the Pit (limestone sport climbing just down the road from Priest Draw), Buffalo Park (in-town basalt bouldering), and Paradise Forks (world-class basalt traditional climbing).

◆OTHER IMPORTANT STUFF

Camping: Primitive camping is available along the dirt road that leads to the bouldering area. Please maintain a low profile and clean up after yourself. For amenities, see the entries under *Showers*.

Nearby phone: There is a pay phone located just outside Macy's European Coffeehouse (see complete listing under *Restaurants*) on Beaver Street.

Showers: Try the Woody Mountain Campground and RV Park (928-774-7727; www.woodymountaincampground.com; 2727 West Route 66) or the Flagstaff KOA (928-526-9926; www.koa.com/where/az/03102.htm; 5803 North US 89).

Water: You will not find water at Priest Draw, and since Flagstaff has been experiencing serious water issues, it could be difficult to find anywhere that will let you fill a big jug. Your best bet is to ask at the campgrounds when you go to shower or to politely inquire at one of the many gas stations in town.

In case of emergency: Call 911 in all emergencies.

Flagstaff Medical Center (928-779-3366; 1200 North Beaver Street). After retracing your drive out to the bouldering area from Flagstaff back onto Old Route 66, proceed to Beaver Street and turn left. Follow Beaver Street for 1 mile.

Nearby Internet hookup: Flagstaff City–Coconino County Public Library (928-779-7670; www.flagstaffpubliclibrary.org; 300 West Aspen Avenue). From Old Route 66 and Humphreys Street, turn north onto Humphreys Street (US 180). After less than .1 mile, turn east onto Aspen Avenue.

Restaurants: Don't leave town without stopping by Macy's European Coffeehouse (928-774-2243; 14 South Beaver Street) for a cup of coffee or a vegetarian treat. If you like to play chess, you might find someone there to challenge you, or you can just relax at one of the well-worn wooden tables and take in the comforting sights and smells of this favorite local hangout. Call for hours, or just stop by.

Across the street you can check your e-mail ($5/hour) while you nosh a bagel or sandwich at Biff's Bagels (928-226-0424; www.biffsbagels.com;

1 South Beaver Street). Inexpensive. Biff's is open Monday through Saturday 7–3 and Sunday 8–2.

You can also have dinner on Beaver Street at the Beaver Street Brewery & Whistle Stop Café (928-779-0079; www.beaverstreetbrewery.com; 11 South Beaver Street #1). Expect hearty American fare, large portions, and decent microbrews. The restaurant specializes in wood-fired pizzas. Meal salads, platters, burgers, and sandwiches are available as well. Inexpensive. Open daily 11:30 AM –midnight.

Box Canyon—Socorro, New Mexico

Each night I've stayed in Box Canyon has brought with it a welcome sense of isolation prompted by the area's desolate but inspiring landscape, with its ruddy, reddish black cliffs and boulders and its shrubby, low-lying vegetation grappling to hold on to the hillsides, sucking whatever bits of moisture it can to survive from the gravelly ground cover. This aura of remoteness always amazes me because Box Canyon is adjacent to US 60 and in close proximity to I-25 (about 80 miles south of Albuquerque, New Mexico), but somehow the place manages to maintain its sense of wildness. Daylight creeps over the eastern walls of the canyon long before sunlight graces the parking and camping area, making it hard to exit the sleeping bag on colder mornings. There's no rush, though—if you've stopped to boulder, a good three-hour session will likely suffice, whether you're waiting for the rock to warm up or for the heat of the day to pass.

The bouldering at Box Canyon sports a diverse array of angles and even rock textures, varying from the porous, sandpaper-rough, overhanging, pocketed tuff of the Streambed area to the smoother, crimpy, sharp-edged vertical faces and overhangs on the porphyritic andesite—a type of water-washed volcanic rock— that makes up the majority of the bouldering. Though Box Canyon and other outlying areas contain a wide range of quality problems suited to challenge almost anyone, this area does not see a ton of out-of-town traffic, probably because of its proximity to the world-renowned bouldering of Hueco Tanks State Historic Site in Texas (see pages 156–163). Nonetheless, Box Canyon is a worthy bouldering destination in its own right, and its easy access from I-25 makes it that much more worthwhile to stop for a day or two to check it out and enjoy some peaceful, quiet camping away from the madding crowds you're likely to find at more "in" bouldering areas.

The Lowdown

◆▶GETTING THERE

Driving directions: From I-25 North or South, take exit 150, which will feed you onto North California Street in Socorro. Follow this for 1.7 miles through town. Turn right onto US 60 West, or Spring Street. Follow this out of town for

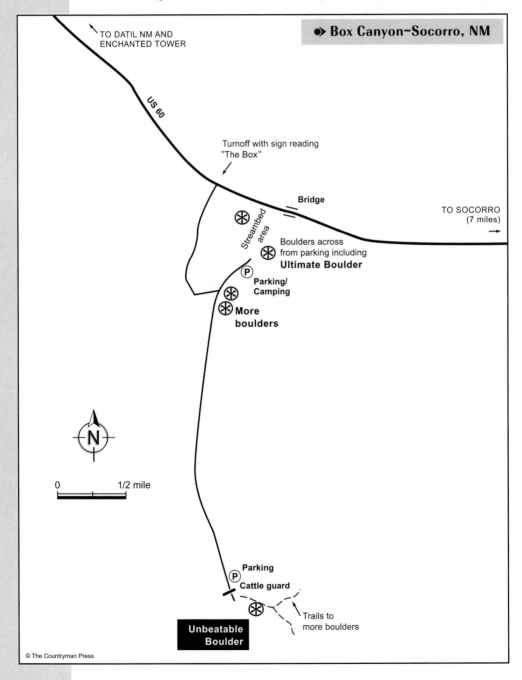

TO DATIL NM AND
ENCHANTED TOWER

◆▶ **Box Canyon—Socorro, NM**

US 60

Turnoff with sign reading
"The Box"

Bridge

TO SOCORRO
(7 miles)

Streambed area

Boulders across
from parking including
Ultimate Boulder

Ⓟ

**Parking/
Camping**

✸ **More
boulders**

N

0   1/2 mile

Parking
Ⓟ
Cattle guard

Trails to
more boulders

**Unbeatable
Boulder**

© The Countryman Press

7.2 miles. Start slowing down just after you cross a small bridge spanning the canyon, or your turn on the left will likely come up before you have time to react. Turn left onto a dirt road at 7.2 miles just after a hill marked by a small—and I mean small—BLM sign that says THE BOX. Proceed .5 mile and then take the left fork of the dirt road. After .1 mile you will see the parking area on your left.

Nearest major airports: The nearest major airport is the Albuquerque International Sunport (505-244-7700; www.cabq.gov/airport; P.O. Box 9948, Albuquerque, NM), about 83 miles from Box Canyon. Socorro has an airport run by the city—the Socorro Municipal Airport (505-838-4477).

Public transportation: There is no public transportation to Box Canyon.

➧CLIMBING CONCERNS

Cost: Free.

Hours: No set hours.

Land manager: The Bureau of Land Management (BLM) Socorro Field Office (505-835-0412; www.nm.blm.gov/sfo/sfo_home.html; 198 Neel Avenue, Northwest, Socorro, NM 87801).

Finding the boulders: From the parking area, a number of boulders are visible, including the Ultimate Boulder. To find the Streambed bouldering area, follow the wash/streambed north out of the parking area for 5 minutes or less—you can't miss it. It lies just before the bridge you drove over on US 60. Another boulder that should not be missed is the Unbeatable Boulder, which is reached by turning left out of the parking lot and following the road for a short distance through two washes and over a hill (driving is suggested, but walking is possible—especially if your auto is fragile or the road is wet). Park on the left side of the road just before a yellow cattle guard. The boulder should be obvious from here. It has an overhanging face and a cool slabby face, and mostly perfect landings. Head down the slight hill following a justly well-beaten path.

Type of rock: Porphyritic andesite or volcanic tuff.

Five good problems: Test your mettle on The Ultimate Boulder Problem (V1, Ultimate Boulder), Pressure Drop (V1, Unbeatable Boulder), High Traverse (V1, Streambed), Right Roof (V3, Streambed), and Jah Lives (V5, Unbeatable Boulder).

Range of grades: Mellow, easy problems for beginners—especially the Streambed's traverse, which can be done in sections and has safe landings—along with some sick pure lines and great contrivances bound to push the strongest boulderer in your group.

Prime season: Best visited in late fall, winter, and early spring. Even in November it can be too hot in the middle of the day. Summers can be blistering.

Dogs: Allowed.

Guidebooks to area problems: See *Online resources*.

Online resources: Box Canyon possesses an amazing online, free bouldering guide, *Socorro Bouldering Guide*, painstakingly put together by local boulderer

Bob Broilo. It is all you need to locate boulders, figure out grades, learn about the area's history and development, and so forth. Color photos with lines drawn on them assist you in finding the problems. The guide is available at www.nmt .edu/~bob/boulder_guide/socorro_boulder_guide.html. If you run into Bob Broilo, please thank him for this monumental work that he's graciously made available free of charge—or drop him an e-mail when you download the guide.

Other resources: The New Mexico Mountain Club (www.swcp.com/~nmmc; P.O. Box 4151, University Station, Albuquerque, NM 87196) runs a technical rock climbing school each spring and outings year-round. REI-Albuquerque (505-247-1191; www.rei.com; 1550 Mercantile Avenue Northeast) has a climbing boulder and a great selection of gear.

Local climbing gyms: Located about an hour away in Albuquerque is Stone Age Climbing Gym (505-341-2016; www.climbstoneage.com; 4201 Yale Avenue Northeast, Suite 1).

Nearby bouldering and climbing areas of note: On the other side of the east wall of Box Canyon is Spook Canyon, another bouldering area worth checking out.

Boulders visible from the parking area at Box Canyon.

Farther down US 60 by the tiny town of Datil is the well-known sport-climbing area of Enchanted Tower, but be sure to have up-to-date access information before you head there for a visit, as access has often been an issue. City of Rocks State Park (see pages 153–156) and Hueco Tanks State Historic Site (see pages 156–163), are nearby bouldering destinations. Northern New Mexico has a number of crags as well, including Cochiti Mesa.

❧ OTHER IMPORTANT STUFF

Camping: Primitive camping is permitted in Box Canyon. There is even a potty, but not water or additional facilities. Please maintain a low profile and be aware that the police may come through and shine a light in your tent or car to make sure no illicit activities are going on, since this place has a reputation as a high-school party spot.

Nearby phone: Socorro has many pay phones to offer, but there are no phones in Box Canyon.

Nate Bancroft sticking the move near Socorro, New Mexico.

Showers: Your best bet is to rent a cheap motel room for a night if you really need to get clean. You can find rates as low as $25 a night, so if you get a few buddies who want showers, too, to chip in and you'll be all set.

Water: None available in Box Canyon. Ask politely at a gas station in town, or fill up when you grab a cheap motel room for a night to shower.

In case of emergency: Dial 911 for all emergencies.

Socorro General Hospital (505-835-1140; 1202 US 60 West) is easily reached from Box Canyon by simply heading back toward Socorro on US 60. Just before US 60 hangs a right onto Spring Street, the hospital will be on your right.

Nearby Internet hookup: Socorro Public Library (505-835-1114; www.sdc.org/~library; 401 Park Street). Coming back into Socorro on US 60, look for Park Street on your left. Take a left and drive .1 mile, passing the intersection with McCutcheon Street West; the library is in the next block of Park Street.

Restaurants: Martha's Black Dog Coffeehouse (505-838-0311; 110 Manzanares Avenue East) is the best place to grab any type of coffee drink. You can also sit

No visit to Box Canyon is complete without a stop at the Unbeatable Boulder (Jordan Fitzgerald climbing).

down for one of its delicious, creative entrées that include a good selection of options for vegans and vegetarians. Desserts (try the Dog Overboard!) and baked goods are great, too. Inexpensive to moderate. Open a little before 7:30 every morning of the week. Closes at 6 on Saturday, 3 on Sunday, 6 on Monday, 9 on Tuesday, and 8 Wednesday through Friday. From Box Canyon, head back into Socorro on US 60, following it as it turns right onto Spring Street and left onto California Street. Turn west onto Manzanares Avenue and park in the large parking lot just east of the restaurant on the south side of the street.

If you're hungry for giant helpings of Mexican or American food any time of day or night, stop at El Camino Restaurant and Lounge (505-835-1180; 707 North California Street). Inexpensive. Open 24 hours, this restaurant will serve you anything from huevos rancheros to spaghetti. From Box Canyon, follow US 60 back to Socorro, turning left onto California Street. The restaurant's bright neon sign on the left after several blocks cannot be missed.

City of Rocks State Park—Deming, New Mexico

While Box Canyon, near Socorro, New Mexico, always imbues me with a sense of delicious isolation despite its proximity to major highways, City of Rocks State Park—tucked away in the southwestern corner of New Mexico between Deming and Silver City—offers a truly isolated bouldering experience for the adventure seeker. With no published guidebook to the problems and no record of ratings or even specific boulder problems established (except possibly in a handful of boulderers' minds), time spent bouldering in City of Rocks must stem from your desire to play on the hundreds of rocks scattered about in this remote locale. In fact, you are unlikely to see another boulderer here, or even another person! For

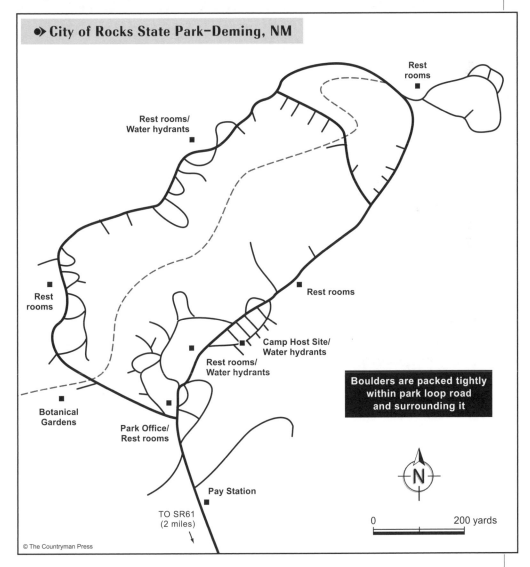

● City of Rocks State Park—Deming, NM

Rest rooms

Rest rooms/
Water hydrants

Rest
rooms

Rest rooms

Camp Host Site/
Water hydrants

Rest rooms/
Water hydrants

Boulders are packed tightly
within park loop road
and surrounding it

Botanical
Gardens

Park Office/
Rest rooms

Pay Station

TO SR61
(2 miles)

N

0   200 yards

© The Countryman Press

those who wish for a break from the scene often associated with popular boul-dering areas like Hueco Tanks and Bishop, or those who prefer to do all of their bouldering without an audience, City of Rocks will prove a veritable haven with its endless supply of edges waiting to be pulled on.

Sculpted by wind and water 30 million years ago, the boulders at City of Rocks range from 10 to 30 feet in height and offer mostly crimpy, often sharp, and often vertical or slightly overhanging problems. With this area frequented by New Mexico climbing legend Bob Murray, it is quite probable that many of the plum hard lines here have already been climbed, but who cares? With no estab-lished listing of problems, your mind and your ability will be the only limitations for whatever pure lines or contrivances you and your partners create. Whether you're just starting out or you've been bouldering forever, the freedom from grades, expectations, and crowds makes the City of Rocks bouldering experience one of the purest available—your only reason to sample this volcanic tuff play-ground should stem from your innate spirit of adventure and playfulness.

The Lowdown

➡ GETTING THERE

Driving directions: From Deming, drive 24 miles northwest on US 180. Exit northeast onto NM 61 and continue 4 miles to the park entrance.

Nearest major airports: El Paso International Airport (915-780-4749; www.elpaso internationalairport.com; 6701 Convair) is the closest major airport, 130 miles from the park. Closer by is the Deming Municipal Airport (505-544-3660; www.cityofdeming.org/airport.html; 310 Airport Drive).

Public transportation: None.

➡ CLIMBING CONCERNS

Cost: Entrance to the park costs $4 a day per vehicle, or $20 for an annual day pass good at all New Mexico State Parks.

Hours: 7 AM–9 PM April 1 through October 31 and 7 AM–6 PM November 1 through March 31.

Land manager: City of Rocks State Park (505-536-2800; www.emnrd.state.nm .us/nmparks/pages/parks/cityrock/cityrock.htm; P.O. Box 50, Faywood, NM 88034).

Finding the boulders: You will see the boulders upon entering the park—there's no way you could miss them!

Type of rock: Wind- and water-sculpted welded volcanic tuff.

Five good problems: You are on your own finding good problems here—use your creativity and imagination.

Range of grades: Easy problems as well as the potential for seriously difficult problems.

Prime season: Spring, fall, and winter can all yield picture-perfect weather, though wind can be an issue here due to the exposed nature of the rocks. Some winter days may be too cold. Summer will almost assuredly be too hot.

Dogs: Must be on a leash not more than 10 feet in length and under your supervision at all times. You cannot leave Fido unattended in the car, and you must dispose of pet waste appropriately.

Special notes: With boulders up to 30 feet in height, finding the way down at City of Rocks should always be taken into consideration before you start up a particular line of holds that you may spy. Creative down-climbing methods might include a stack of crash pads to cushion your landing or a jump from the top of one boulder to another with an easier descent. If need be, bring a rope to rappel. Just be sure you won't be "treed," as this has been a problem in the past. Also, try to limit your use of chalk and brush it off when you leave. This will help ensure future access.

Guidebooks to area problems: None.

Online resources: Aside from the official Web site listed under *Land Manager*, there are precious few helpful listings on the Web for boulderers interested in adventuring here. Look on RockClimbing.com (www.rockclimbing.com) for a brief discussion of the area.

Other resources: The New Mexico Mountain Club (www.swcp.com/~nmmc; P.O. Box 4151, University Station, Albuquerque, NM 87196) runs a technical rock climbing school each spring and outings year-round.

Local climbing gyms: No reasonably close indoor climbing facility.

Nearby bouldering and climbing areas of note: Hueco Tanks State Historic Site (see pages 156–163), one of the country's top bouldering destinations, is 130 miles south just outside of El Paso. Also less than 200 miles away is the isolated traditional climbing of Cochise Stronghold in southern Arizona.

➧OTHER IMPORTANT STUFF

Camping: Available in the park for $10 a night per site.

Nearby phone: No public phones are available in the park. In an emergency, the rangers in the visitor center should be contacted. For other phone needs, you'll need to drive south to Deming or north to Bayard or Silver City.

Showers: Available in the park.

Water: Available in the park.

In case of emergency: Dial 911 for all emergencies.

Medical help is available at Mimbres Memorial Hospital (505-546-2761; 900 West Ash Street, Deming). Follow US 180 south to Deming. Turn right onto West Pine Street (I-10 Business Loop West). Proceed .5 mile and then turn left onto South Eighth Street. Drive .4 mile and turn left onto West Ash Street, where you will see the hospital.

Nearby Internet hookup: Marshall Memorial Library (505-546-9202; www.zianet
.com/demingpl; 301 South Tin Street). Follow US 180 south to Deming. Turn
right onto West Pine Street (I-10 Business Loop West). After .2 mile, turn left onto
South Tin Street and proceed .1 mile to the library. Alternatively, log on at the
Silver City Public Library (505-538-3672; http://townofsilvercity.org/publibrary;
515 West College Avenue). Drive north on US 180 to Silver City. Turn right onto
West College Avenue and proceed .1 mile to the library.

Restaurants: You can find restaurants south of the park in Deming or north in
Silver City. For a treat try Silver City's Diane's Restaurant and Bakery (505-538-
8722; www.dianesrestaurant.com; 510 North Bullard), where you can choose
from a menu offering basics like salad and spaghetti to much more exotic cre-
ations. Moderate to expensive. Open for lunch Tuesday through Sunday 11–2;
for dinner Tuesday through Saturday 5:30–9; and for brunch Saturday and
Sunday 9–2. Take US 180 north to Silver City. Turn left onto West College Avenue. Less than .1 mile later, turn right onto Bullard Street and proceed .1 mile
to the restaurant.

Stroll down the block to Alotta Gelato (505-534-4995; www.alottagelato.com;
619 North Bullard Street) to finish your meal with a delicious homemade Italian
ice cream available in flavors such as chocolate hazelnut or sour cherry. Open
Sunday through Thursday 12–9; Friday and Saturday 12–10 or later.

Hueco Tanks State Historic Site—El Paso, Texas

I first visited Hueco Tanks in 1994. I had been climbing for less than two years at
the time, and I had never really bouldered before. Nonetheless, I'd heard of
Hueco, and I needed to get out of New England and go somewhere warmer for
my college winter break. When a climbing buddy who had gone on the road said
he'd meet up with me there, I booked a flight and headed south, little knowing
that my destination possessed some of the highest-quality bouldering available in
this country in a stunningly lovely setting. I also didn't know that during the subsequent years, climbing and bouldering in Hueco Tanks would become the target
of serious controversy as a host of interested parties became involved in some un-
pleasant wrangling concerning whether or not climbers and boulderers should be
allowed to utilize the park for their preferred recreational activity.

Instead of rehashing the whole debate and the results, suffice it to say that
the Hueco Tanks experience for the huge numbers of boulderers who still flock
to the park every winter is by no means the same as the experience of those who
visited prior to the imposition of current regulations stipulated in the Public Use-
Restriction Plan—2000 (PURP), such as limiting the number of people on North
Mountain to 70 a day and making East and West Mountains accessible only via

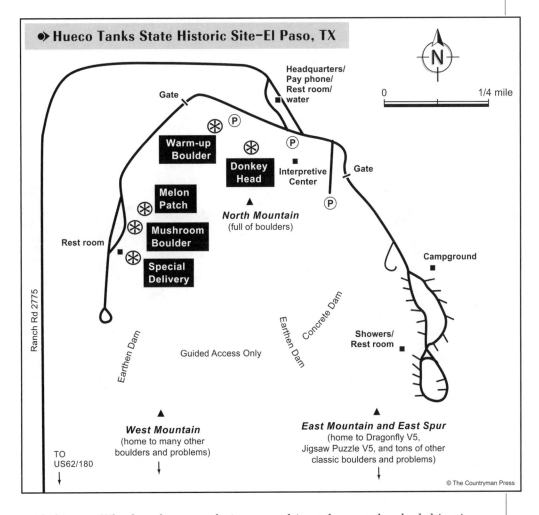

Hueco Tanks State Historic Site–El Paso, TX

0   1/4 mile

Headquarters/
Pay phone/
Rest room/
water

Gate

Warm-up
Boulder

Donkey
Head

Interpretive
Center

Gate

Melon
Patch

▲
North Mountain
(full of boulders)

Rest room

Mushroom
Boulder

Special
Delivery

Campground

Ranch Rd 2775

Earthen Dam

Concrete Dam

Earthen Dam

Showers/
Rest room

Guided Access Only

TO
US62/180

▲
West Mountain
(home to many other
boulders and problems)

▲
East Mountain and East Spur
(home to Dragonfly V5,
Jigsaw Puzzle V5, and tons of other
classic boulders and problems)

© The Countryman Press

guided tours. Whether these regulations are ultimately a good or bad thing is not for me to judge—but for now, the park remains open to bouldering, and I think this is proper, since Hueco Tanks not only holds historical and cultural value to Native Americans and is home to a diverse array of flora and fauna but also has significant historic value in the world of bouldering. After all, Hueco Tanks is the place that spawned the "V" grading scale used to rate boulder problems' difficulty, and it is still home to some of the country's most challenging problems.

I believe that every boulderer should have the opportunity to repeat classic problems established by the past masters whose footsteps still seem to echo among the amazing formations found at Hueco Tanks. Hueco's unique volcanic rock, though notoriously tough on the skin, has some of the finest, most aesthetic boulder problems to be found anywhere, from the El Murrays on North Mountain's Mushroom Boulder (heck, practically everything on the Mushroom

Boulder) to the remarkably near-horizontal insanity of the Martini Roof. Even more amazing is that new problems—and even entire new bouldering areas like New North Meadow—continue to be developed with visits from each season's crop of the latest mutants (boulderers with unbelievable natural talent and strength) to hit the scene. And don't be discouraged if pulling hard isn't your game or you're just getting started bouldering—Hueco's easy problems number in the hundreds as well.

Alli, How Cilley Can You Get, Hueco, Texas. PHOTO BY MATT WENDLING

The Lowdown

❧ GETTING THERE

Driving directions: Take US 62/180 32 miles east of El Paso. Watch for signs for the park, and turn left (north) onto Ranch Road 2775. Follow this for roughly 6 miles to the park entrance.

Nearest major airports: El Paso International Airport (915-780-4749; www.elpasointernationalairport.com; 6701 Convair) is the closest major airport, less than 30 miles from Hueco.

Public transportation: None.

❧ CLIMBING CONCERNS

Cost: $4 per person per day, or you can purchase an annual Texas Park Pass for $60 at any state park or by calling 800-895-4248, which takes 7–10 days to process. The pass covers up to 15 people in two cars entering at the same time.

Hours: Open 8 AM–6 PM daily October 1 through April 30; 8–6 Monday through Thursday and 7–7 Friday through Sunday May 1 through September 30.

Land manager: Texas Parks and Wildlife Department (TPWD; 800-792-1112 or 512-389-4800; www.tpwd.state.tx.us; 4200 Smith School Road, Austin, TX 78744). The park has its own office as well (915-857-1135 or 915-849-6684; www.tpwd.state.tx.us/park/hueco/hueco.htm; 6900 Hueco Tanks Road Number 1, El Paso, TX 79938).

Finding the boulders: For the boulders on North Mountain, the map on page 157 can get you started, but it's a maze out there, so it's best to follow the extensive descriptions in John Sherman's guidebook or the Dr. Topo free topo, to tag along with another group, or simply to look for chalk left by other climbers, taking care to respect the NO CLIMBING signs. All other areas of the park are accessible via tour only. You can sign up for free tours led by volunteers at the park office by calling or signing up when you get there, or you can hire a private guide at the Hueco Rock Ranch (see *Camping*).

Type of rock: A volcanic rock called syenite porphyry.

Five good problems: Hueco is a bouldering Mecca, but here are five recommendations in the easy-to-moderate range on North Mountain: The Melon Patch (V0, near the Mushroom Boulder), The Local Flakes (V2, Mushroom Boulder), Namedropper (V3, Warm-Up Boulder), Donkey Head (V4, across from the park headquarters), and Special Delivery (V6, Deliverance Boulder).

Range of grades: A great many easy problems and a large concentration of problems harder than V8, with a fair assortment of problems through the mid grades as well.

Prime season: Mid-autumn through mid-spring. Beware the almost eternally blowing wind, and note that though this is a well-known winter-climbing destination, it can be quite, quite cold and cloudy on any given day in winter, so bring the proper attire.

Jason Bennett, Crash Dummy, Hueco Tanks, Texas. PHOTO BY MATT WENDLING

Dogs: It's best to leave your dog at home. Dogs are allowed in the park only on a leash and only in the picnic and camping areas—not where you will be climbing. Leaving your dog in the car can get you a ticket for animal endangerment.

Special notes: IMPORTANT: Be sure to visit HuecoTanks.com (www.huecotanks.com) before planning your trip for the latest on access restrictions and regulations, and make reservations in advance—don't just show up, or you might never touch the boulders. Use your common sense, following all of the "rules" included in the *Ethics* section of chapter 1.

Reservations are *highly* recommended (read—make reservations if you want to ensure that you will boulder), especially during prime seasons such as winter weekends, winter break, spring break, and so forth. Make reservations early for peak periods, and be aware that this will involve calling several different numbers as you wend your way through the convoluted system that has evolved. Start by calling central reservations in Austin (512-389-8900), and good luck!

Matt Hoch, Slim Pickin's, Hueco Tanks, Texas. PHOTO BY MATT WENDLING

A full explanation of the bureaucratic maze you'll go through is available by clicking on "Hueco Info" at HuecoTanks.com (www.huecotanks.com).

Please respect all area closures and go out of your way to maintain good relationships with the park staff, obeying all of the rules and guidelines. This will help protect against the imposition of further restrictions.

Guidebooks to area problems: Still the best guide out there is *Hueco Tanks Climbing and Bouldering Guide*, 2nd edition, by John Sherman (Falcon, 1995).

Online resources: By far the best online resource for Hueco Tanks is HuecoTanks.com (www.huecotanks.com), where you will find details on how to make reservations, hiring a guide, the latest access crises, and the latest spray. You can download *A Little Bouldering Guide of Hueco Tanks North Mountain* free from Dr. Topo (www.drtopo.com). You should also visit the Hueco Rock Ranch's Web site (www.huecorockranch.com) for information on where to stay, commercial tours, and the bouldering community in Hueco. The Texas Climbers Web site also has a section on Hueco Tanks (www.texasclimbers.com/crags/hueco).

Other resources: Climbers of Hueco Tanks is a group dedicated to improving access to Hueco Tanks. Contact the Hueco Rock Ranch for details (915-855-0142; www.huecorockranch.com).

Local climbing gyms: None.

Nearby bouldering and climbing areas of note: The unique limestone sport-climbing area called Sitting Bull Falls, near Carlsbad, New Mexico, is a bit shy of 100 miles north and east of Hueco Tanks. City of Rocks State Park (see pages 153–156), near Deming, New Mexico, is about 130 miles from Hueco.

◆OTHER IMPORTANT STUFF

Camping: Most boulderers stay at the Hueco Rock Ranch (915-855-0142; www.huecorockranch.com; 17498 Bettina Avenue). The cost is $5 per person per night, or $4 per person per night for stays longer than 14 days. After passing a distinctive Quonset hut (formerly Pete's, where climbers used to stay) on your left, turn left onto Hueco Mountain Road, the first paved road after Pete's. After .1 mile turn right onto Woodrow Road. Proceed less than 2 miles until Woodrow ends at Bettina, and turn left. HRR will be on the left side of the road after less than .5 mile. There are HRR signs that will help guide you to the campground.

Camping is also available in the park for $10 a night per site. Call the park headquarters for reservations and details.

Nearby phone: There is a pay phone located just outside the entrance to the park office.

Showers: Available at the Hueco Rock Ranch (see *Camping*) for $2. Do *not* poach showers in the park—this will get you thrown out and will portray boulderers as an irresponsible user group. Showers in the park are only for those who camp in the park.

Water: Available in the park.

In case of emergency: Call 911 for all emergencies.

Head for Del Sol Medical Center (915-595-9000; 10301 Gateway West). From the park, head back to US 62/180. Turn right and drive 17.3 miles. Turn left onto McRae Boulevard. After 2.5 miles, turn left onto Gateway Boulevard East. Turn left to cross under I-10, and then left again onto Gateway Boulevard West, where you will find the hospital.

Nearby Internet hookup: You can log on for free at the Irving Schwartz Branch Library (915-857-0594; www.elpasotexas.gov/library/ourlibraries/branches/irving _schwartz.asp; 1865 Dean Martin). From the park, head back to US 62/180.

Turn right and drive 14.1 miles. Turn left onto George Dieter Drive. After 2.6 miles, turn left onto Trawood Drive. Go .1 mile and then turn right onto Dean Martin Drive.

Restaurants: El Paso has tons of eateries both far away and near to the park—all you need to do is drive toward town to find a place to eat. Since you're in a border town, I've chosen to recommend a couple of Mexican restaurants (in El Paso), but there are plenty of other options to choose from as well.

Lots of boulderers nosh nearby at El Rancho Escondido (915-857-1184; 14261-A Montana), where you'll find large portions of hearty Mexican fare, as well as margaritas and cold beer. Specialties include thick, hand-cut steaks and a variety of fajitas, including beef, chicken, and ostrich. The chile rellenos also come recommended. Inexpensive to moderate. Open Tuesday through Saturday 4–10. From Hueco Tanks State Historical Site, go back to US 62/180. Go right, and after about 7 miles, the restaurant will be on your right.

Another suggestion a bit further away is Kiki's (915-565-6713; www.kikisrestaurant.com; 2719 North Piedras). Renowned for its great Mexican food, Kiki's also stays open until 10 PM every day of

Matt Hoch, Slim Pickins, Hueco Tanks, Texas.
PHOTO BY MATT WENDLING

the year except for Thanksgiving and Christmas. Inexpensive to moderate. Open 10:30–10 every day of the week. From the park, head back to US 62/180. Turn right and drive 21.5 miles. Turn right onto US 180 (Gateway Boulevard West) and merge onto I-10 West. Go 1.7 miles before taking exit 21 toward Piedras Street. Take a slight left onto Gateway Boulevard West and go .3 mile. Turn right onto North Piedras Street and proceed 1.4 miles to the restaurant.

MIDWEST

FIELDS OF WHEAT, CORN, and other such grains carpet the ground for miles at a time, a ground so flat that you can't even tell how far you can see, with the horizon never changing . . . yes, this is America's heartland, the breadbasket of our nation, a place where you'd probably think it unlikely to find any sort of climbable surface. But the midwestern United States covers a huge swath of the nation, encompassing a dozen states more varied in their topographies than you might expect. Though this region is home to agricultural endeavors aplenty, it is also home to incredible diversity, including major cities, lakes, forests, and some undeniably worthwhile climbing destinations, including both developed and developing bouldering areas of note.

I've been able to explore the bouldering opportunities of only a scant two midwestern states—South Dakota and Kansas—though I've caught wind of worthy places elsewhere in the region, including southern Illinois and Minnesota, among others. South Dakota's Mount Baldy provides the much-needed drive-buster for boulderers in need of a session while journeying along I-90—in fact, you might even stay for a while. Mount Baldy's coarse granite rocks will challenge your climbing skills (and your finger skin, especially on a warmer day), with its array of midrange to harder problems along with plenty of easier stuff, all tucked in an idyllic setting of thick ponderosa pines seemingly far from the madding crowds of Mount Rush-

*The Seul Avec Dieux Boulder sports some area classics
(Matt Wendling climbing).*

more's tourists. The bouldering of Rock City, Kansas, on the other hand, should not be missed by any boulderer or climber crossing the country on I-70. Not only is it a treat for sore eyes after miles on the interstate, but it also features incredibly bizarre rock formations of a type of stone—sandstone concretions—that you are unlikely to climb on anywhere else, so who cares if all of the problems are easy?

Mount Baldy—Keystone, South Dakota

Even if you're not paying attention to the scenery outside your window while you motor across the northern United States on I-90, upon entering the Black Hills of South Dakota, you'll be hard-pressed not to register the dramatic change. To a climber's eyes, the place is pure magic, with grayish granite needles and rounded humps of stone—often striped in dazzling shades of green, orange, yellow, or

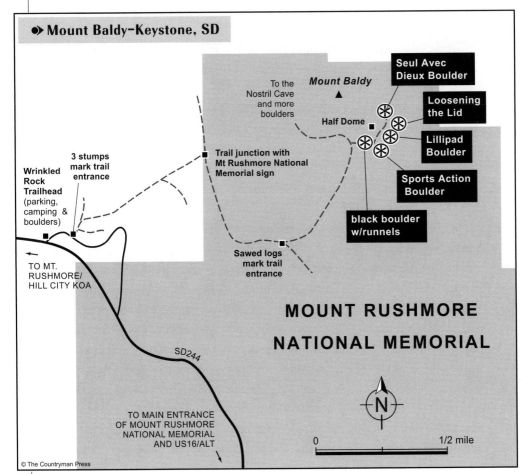

black—thrusting upward through thick stands of ponderosa pines as far as the eye can see. Without even getting out of the car, you will know you've entered an area that has been a playground for rock climbers for years, from the original masters who put up some of the area's ballsy test pieces in the Needles of Custer State Park to the present-day pioneers and enthusiasts working to discover, develop, and promote the Rushmore area's mostly untapped bouldering potential.

Mount Baldy's bouldering reflects the efforts of a dedicated group of South Dakota locals to begin a process that could consume several lifetimes of exploration—to locate, develop, and spread the word about the numerous boulder gardens undoubtedly secreted away among the taller, more visible granite formations throughout the Black Hills. This process is made more difficult by the area's incredibly dense pine forests, which also provide the pervasive and aromatic woodsy fragrance that permeates your very being as you walk along the trail leading you to Mount Baldy's hidden cache of bouldering gems. And while you may find your fingertips shredded after a few scant hours of play on the mostly rough and abrasive stone, this area wins top honors for its unbeatable setting, especially when you consider the veritable tourist mayhem taking place nearby as people flock from all over to see the silent, giant, and, to me, eerily bizarre heads of our former presidents enshrined in the stone at Mount Rushmore National Memorial.

The Lowdown

◆▶GETTING THERE

Driving directions: From I-90 East or West, go south out of Rapid City on US 16 (Mount Rushmore Road), following US 16 for about 18 miles. Turn left (south) onto US 16 Alternate, and follow this for about 2.5 miles. Turn right onto SD 244, go 3.2 miles (driving past the main parking area at Mount Rushmore National Memorial), and park either at Wrinkled Rock Trailhead on the right or, alternatively, on the right or left just before Wrinkled Rock Trailhead, in the pullout just after the Mount Rushmore National Memorial/Black Hills National Forest sign.

Nearest major airport: Rapid City Regional Airport (605-394-4195; www.rcgov.org/airport/pages; 4550 Terminal Road, Suite 102), about 40 miles from Mount Baldy.

Public transportation: None.

◆▶CLIMBING CONCERNS

Cost: There is no entrance fee to walk in from Wrinkled Rock Trailhead. There is an annual (calendar year), one-time $8 parking fee per vehicle to visit Mount Rushmore National Memorial.

Hours: Dawn through dusk.

Matt samples Frogonious (V4) at Mount Baldy's Lillipad Boulder.

Land manager: Mount Rushmore National Memorial (605-574-2523, www.nps .gov/moru; 13000 Highway 244, Building 31, Suite 1, Keystone, SD 57751) and Black Hills National Forest (605-673-9200; www.fs.fed.us/r2/ blackhills; 25041 North Highway 16, Custer, SD 57730).

Finding the boulders: For best results, refer to the map as well. This is less con-fusing than it sounds . . . I found the boulders with less detailed instructions, and

I'm not the most directionally inclined individual. From the parking at Wrinkled Rock Trailhead, walk back on the road toward the entrance from SD 244. On your left (southeast), you will see an obvious trail dropping down off the road. Follow this trail for a short distance as it makes a semicircle. Just before a large granite buttress on the left, you will see a trail leading down the hill, with three stumps at the entrance. Head down this trail, ignoring the first trail off it to the right. Go right between two granite formations at the second opportunity to turn (you can see an aspen with multiple trunks in the middle of this trail). This trail winds down between the granite formations. At a faint trail junction, continue going straight on the well-beaten trail until you encounter an obvious north–south trail marked with a sign reading MOUNT RUSHMORE NATIONAL MEMORIAL. Turn right (south), and follow this trail past several chossy granite buttresses. When you reach a Y in the trail with some split logs on the ground, take the left path, which leads uphill toward more granite formations. Continue up this path as it dips down and then heads more steeply uphill between two chossy granite formations. You will be deposited in front of an obvious black boulder with vertical runnels that has one established problem and a project. Just before this boulder, look for trails leading off in either direction—these will take you to the main boulders.

To the right, you'll find Seul Avec Dieux, Sports Action, and Lillipad, among others; to the left, you'll find the Nostril Cave and more. Baldy is the large granite formation on your left, and Half Dome is the smaller formation on your right. If you feel disoriented or can't find the exact trail, a few minutes of poking around the base of either formation should result in you finding boulders with established problems quite readily. Expect the total approach time to be 15 to 20 minutes.

Type of rock: Granite.

Five good problems: Test yourself on Frogonius (V4, Lillipad Boulder), 4 on 6 (V5, Seul Avec Dieux), Sports Action (V5, Sports Action), Loosening the Lid (V6, Loosening the Lid Boulder), and The Prow (V10, Seul Avec Dieux). Baldy also features many easier problems in the V0–V3 range that are fun outings.

Range of grades: Everything from VB to double-digit problems, with ample room for development.

Prime season: Best visited in spring and fall. Winter can have some passable days, while hot summer days will undoubtedly tear your fingers into mincemeat in seconds.

Dogs: Allowed in Black Hills National Forest, but they must be leashed at all times. Dogs are not allowed in the visiting area or developed areas at Mount Rushmore National Memorial, so be aware that if you want to go and see the giant heads close up, you'll need to leave your pooch behind.

Special notes: Check the Climbing Black Hills and the Black Hills Climbers Coalition Web sites (see *Online resources*) before your visit for any access issues or concerns. Obey all posted regulations and interact politely with rangers to help keep a solid and positive relationship between climbers and land managers. No campfires are allowed outside of developed campgrounds, so don't have a fire at Wrinkled Rock Trailhead if you choose to stay there. Do not camp within Mount Rushmore National Memorial boundaries; this is strictly prohibited. Pack out your trash.

Guidebooks to area problems: None at press time, but local boulderer Dan Dewell—who provided much of the information for this guide and graciously gave me a tour of the place despite a busted thumb—plans to have one out in both written and online formats by spring of 2005. Check the Climbing Black Hills Web site for details and more information.

Online resources: A good online resource is Climbing Black Hills (www.climbing blackhills.com), which includes beta on not only Mount Baldy (complete with photos with topos of some of the area's primo boulders) but also numerous other South Dakota bouldering and climbing destinations.

The Friction Addiction Web site (www.frictionaddiction.net) includes photos of area boulder problems and information on how to order the Kurt Smith film *Friction Addiction—Black Hills Gold*, which includes footage of bouldering at Mount Baldy and more. RockClimbing.com (www.rockclimbing.com) has a listing for Mount Baldy as well as numerous other South Dakota bouldering and climbing destinations.

The Black Hills Climbers Coalition(www.bhclimbers.com) provides helpful information about climbing in the Black Hills area (including Mount Baldy and Mount Rushmore), as well as working as a liaison between climbers and land managers.

Other resources: If you've never rock climbed or bouldered before and you want to hire a guide, contact Sylvan Rocks Climbing School & Guide Service (605-574-2425; www.sylvanrocks.com; P.O. Box 600, Hill City, SD), Tower Guides (888-345-9061; www.towerguides.com; 157 Highway 24, Devils Tower, WY), or Exum Mountain Guides (307-733-2297; www.exumguides.com/special/needles .shtml; Box 56, Moose, WY 83012); the latter two also provide climbing guide services in the Black Hills area of South Dakota.

You will find a wide selection of camping and climbing supplies at Granite Sports (605-574-2425; www.sylvanrocks.com/gsports.shtml; 301 Main Street, Hill City). Rapid City also has a number of outdoor suppliers, including Adventure Sport (605-341-6707; 900 Jackson Boulevard) and Scheels All Sports (605-342-9033; www.scheelssports.com; 2200 North Maple, in the mall).

Local climbing gyms: You can climb indoors at the Athletic Club (605-343-0744; 7800 Albertta Drive, Rapid City).

Nearby bouldering and climbing areas of note: Though often overlooked by boulderers and rock climbers, South Dakota's vast quantity of climbable rock should probably get much more notice from the climbing community at large. The Mount Rushmore area has additional bouldering besides Mount Baldy—including a few problems at Wrinkled Rock Trailhead—as well as sport climbing and traditional climbing.

Just south of Mount Rushmore in Custer State Park, you'll find South Dakota's famous Needles, one of bouldering master John Gill's haunts, which includes the famous highball problem The Thimble, among a number of other classics. Custer State Park also has route climbing. Nearby Spearfish Canyon has gained recognition for its steep, limestone sport climbing. Rapid City has some small bouldering and route-climbing areas. The well-known traditional-climbing destination of Devils Tower is located just across the border in eastern Wyoming.

●▶OTHER IMPORTANT STUFF

Camping: Mount Rushmore National Memorial does not have camping facilities. You can camp for free at Wrinkled Rock Trailhead. There is an outhouse but no water or additional facilities.

There are numerous privately operated campgrounds nearby offering more amenities. One of the closest is the Mt. Rushmore/Hill City KOA (800-562-8503; www.koa.com/where/sd/41125.htm; 12620 Highway 244, Hill City), located 5 miles west of the memorial on SD 244. You will pay at least $25 a night for a tent site, but you can also partake of the hot tubs, swimming pools, showers, and other amenities. Open May 1–October 1. For information on other nearby options, visit www.keystonechamber.com/lodging.html.

Though more of a drive, you can also camp year-round in Custer State Park (605-255-4515;

The Seul Avec Dieux Boulder sports some area classics (Matt Wendling climbing).

www.custerstatepark.info; HC 83, Box 70, Custer) for $13–$18 a night ($6 for limited facility sites in off-season), which includes showers and flush toilets. Making reservations in advance is highly recommended May through October, or you might find yourself siteless. Call 800-710-CAMP or make online reservations at www.campsd.com. From the parking area at Mount Baldy, drive east on SD 244 back to US 16 Alternate. Go south on US 16 Alternate for about 15 miles. Turn right (west) onto SD 36 (still US 16 Alternate) and proceed several miles to the Peter Norbeck Visitor Center or your campground of choice.

Nearby phone: You'll find pay phones in the building opposite the Mount Rushmore Information Center. Proceed east on SD 244 less than 2 miles from the parking area to find the main parking area for Mount Rushmore National Memorial and the phones. If you don't want to pay the entrance fee, proceed east on SD 244 for 3.2 miles from Wrinkled Rock Trailhead. Turn left onto US 16 Alternate and proceed about .8 mile to Keystone, where you'll find plenty of pay phones.

Showers: See *Camping*.

Water: Available in the building opposite the Mount Rushmore Information Center. Proceed east on SD 244 less than 2 miles from the parking area to find the main parking area for Mount Rushmore National Memorial and water (and vending machines). If you don't want to pay the entrance fee, proceed east on SD 244 for 3.2 miles from Wrinkled Rock Trailhead. Turn left onto US 16 Alternate and proceed about .8 miles to Keystone.

In case of emergency: Dial 911 for all emergencies.

Drive to Rapid City Regional Hospital (605-719-1000; www.rcrh.org; 353 Fairmont Boulevard). From the parking area, drive east on SD 244 back to US 16 Alternate. Take US 16 Alternate east for 3.4 miles, and then join US 16 East and continue for 16.5 miles. Turn right onto Cathedral Drive and proceed .3 mile to the hospital (the street name changes to Fairmont Boulevard).

Nearby Internet hookup: Keystone Town Library (605-666-4499; http://kcclib .sdln.net; 1101 Madill Street), located at the Keystone Community Center. From the parking area, drive east on SD 244 3.2 miles back to US 16 Alternate. Go east on US 16 Alternate for 1.2 miles. Turn right onto SD 40 (Holy Terror Trail) and proceed 1 mile to find the library (the street name changes).

Restaurants: In addition to the concessionaire at Mount Rushmore National Memorial (operating a restaurant, snack shop, and fudge and ice cream shop), you have many additional dining options in the area, but be aware that many restaurants (and lodging options) operate only seasonally, May through September or October.

For fantastic pizza, head for Big Time Pizza, located in the Roosevelt Inn (605-666-4443; www.rosyinn.com/3000.htm; 206 Old Cemetery Road, Keystone), where they make pizzas piled high with toppings and tons of cheese or savor an oven-roasted sub in flavor combos like tender roast beef and pastrami, veggie lovers', or smoked ham and meaty bacon. Inexpensive to moderate.

Hours vary seasonally. From Wrinkled Rock Trailhead, proceed 3.2 miles east on SD 244. Go left (east) on US 16 Alternate for about .8 miles to find the restaurant, located within the Roosevelt Inn on the right side of the street.

For a reasonably priced, all-American meal, one option is to drive to the Wrangler Restaurant (605-673-4271; 302 Mount Rushmore Road, Custer). The Wrangler specializes in buffalo but also offers chicken and salads, among other selections. Inexpensive. Open 5 AM–7 or 8 PM. From Wrinkled Rock Trailhead, go 7.3 miles west on SD 244. Turn south (left) onto US 16 and go 11 miles. Turn right onto US 16 Alternate and proceed .1 mile to find the restaurant on the left.

Rock City—Minneapolis, Kansas

Deep in America's heartland, with nary a cliff—much less a mountain—in sight for miles and miles, you'll find a treasure trove of boredom-alleviating boulders if you follow those signs off the interstate that advertise a random tourist attraction, or trap, as is often the case. In this case, if you're a boulderer or rock climber cruising along I-70 through Kansas, by following the signs near Minneapolis to Rock City, you'll find yourself wowed by one of rural Kansas's greatest sights to behold—a field filled with more than 200 boulders strewn about in close proximity to one another. Though most are too small to climb on, the handful of boulders large enough to be of interest to the traveling climber range from two- or three-move shorties to those tall enough to almost qualify as highballs.

Classified as sandstone concretions, these seemingly out-of-place boulders were actually hewn from Dakota sandstone that used to be underground. The concretions are what is left behind from a geological process and subsequent erosion that took place millions of years past when Kansas sported its own sea. (For a complete explanation in scientific terms as to their formation, please visit www.washburn.edu/cas/art/cyoho/archive/KStravel/rockcity; for your sake and mine, I'm not even going to try my nonscientific hand at explaining these formations in detail.) Remarkably, this is the largest place—in both quantity and size of the boulders—known in the world where these geological formations occur. Luckily for climbers and boulderers, they happen to sit practically right in the middle of the United States in a place otherwise virtually devoid of rock worth climbing—what a treat!

The boulders themselves feature a texture so pleasing and sticky that you might as well leave your chalk bag in the car. Not only is chalk unnecessary, but the absence of chalk on the boulders will help protect against any future potential problems with access, since many visitors to this attraction come simply to

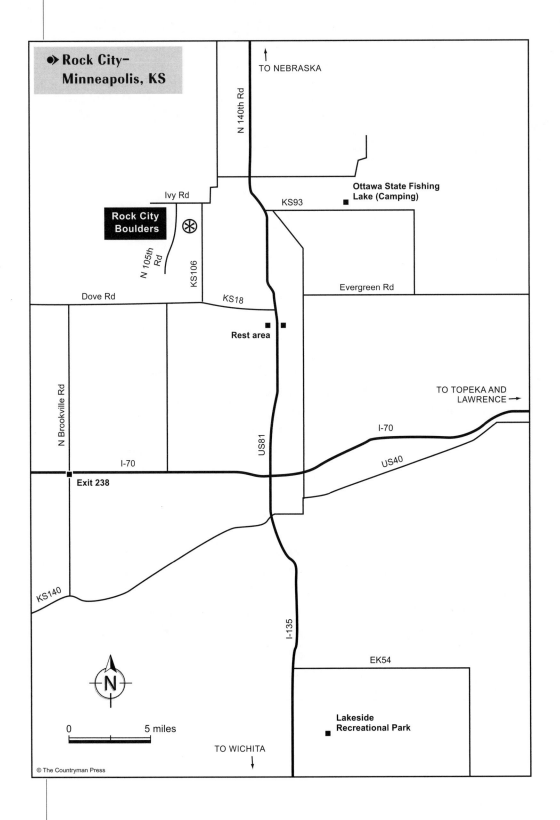

Rock City-
Minneapolis, KS

TO NEBRASKA

N 140th Rd

Ivy Rd

KS93

Ottawa State Fishing
Lake (Camping)

Rock City
Boulders

N 105th Rd

KS106

Evergreen Rd

Dove Rd

KS18

Rest area

N Brookville Rd

TO TOPEKA AND
LAWRENCE →

I-70

US81

US40

I-70

Exit 238

KS140

I-135

EK54

N

Lakeside
Recreational Park

0   5 miles

TO WICHITA

© The Countryman Press

see the rocks, not to climb on them. Though you can certainly make up challenging eliminates if you feel so inclined, most of the boulders here don't have specific, clearly defined problems, since they are riddled with excellent holds. Add to that the perfect landings and mostly easy top outs, and Rock City makes an ideal destination for beginning boulderers or for anyone who needs to break up the monotony of a long, cross-country drive.

The Lowdown

➥GETTING THERE

Driving directions: From I-70 East or West, take I-135/US 81 North toward Concordia for 9.8 miles. Take the KS 18 exit for Lincoln/Junction City and turn left. Go 4.5 miles, and then turn right onto KS 106. Go 5 miles, and then turn left onto Ivy Road. Go .5 miles to find Rock City. Signs will guide your way as well (though they will take you through Minneapolis if you follow them off the interstate), and you can actually find Rock City marked in many road atlases.

Nearest major airports: The Wichita Mid-Continent Airport (316-946-4700; www.flywichita.org; 2173 Air Cargo Road) is about 110 miles south of Rock City.

Public transportation: None.

➥CLIMBING CONCERNS

Cost: From May 1 through September 1, admission is $3 a day per person. For the remainder of the year, money collected in a donation deposit box goes toward the upkeep of the area, so please be sure to contribute.

Hours: Open dawn through dusk year-round.

Land manager: Rock City (www.ourks.com/rockcity.html; 1051 Ivy Road, Minneapolis) is privately owned and managed by Rock City, Inc. For information, contact the Minneapolis Chamber of Commerce (785-392-3068; www.minneapolisks.org; 213 West Second, Minneapolis, KS 67467).

Finding the boulders: You will have no problem finding the boulders!

Type of rock: Sandstone concretions.

Five good problems: Rock City is truly a place where you can—and should—let your imagination dictate what you climb instead of trying to follow any sort of established lines. The boulders sizable enough for climbing are veritably teeming with holds allowing you to climb them straight up, traverse around them, or randomly select specific holds to create your own challenges.

Range of grades: I would guess that most of Rock City's pure lines (with no holds eliminated) are in the VB–V1 range, with perhaps a few problems as hard as V4 or 5. The potential for more challenging eliminates exists, of course.

Prime season: Spring and fall. Rock City is best visited anytime you happen to be passing through Kansas and need a break from driving, but probably you will find it pretty bone-chilling in the middle of winter and quite sweltering in the heat of the summer.

Dogs: Allowed, but please keep your dog leashed and pick up after it.

Special notes: Please be respectful of other visitors to this area, most of whom are not boulderers—though they will often climb on the rocks nonetheless. Leave your chalk in the car, since it is entirely unnecessary.

Guidebooks to area problems: To my knowledge, no such guide currently exists.

Online resources: There are several Web sites featuring information about and photos of Rock City, including www.ourks.com/rockcity.html, www.washburn.edu/ cas/art/cyoho/archive/KStravel/rockcity, and www.lasr.net/pages/city.php? City_ID=KS0809014&VA=Y&Attraction_ID=KS0809014a001. RockClimbing.com (www.rockclimbing.com) and Climbingsource.com (www.climbingsource.com) both have listings on Rock City as well.

The Kansas City Outdoor Calendar (www.cirrus.kcsky.net/outdoor.html) is an excellent resource with a variety of links to outdoor-oriented organizations in the area. Also check out the Kansas City Climbing Club (www.kcclimbingclub .com).

Other resources: From May 1 through September 1, the Rock City Gift Shop, located at the boulders, sells items handcrafted by local artisans.

If you've never climbed before and you want to take a class or hire a guide, see *Local climbing gyms* for more information.

If you need camping supplies, your best bet near Rock City is probably the Salina Wal-Mart (785-825-6800, www.walmart.com; 2900 South Ninth Street). For climbing supplies, if you approach Rock City from the south, check out Backwoods Equipment Company, Inc. (316-267-0350; www.backwoods.com; 111 North Mosley Street, Suite 2, Wichita, KS), about 100 miles from Rock City. If you approach from the east, try Backwoods Equipment Company, Inc. (785-331-3772; www.backwoods.com; 916 Massachusetts Street, Lawrence, KS), about 160 miles from Rock City.

For communion with other area climbers and outdoor enthusiasts, consider attending a meeting or joining the Kansas City Outdoor Club, Inc. (www.kcoc .info; P.O. Box 95, Shawnee Mission, Kansas, 66201).

Local climbing gyms: About 200 miles east on I-70, you can play on plastic—or take a climbing class—at Ibex Climbing Gym (816-228-9988; www.climbibex.com; 801 South Outer Road, Blue Springs, MO) or at the Emerald City Gym's Monster Mountain (913-438-4444; www.emeraldcitygym.com/monster_mountain.htm; 9063 Bond, Overland Park, KS). If you are headed south through Oklahoma, 300 miles away in Tulsa you'll find New Heights Rock Gym (918-439-4400; www.new heightsgym.com; 1140 South 107th East Avenue), which offers indoor climbing as well as classes and outdoor guiding. About 110 miles south in Wichita, try the Kansas Cliff Club (316-612-2369; 4456 South Clifton Avenue).

Nearby bouldering and climbing areas of note: Due to its location smack-dab in the middle of the heartland, Rock City stands alone as an area of note in the state of Kansas, unless the locals are keeping some great secrets. You'll find worthy bouldering (such as Chandler Park in Tulsa) and rock climbing (notably the Wichita Mountains Wildlife Refuge) to the south in Oklahoma; to your west is Colorado with all its well-known climbing and bouldering destinations, and to the east, Missouri is gradually gaining notice for quality limestone sport climbing, among other climbing opportunities. To the north is Nebraska, which has less climbable rock than Kansas.

◆▶OTHER IMPORTANT STUFF

Camping: If you want to spend the night, primitive free camping can be found at the Ottawa State Fishing Lake (785-628-8614, www.naturalkansas.org/ottawa.htm). From Rock City, drive east on Ivy Road for .5 mile. Turn left (north) onto KS 106 and go 2.7 miles. Turn right onto KS 106/West First Street and go .4 mile. Stay on KS 106 as it turns right (Rothsay Avenue) for .2 mile and then left (Laurel Street) for 1.8 miles to join up with I-81/135. Turn right onto I-81 South and go 1.2 miles before exiting for KS 93. Go east on KS 93 for 4 miles to find the lake.

If you want more amenities, one option is to camp south of Salina at Lakeside Recreational Park (785-667-5795; www.lakesiderec.org; 1288 East Lapsley Road, Assaria). A tent site costs $10 per night, including showers. From Rock City, drive east on Ivy Road for .5 mile. Turn right onto KS 106 and go 5 miles. Turn left onto KS 18 East and go 4.3 miles. Turn right onto I-81/135 South and go 23.5 miles. Take exit 32 (KS 4 East/Falun Road) and turn left. Proceed .5 mile and turn right onto KS 104/South Old Highway 81. Go 2 miles, and turn left onto East Lapsley Road. Proceed 1.1 miles to find the park.

Another camping option—with more wacky boulders nearby to explore—is to drive a bit further to Kanopolis State Park (785-546-2565; www.kdwp.state.ks .us/pmforum/kanopolis.html; 200 Horsethief Road, Marquette), where you can camp for $7 or $8 a night, depending on the season. It is recommended that you call before you visit October 1–March 31 to ensure accessibility to camping, particularly if you want a guaranteed hot shower. From Rock City, drive east on Ivy Road for .5 mile. Turn right onto KS 106 and go 5 miles. Turn left on KS 18 East and go 4.3 miles. Turn right onto I-81/135 South and go 9.5 miles. Merge onto I-70 toward Hays and go 12.2 miles. Take exit 238, turn left onto North Brookville Road, and go 7.3 miles. Turn right onto KS 140 and go 5.7 miles. Turn left onto KS 141 and go about 8 miles before turning right into the park. And about those rocks . . . you'll drive right by them on your way to Kanopolis State Park—just turn at the signs for Mushroom Rock State Park (no camping) off KS 141 (785-546-2565; www.kdwp.state.ks.us/pmforum/mushroom .html). Happy hunting!

Nearby phone: You can find pay phones nearby in Minneapolis. From Rock City, drive east on Ivy Road for .5 mile. Turn left (north) onto KS 106 and go

2.7 miles. Turn right onto KS 106/West First Street to enter Minneapolis proper.

Showers: See *Camping*.

Water: Stop at one of the rest areas (north, south, east, and west) outside of Salina along I-70 or I-81/135 for a quick fill-up of your water bottles. I have heard that the rest area by exit 225 along I-70 has a couple of climbable boulders.

In case of emergency: Dial 911 for all emergencies.

Salina Regional Health Center (785-452-7000; www.srhc.com; 400 South Santa Fe Avenue) has a 24-hour emergency room. From Rock City, drive east on Ivy Road for .5 mile. Turn right onto KS 106 and go 5 miles. Turn left onto KS 18 East and go 4.3 miles. Turn right onto I-81/135 South and go 11.9 miles. Take exit 93 (KS 140/State Street), and turn left onto KS 140/West State Street. Go 1.4 miles and turn right onto North College Avenue. After less than .1 mile, turn left onto West Iron Avenue. Go .5 mile and turn right onto Santa Fe Avenue. Go .4 mile to find the hospital.

Nearby Internet hookup: Minneapolis Public Library (785-392-3205; www.ckls .org/members/Minne/MinneapolisLibrary.html; 519 Delia Avenue). From Rock City, drive .5 mile east on Ivy Road. Turn left (north) onto KS 106 and go 2.7 miles. Turn right onto KS 106/West First Street and go .2 mile. Turn left onto North Rock Street and go .2 mile. Turn right onto East Fifth Street and go .1 mile. Turn left onto Delia Avenue and proceed less than .1 mile to find the library.

Restaurants: For reasonably priced pizza, burgers, chicken baskets, or just an ice cream cone, head for KT's Grill and Pizza Parlor (785-392-2322; 202 North Rock Street, Minneapolis). Inexpensive. Open 9–9 daily. From Rock City, drive .5 mile east onto Ivy Road. Turn left (north) onto KS 106 and go 2.7 miles. Turn right onto KS 106/West First Street and go .2 mile. Turn left onto North Rock Street and go less than .1 mile to find the restaurant.

If you're headed back toward I-70 or to camp south of I-70, consider dining in Salina. One option is Martinelli's Little Italy (785-826-9190; www.ebclink .com/restaurants/mli; 158 South Santa Fe Avenue, Salina), where you'll find ample portions of Italian favorites, including plenty of choices for vegetarians and diet-minded souls. Choose from a variety of pastas, salads, or full entrées such as shrimp and herbs or veal Parmesan. Inexpensive to moderate. Open Monday through Saturday 11–10; Sunday 11–4. From Rock City, drive east on Ivy Road for .5 mile. Turn right onto KS 106 and go 5 miles. Turn left onto KS 18 East and go 4.3 miles. Turn right onto I-81/135 South and go 11.9 miles. Take exit 93 and turn left onto West State Street/KS 140. Go 1.4 miles, and turn right onto North College Avenue. After less than .1 mile, turn left onto West Iron Avenue. Go .5 mile and turn right onto Santa Fe Avenue. Proceed less than .1 mile to find the restaurant.

If you want a good cuppa joe in the morning as well as some tasty break-fast fare, try Capers Café and Bakery (866-823-7177 or 785-823-7177; www .capersonline.com; 109 North Santa Fe Avenue, Salina). Fresh-brewed coffee in basic or endless varieties, including a full coffee press, will start you off, and then you can select from a number of pastries and baked goods. Capers also has lunch fare, including sandwiches, salads, and soups. Open Monday through Saturday 7 AM–6 PM; Sunday 8 AM–3 PM. From Rock City, drive east on Ivy Road for .5 mile. Turn right onto KS 106 and go 5 miles. Turn left onto KS 18 East and go 4.3 miles. Turn right onto I-81/135 South and go 11.9 miles. Take exit 93 and turn left onto   West State Street/KS 140. Go 1.4 miles and turn right onto North College Avenue. After less than .1 mile, turn left onto West Iron Avenue. Go .5 mile and turn left onto Santa Fe Avenue. Go less than .1 mile to find the café.

chapter 8

Northeast

AUTUMN IN THE NORTHEASTERN UNITED STATES can yield perfectly crisp, sunny days ideal for bouldering, made even lovelier by the scents and sights of trees with leaves turning for the season. Brilliant reds, oranges, and yellows make entire valleys dance in a cacophony of colors pleasing to the eye, while cooler days and nights bring with them lower humidity and fewer bothersome, biting bugs—making fall the best season to plan a bouldering adventure to this area of the country. Still, before you pack your bags and head this way, you should watch the weather if you can, since you don't want to go during a rainy spell. Of course, you could luck out and spend two weeks basking in a brilliant autumn sunny spell and return home confused about why people ever complain about the weather in this region.

Northeastern bouldering has much variety to offer the traveler, from the urban bouldering experiences of Lincoln Woods State Park and Hammond Pond Reservation to the more pastoral areas of the Shawangunks (or the Gunks) and Rumney. No matter where you choose to drop your crash pad, though, you're likely to be close to a population center, be it a large one like Boston or a tiny, classic New England hamlet like Rumney. This means you are likely to have the company of friendly local or regional boulderers on any given day. Whatever your tastes in bouldering, you will find problems that will cater to your strengths or exploit your weaknesses

Rumney's classic Zig-zag Crack, located in the Black Jack Boulders.

depending on where you go (unless your skills are equally solid on all sorts of angles and holds). From the more technical granite of Lincoln Woods to the slopers and steep problems at the Gunks, a visit to the Northeast will expose you to a diverse variety of bouldering styles and areas.

Rumney, New Hampshire

If you know anything about New England rock climbing, you've probably heard of Rumney. In recent years this collection of crags poking out of the woods across the side of Rattlesnake Mountain has gained national notoriety not only for its high concentration of difficult sport climbs but also for spawning some young, talented "rock stars" who cut their teeth on the unusual schist routes of the area (up to 5.14d —the upper end of difficulty for route climbing). However, what you may not know is that Rumney contains two fun and concentrated bouldering areas featuring the same quality schist—the Black Jack Boulders and the Pound—both of which have plenty of moderate problems suitable for beginning to intermediate boulderers, as well as a handful of challenging test pieces for experts.

The Black Jack Boulders lie just off one of the trails to one of Rumney's finest sport crags, Waimea. A short jaunt brings you to the first boulder, the classic Umbrella Traverse, and numerous other boulders with a network of trails connecting them will greet your eyes as you round the side of the Umbrella Traverse—which stays dry in most inclement weather. Don't let the muddy puddles ringing the bases of some of these boulders (in particular the aptly named Moat Boulder)

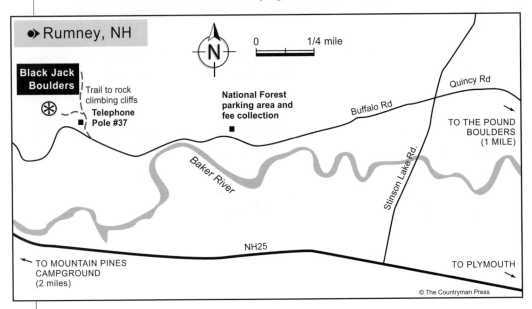

deter you from climbing here, unless you visit in spring or early summer, when the blackflies and mosquitoes are sure to drive you away. Otherwise, Black Jack Boulders should prove a worthy spot to drop your pad for a while—and you can get downright creative about how to avoid a penalty splashdown if you fall from the starting holds!

No boulderer's visit to Rumney would be complete without a stop at the Pound. Though a bit removed from the main climbing area, this location contains a superb, small cluster of boulders with numerous easy problems—many of which are highballs—and a few more difficult ones as well. Quick access and a high concentration of problems make this a great spot if your time is limited. Close proximity to the road means that local traffic will be apparent—and that you should be careful to stay off the road when a vehicle approaches, as some of the boulders hug the shoulder.

The Lowdown

➡️ GETTING THERE

Driving directions: From I-93, take exit 26 onto US 3/NH 25/NH 3 Alternate toward Plymouth/Rumney for almost .5 mile. Merge onto NH 25 West/NH 3 Alternate South—the Tenney Mountain Highway—and follow this for 3.9 miles before veering right at a roundabout to continue on NH 25 toward Rumney for 3.4 miles. When you reach the second flashing yellow light, turn right onto Stinson Lake Road in Rumney. After about .5 mile, turn right onto Quincy Road and proceed about 1 mile to reach the Pound boulders. They lie on both sides of the road, with the large boulder on the right nearly on the road. Be sure to park your vehicle completely off the road on the right past this first huge boulder. Watch for cars when opening your doors, and give all cars the right of way when crossing the road or bouldering. For Black Jack Boulders, turn left onto Buffalo Road (the same road as Quincy Road with a different name) and proceed about 1 mile to the obvious National Forest parking area on the right.

Nearest major airports: Manchester Airport in New Hampshire will land you 70 miles from the crags. Another option is Boston's Logan International Airport, which is about two hours' drive (or 120 miles) from Rumney.

Public transportation: None.

➡️ CLIMBING CONCERNS

Cost: The parking areas for all of Rumney except for the Pound are included in the "national recreation fee demonstration program," meaning that you are required to purchase a $3 daily parking pass (self-serve stations are located in the parking area) or you will receive a ticket. You can also purchase a pass for up to seven consecutive days for $5 or an annual pass for $20.

Hours: Dawn through dusk.

Land manager: Rumney lies in the White Mountain National Forest. Contact the Pemigewasset/Ammonoosuc Ranger District (603-536-1310; www.fs.fed.us/r9/white; RFD #3, Box 15, Route 175, Plymouth, NH 03264).

Finding the boulders: For the Pound, see *Driving directions*. For Black Jack Boulders, walk west on Buffalo Road from the main parking area until you reach telephone pole 37, making sure that you yield to all automobile traffic. Head up the trail, keeping your eyes peeled for the first split, where the main trail continues up and right and a small spur trail dips left at a 90-degree angle behind a not-so-appealing boulder. Take the spur trail and you should come upon the obvious and aptly named Umbrella Traverse within about 30 seconds. Trails continue from here, weaving in and out of the boulders—have fun exploring! If you reach the trail junction where the trail splits for Waimea and Monsters, you have gone too far.

Type of rock: Schist.

Five good problems: Grab a good spotter and check out Pound Crack (V0, Pound) and Zig-zag Crack (V0+, Black Jack Boulders). Less frightening will be Umbrella Traverse (V2, Black Jack Boulders), Ricochet (V3, Black Jack Boulders), and the Stone Wall boulder problems (many variations, Pound).

Range of grades: Grades range from VB to V10 or possibly harder.

Prime season: Autumn is undoubtedly the best time to visit Rumney. Warmer, drier winter days can bring tolerable temps as well. As in all New England areas, spring here tends to be wet, buggy, and muggy, and summer brings with it soaring humidity. This doesn't mean you won't find a decent day here or there in spring and summer, though.

Dogs: Allowed, but please keep your dog on a leash and clean up after it.

Special notes: Please be sure to yield to all automobiles when walking on roads—this means you need to move off the road. Inconsiderate climbers could lead to access issues in the future, particularly at the Pound, due to the close proximity of the boulders to the road. Drive courteously and park only in permitted areas.

Guidebooks to area problems: The best guidebook (which also includes all of the sport-climbing areas) is *Rumney*, by Ward Smith (© Ward Smith, 2001).

Online resources: RumneyGuides.com (www.rumneyguides.com) will provide you with information about the Rumney area as well as where to purchase Ward Smith's guidebook locally (it's also available for purchase on the site). NERock .com (www.nerock.com) sells the guidebook and has information about New Hampshire and Maine rock climbing. Climb New Hampshire (www .climbnh.com) provides extensive information on climbing in the area. Also check out New England Climbs (www.neclimbs.com) and New England Bouldering (www.new englandbouldering.com). The Rumney Climbers' Association, responsible for helping with the purchase and donation of Rumney to the National Forest Service and the maintenance of the climbing area, has a Web site (http://oz.plymouth.edu/~rbruemme), but it had not been updated in several

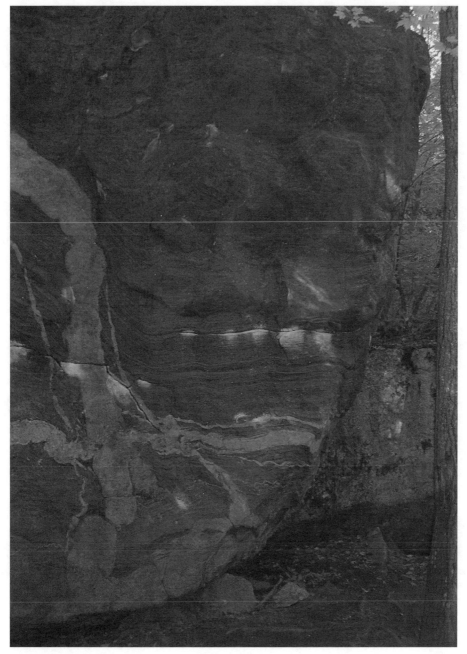

This is the place the right side of the Umbrella Traverse—that marks the entrance to Black Jack Boulders.

years as of this writing. Dr. Topo (www.drtopo.com) has a small, free guide to a few of Rumney's sport crags.

Other resources: The Appalachian Mountain Club's New Hampshire chapter (www.amc-nh.org) is a great organization if you want to meet local folks interested in rock climbing and other outdoor endeavors. For membership information, go to the AMC's main Web site (www.outdoors.org), call 617-523-0636, or write the main office at AMC Main Office, 5 Joy Street, Boston, MA 02108. If you want to climb some of Rumney's bigger rocks but lack the technical knowledge and skills to do so safely, consider hiring a guiding service such as Rhinoceros Mountain Guides (603-726-3030; www.navbuoy.com/rhino) or Eastern Mountain Sports Climbing School (800-310-4504; www.emsclimb.com/rumney.htm).

Local climbing gyms: New Hampshire has a number of indoor climbing facilities. The closest one to Rumney is the Rock Barn (603-536-2717; www.navbuoy .com/rhino), operated by Rhinoceros Mountain Guides, located conveniently on the Tenney Mountain Highway on the way to Rumney. The Rock Barn is open most rainy days, so if you find the weather disagreeable and still want a workout, check here before you give up. For a complete listing of New Hampshire's indoor climbing facilities, visit IndoorClimbing.com (www.indoorclimbing .com/newhampshire.html).

Nearby bouldering and climbing areas of note: Pawtuckaway State Park, located in New Hampshire near the town of Raymond (about 80 miles from Rumney), is rapidly gaining a reputation as one of New England's finest up-and-coming bouldering areas. New England Bouldering (www.newengland bouldering.com) lists several other bouldering areas for the state. In addition, New Hampshire has tremendous sport and traditional climbing opportunities, including the sport climbing at Rumney and at scattered crags along the Kancamagus Highway and the traditional climbing at Cathedral and Whitehorse Ledges and Cannon Mountain.

❖ OTHER IMPORTANT STUFF

Camping: Camping and overnight parking are not allowed. Call Mountain Pines (603-786-9934; 2759 Rumney Route 25) or Baker River Campground (603-786-9707; 56 Campground Road), both in Rumney, for rates and reservations, or try Plymouth Sands Campground five minutes away in Plymouth (603-536-2605; 3 Quincy Road). See map for driving directions to all three campgrounds.

Nearby phone: No pay phones are currently available in Rumney, so bring your cell phone in the event of an emergency—Verizon cell phones pick up service on at least some of the crags. Otherwise, plan to dine on the town in Plymouth and make your calls there.

Showers: See *Camping*.

Water: No water is available at the crags. See *Camping*, buy some at the Rumney Village Store (603-786-9800; 453 Main Street—just beyond the Buffalo Road/Quincy Road turnoff for both bouldering areas), or try your luck at one of several nearby gas stations—but please be sure to ask before filling your containers.

In case of emergency: Call 911 for all emergencies.

Drive to Speare Memorial Hospital (603-536-1120; www.spearehospital.com; 16 Hospital Road, Plymouth). From Stinson Lake Road in Rumney, turn left onto NH 25, heading east. After 3.4 miles, stay on NH 25 as it curves through a roundabout, continuing for another 2 miles to Highland Street. Take a slight right onto Highland and proceed 1.7 miles to turn onto Hospital Road.

Nearby Internet hookup: In nearby Plymouth, check your e-mail at the Pease Public Library (603- 536-2616; www.worldpath.net/~pease/Home.htm; 1 Russell Street). From Stinson Lake Road in Rumney, turn left onto NH 25, heading east. After 3.4 miles, stay on NH 25 as it curves through a roundabout, continuing for another 2 miles before turning right onto Highland and proceeding 2 miles. The library is on the corner of Highland and Russell.

Restaurants: Steve's Restaurant (603-786-9788), located on Stinson Lake Road in Rumney, serves up steaks, seafood, and other well-prepared American food at moderate prices. Open daily 11–9; closed Monday. The restaurant also serves brunch on Sunday from 9–3.

For an old-fashioned and inexpensive roadside diner experience, stop for breakfast at Plain Jane's Diner (603-786-2525; 897 Rumney Route 25, Rumney), where you will find yourself choosing from a menu that includes all of the usual suspects for down-home American cooking. Open 6 AM–8 PM daily. Free coffee refills will make you shake off the rocks if your laden belly doesn't pull you off first!

Many additional dining options are available nearby in Plymouth as well.

Hammond Pond Reservation—Newton, Massachusetts

The appeal of Hammond Pond's bouldering has less to do with sheer quality and more to do with its remarkable accessibility, given that getting there involves a short stroll from a Massachusetts Bay Transportation Authority (MBTA, or "T") stop. This is not to say that bouldering at Hammond Pond is not worth your while if you live in Boston or if you're visiting and have only an afternoon to spare, particularly if you're carless, since parking and driving in Boston can be notoriously difficult.

Located on Hammond Pond Reservation, behind the Chestnut Hill Shopping Center in Newton, the puddingstone boulders of Hammond Pond offer plenty of challenges for beginning to intermediate boulderers, while more advanced boulderers will likely have to come up with some creative eliminate problems to keep themselves entertained. In addition to numerous easy-to-moderate boulder problems scattered through the woods, some of the taller walls (20–25 feet) make for great roped outings on easy ground. No matter what your ability level, however, Hammond Pond offers a decent and relatively easy-to-access good-weather escape from the bustle of nearby city life—a fact that may be abundantly clear on nicer autumn afternoons, when the local after-work crowd shows up for some evening bouldering.

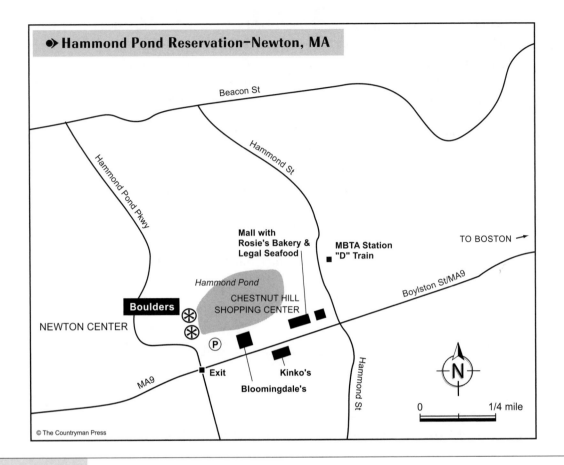

Hammond Pond Reservation–Newton, MA

The Lowdown

GETTING THERE

Driving directions: From Boylston Street/MA 9 in Boston, head west for roughly 5 miles (depending on where you start) to the Hammond Pond Parkway exit. The reservation parking lot lies just north of the parkway on the left as you enter the Chestnut Hill Shopping Center.

Nearest major airports: Boston's Logan International Airport (617-561-1800; www.massport.com/logan; Massport, One Harborside Drive, Suite 200S, East Boston).

Public transportation: Take the MBTA (800-392-6100; www.mbta.com) Green Line (D) to Chestnut Hill. Be sure you take the D Train—the B Train has a stop called Chestnut Hill Avenue, but that is not where you want to go. The fare is $1.25 outbound if you board the train from Park Station in downtown Boston, and $3 for the return trip. From the Chestnut Hill T stop, walk up the stairs from the parking lot to the street level. Turn left onto Hammond Street and walk across a bridge. Walk for two blocks until the Chestnut Hill Shopping Center is on your right. Walk through the parking lot behind the mall. The 64-acre reservation and its parking area lie behind Bloomingdale's.

◆ CLIMBING CONCERNS

Cost: Free.

Hours: Dawn to dusk.

Land manager: The Massachusetts Department of Conservation and Recreation Division of Urban Parks and Recreation (formerly the Metropolitan District Commission) (617-698-1802; www.state.ma.us/mdc/HAMMOND.HTM).

Finding the boulders: Facing the information sign in the parking area, to access the Alcove, turn left and head up a hill on a well-worn trail toward a cluster of boulders—the abundant amount of chalk should indicate when you've reached your destination. Taking the trail straight behind the sign will lead you to the Lower Wall, a popular roped climbing area.

Type of rock: The rock here is called puddingstone, or Roxbury conglomerate. It can be sharp and greasy to climb on, particularly when it's humid. Named for its puddinglike appearance, the rock is actually a colorful mishmash of Dedham granite, Westborough quartzite, and Mattapan volcanic rocks set in a background of solidified mudstone. Puddingstone is the official rock of the Commonwealth of Massachusetts.

Five good problems: From easiest to hardest, the following five problems can all be found in the Alcove—OJ (VB), Over Easy (VB), Snap (V0-), Breakfast of Champions (V2/3), and Hammond Eggs (V4/5). Easy traverses and straight-up problems are available on the wall to the right as well.

Range of grades: The range of grades at Hammond Pond is VB—V7 or thereabouts, unless you create some eliminate problems—or ask locals for their favorites.

Prime season: Autumn is undoubtedly the best time to visit. Warmer, drier winter days can bring perfect temps as well. As in all New England areas, spring here can be wet, buggy, and muggy, and summer brings with it soaring humidity. This doesn't mean you won't find a decent day here in any season.

Guidebooks to area problems: Just out is the new *Boston Rocks*, 2nd edition (© Richard Doucette and Susan Ruff). See www.bostonrocksonline.com for information about where to purchase the book.

Dogs: Must be on a leash at all times.

Online resources: Boston Rocks (www.bostonrocksonline.com)—be sure to explore the "climbing resources and links" section; New England Climbs (www.neclimbs.com); and New England Bouldering, (www.newenglandbouldering.com).

Other resources: The Boston chapter of the Appalachian Mountain Club (617-523-0655; www.amcboston.org; located at 5 Joy Street, Boston, MA 02108) offers organized rock climbing instruction and outings. The Nth Pitch, the American Alpine Club's New England Section (www.americanalpineclub.org/community/section_new_england.asp or www.atkinsopht.com/mtn/aacnesct.htm), offers climbers' socials, lectures, and other events. You can meet all of your bouldering gear needs by stopping by REI-Boston (617-236-0746; www.rei.com; 401 Park Drive, Boston) or REI-Framingham (508-270-6325; www.rei.com; 375 Cochituate Road, Framingham; this location has an in-store climbing wall). You can also shop for gear at Bob Smith's Wilderness House

Half of the Alcove at Hammond Pond.

(617-277-1519; 1048 Commonwealth Ave, Boston) or pop across the street to Eastern Mountain Sports (617-254-4250; www.ems.com; 1041 Commonwealth Avenue, Boston).

Local climbing gyms: The nearest indoor facility is Boston Rock Gym (781-935-7325; www.bostonrockgym.com; 78G Olympia Avenue, Woburn), about 12 miles north of Boston.

Nearby bouldering and climbing areas of note: Eastern Massachusetts is home to an abundance of small but worthy climbing areas in addition to Hammond Pond, such as Crow Hill, College Rock, and Quincy Quarries—all of which and many more are thoroughly described in *Boston Rocks*. The Northeast offers myriad notable climbing destinations, from the sport climbing at Rumney (see pages 182–187) to the traditional climbing of the Shawangunks (see pages 198–203). Cathedral and Whitehorse Ledges near North Conway, New Hampshire; Acadia National Park in Maine; and Pawtuckaway in New Hampshire are just a handful of the other terrific climbing destinations around the Northeast.

Other half of the Alcove at Hammond Pond.

●▶OTHER IMPORTANT STUFF

Camping: No camping is allowed in the reservation, and there are no valid free—or even inexpensive—options nearby. In addition, many campgrounds are open only seasonally. For state-run camping facilities, contact the Massachusetts Department of Conservation and Recreation Division of State Parks and Reservation (877-422-6762; www.state.ma.us/dem/recreate/camping.htm). For other ideas, contact the Massachusetts Campground Owners Association (781-544-3475; www.campmass.com).

Nearby phone: Chestnut Hill Shopping Center has pay phones.

Showers: None are available anywhere close. See *Camping* if you are in desperate need, but expect to drive a long way.

Water: Chestnut Hill Shopping Center has water.

In case of emergency: Call 911 for all emergencies.
Newton-Wellesley Hospital (617-243-6000; www.nwh.org; 2014 Washington

Street, Newton) is easily accessed from Hammond Pond Reservation. By car, take the Hammond Pond Parkway back to MA 9/Boylston Street. Go west on MA 9. After 3 miles, merge onto I-95 North and proceed 1.4 miles. Take the exit for MA 16 (exit 21a), heading east toward Newton/Wellesley. After less than .4 mile, the hospital entrance will be on your right. By T, take the Green D Line from Chestnut Hill outbound to Woodland. Walk out to Washington Street and turn left. Walk two short blocks; the hospital is on the left.

Nearby Internet hookup: For a small fee, you can connect at Kinko's (617-731-8800; www.kinkos.com; 1244 Boylston Street, Chestnut Hill, MA 02467, or across MA 9 from the Chestnut Hill Shopping Center)

Restaurants: Chestnut Hill Shopping Center has a number of choices, depending on your budget and mood. Rosie's Bakery (617-277-5629; www.rosiesbakery .com; 9 Boylston Street, Chestnut Hill) offers coffee and coffee-based drinks, pastries, smoothies, cookies, brownies, cake, ice cream, and yogurt. Open Monday through Thursday 8−7; Friday and Saturday 8 AM−9 PM; Sunday 9−6.

If you're hungry for dinner, like seafood, and don't mind dropping a decent amount of cash—stop at Legal Sea Foods (617-277-7300; www.legalseafoods .com; 43 Boylston Street, Chestnut Hill). Expect moderate to expensive prices for dinner entrées such as lobster ravioli or banana-leaf-steamed cod. Open Monday through Thursday 11−10; Friday and Saturday 11−11; Sunday 12−10.

Lincoln Woods State Park—Lincoln, Rhode Island

On any sunshine-kissed day in autumn, Lincoln Woods may make you feel as though you have entered a magical alternate reality, especially due to the fact that the park springs up seemingly out of nowhere. You're driving through a mundane urban setting one minute only to suddenly enter a preserved natural area that includes some of the finest bouldering in New England. There is nothing quite like wandering through a thick deciduous forest on a crisp autumn day with the wind lightly rustling the leaves and the sound of their fallen brethren crunching under your feet until you happen upon a boulder or two—not too high, but high enough—with perfect landings and eye-catching features in the form of cracks—both horizontal and vertical—pockets, crimpers, and slopers.

The boulders of Lincoln Woods seem to beckon, "Climb me," and you can hardly imagine the excitement that must have crackled in the air when the original lines were discovered by the first climbers to grace this stone. Despite all of the subsequent traffic on some of the more popular rocks, the holds on these boulders have still managed to retain their texture for the most part, resisting that slick sheen of polish that so often mars once-classic problems, transforming them into mere shadows of their formerly glorious incarnations. To add to the appeal

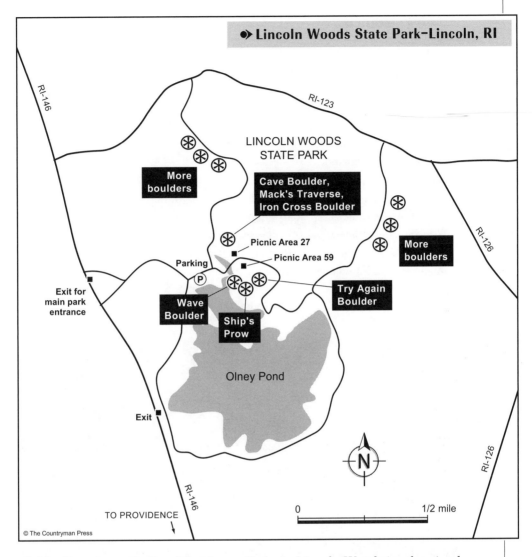

◆ Lincoln Woods State Park–Lincoln, RI

LINCOLN WOODS STATE PARK

More boulders

Cave Boulder, Mack's Traverse, Iron Cross Boulder

More boulders

Picnic Area 27

Picnic Area 59

Parking

Try Again Boulder

Wave Boulder

Ship's Prow

Olney Pond

Exit for main park entrance

Exit

TO PROVIDENCE

RI-146

RI-123

RI-126

RI-126

RI-146

N

0   1/2 mile

© The Countryman Press

of this place, the majority of the down climbs in Lincoln Woods involve simply walking off the back of the boulder as it slopes gently to the ground. It's as though the boulders were deposited in the woods by some higher power that understood how to create a perfect boulderers' playground.

Lincoln Woods, then, is well worth a visit for any level of boulderer, from the complete beginner who will revel in the slew of easy and safe problems to the expert who will find a number of hard problems and undone projects. Most of the problems are within easy walking distance of one another, making it possible for boulderers of all ability levels to put in a good day of climbing together, meaning you're not likely to waste your time sitting off to the side feeling boredom approach as you wait for a weaker or stronger partner to finish a problem that is too easy or too hard for you—you'll be too busy with your own problem!

The Lowdown

◆▶GETTING THERE

Driving directions: Lincoln Woods State Park lies in Rhode Island just east of
RI 146, less than 5 miles north of Providence. Large signs indicate the exit off
RI 146 for the park's main entrance. Depending on the season, parking for the
boulders varies, due to closure of the park's loop road. Parking is always available at the main entrance, and walking to most of the boulders from here is not
a massive undertaking.

Nearest major airports: T.F. Green Airport (888-268-7222; www.pvdairport.com;
2000 Post Road, Warwick, RI) and Boston's Logan International Airport (617-
561-1800; www.massport.com/logan; Massport, One Harborside Drive, Suite
200S, East Boston—about 50 miles away).

Public transportation: From Boston, the Massachusetts Bay Transportation
Authority (MBTA) Attleboro/Stoughton commuter rail will deposit you less than
6 miles from Lincoln Woods for a one-way ticket of $4.50. Depart from South
Station in Boston and debark in South Attleboro—from there, you can call a cab

Unknown boulderer on Iron Cross Boulder, Lincoln Woods, Rhode Island.

to take you the rest of the way. Visit www.mbta.com or call 1-800-392-6100 for schedules and to double-check fares. Check www.ripta.com or call 401-781-9400, the Rhode Island Public Transit Authority, for potential bus service to Lincoln Woods (not available at the time of this writing).

❖CLIMBING CONCERNS

Cost: Free.

Hours: Open daily year-round, sunrise to sunset.

Land manager: Lincoln Woods State Park (401-723-7892; www.riparks.com/lincoln.htm; 2 Manchester Print Works Road, Lincoln, RI 02865).

Finding the boulders: You can find many of the boulders here by simply walking along the park roads and keeping an eye out for them. The area containing Mack's Traverse and the Iron Cross Boulder is perhaps the best place to start your bouldering day, since it has a good concentration of easy and moderate problems as well as a few test pieces. If you are parked at the RI 146 entrance parking area, head east on the paved road toward a gate (which may be open or shut, depending on the season). Just after the gate, the road splits. Take the right fork and look on your left for picnic area 27, which is across the street from picnic area 59. Follow the obvious, well-worn trail uphill from picnic area 27 and you'll find (left to right) the Cave Boulder, Mack's Traverse, Iron Cross Boulder, and Warm-Up Boulder. This whole journey from the parking area should take you about five minutes. With problems from V0 to undone projects, this area is a great place to start out at Lincoln Woods no matter what level you climb at. Wandering along the trails leading out of picnic area 59 will bring you to other classic boulders such as the Wave, Try Again, and Ship's Prow.

Type of rock: Granite.

Five good problems: Be sure not to miss Beginner's Delight (V0, Iron Cross Boulder), Mack's Traverse (V2), Wave Traverse (V2), Iron Cross (V4), and Loadies Dream (V8, Iron Cross Boulder).

Range of grades: Something that will challenge everyone, from the total beginner to the elite boulderer.

Prime season: Autumn is undoubtedly the best time to visit Lincoln Woods. Warmer, drier winter days can bring perfect temps as well. As with all New England areas, spring here can be wet, buggy, and muggy, and summer brings with it soaring humidity. This doesn't mean you won't find a decent day here or there in spring and summer, though.

Dogs: Must be on a leash no longer than 6 feet in length. You are responsible for cleanup and disposal of all waste. Dogs must have a collar with a valid license tag and may not be left unattended in a vehicle.

Special notes: Please carry out all of your trash.

Guidebooks to area problems: Pick up a copy of *A Bouldering Guide to Lincoln Woods, RI,* by local expert Joe McLoughlin (© Joe McLoughlin, 2002).

Online resources: The premier online resource for all New England bouldering is www.newenglandbouldering.com, run by guidebook author Joe McLoughlin. Also check out Rhode Island Climbing (www.climbri.com) for more state-specific information and New England Climbs (www.neclimbs.com) for regional information.

Other resources: The Narragansett chapter of the Appalachian Mountain Club (www.amcnarragansett.org; 15 Brayton Street, Johnston, RI 02919) is Rhode Island's local affiliate of the Boston-based club The Rhode Island Rock Gym (see *Local climbing gym*) offers rock climbing instruction both indoors and outside.

Local climbing gyms: Indoor climbing facilities can be found nearby at the Rhode Island Rock Gym (401-727-1704; www.rhodeislandrockgym.com; 100 Higginson Avenue, Lincoln).

Nearby bouldering and climbing areas of note: The Northeast offers an abundance of notable climbing destinations, from the sport climbing at Rumney (see pages 182–187) to the traditional climbing of the Shawangunks (see pages 198–203). Cathedral and Whitehorse Ledges near North Conway, New Hampshire; Acadia National Park in Maine; and Pawtuckaway in New Hampshire are just a handful of the other terrific climbing destinations around the Northeast.

➧OTHER IMPORTANT STUFF

Camping: No camping is allowed in the park, and there are no valid free—or even inexpensive—options nearby. In addition, many of the campgrounds in Rhode Island operate only on a seasonal basis. For ideas, go to www.visit rhodeisland.com/recreation/camping.html, which contains a list of campgrounds and contact information. One possibility is the Holiday Acres Campground (401-934-0780), due to its relatively close proximity—it is at 591 Snake Hill Road in Glocester, about 15 miles from the park. This campground allows pets and is open year-round. Call in advance for rates and reservations.

Nearby phone: Pay phones are located in the park.

Showers: Coin-operated showers are available in the park.

Water: Available in the park.

In case of emergency: Call 911 for all emergencies.

Providence has a number of hospitals, including Rhode Island Hospital (401-444-4000; www.lifespan.org/partners/rih; 593 Eddy Street, Providence). From the park, take RI 146 south for 4.5 miles to join I-95 South. Stay on I-95 for almost 2 miles. Take exit 19 and bear right. At the end of the exit ramp there is a traffic light at the intersection of Eddy and Dudley streets. Continue straight onto Dudley Street and follow the signs to the Davol emergency department.

Nearby Internet hookup: Head for FedEx Kinko's (www.kinkos.com; 401-273-2830; 236 Meeting Street, Providence). From the park, drive south on RI 146 for

5 miles before merging onto I-95 for another .4 mile. Take exit 22 C-B-A (US 6/RI 10 west), taking the 22A exit on the left after .2 mile onto Memorial Boulevard (toward downtown). After a little less than .7 mile, turn left onto Washington Place, following it for .5 mile (it becomes Waterman Street). Turn left onto Brook Street and proceed .1 mile. Turn left onto Meeting Street. Your total travel time will be about 15 minutes.

Restaurants: The Providence area has far too many good, inexpensive eateries to list them all. One option is Paragon (401-331-6200; www.vivaparagon.com; 234 Thayer Street, Providence), where you can dine inexpensively on hamburgers and fries or go upscale with a baked, stuffed veal chop. From the park, drive south on RI 146 for 5 miles before merging onto I-95 for another .4 mile. Take exit 22 C-B-A (US 6/RI 10 west), taking the 22A exit on the left after .2 mile onto Memorial Boulevard (toward downtown). After a little less than .7 mile, turn left onto Washington Place, following it for .4 mile (it becomes Waterman Street). Turn left onto Brown Street and then make a quick right onto Olive Street and another right after .1 mile onto Thayer Street. Paragon is at the corner of Thayer and Angell. The drive should take about 15 minutes. Open Sunday through Thursday 11 AM−1 AM; Friday and Saturday 11 AM−2 AM (kitchen closes at 11:45 every night).

Grab a cup of coffee at the Brooklyn Coffee & Tea House (401-575-2284, www.brooklyncoffeeteahouse.com; 209 Douglas Avenue, Providence), about 4 miles from the park. This unique destination is located in a historic brick building that local artist Anthony Demings purchased with the intent of transforming it into a coffeehouse. Not only can you have coffee, tea, and pastries, but also you can enjoy walking through the gallery that showcases Demings's artwork. Take RI 146 south for 3.9 miles, and then take the Admiral Street exit, following Admiral Street for .2 mile. Make a slight right onto Whipple Street and continue for .3 mile before turning right onto Douglas and proceeding .1 mile to the coffeehouse. Open Monday through Tuesday 7 AM−1 PM; Wednesday through Friday 7 AM−1 PM and 6 PM−10 PM; Saturday 8 AM−1 PM and 6 PM−10 PM; Sunday 8 PM−1 PM.

The Gunks—New Paltz, New York

If you're looking for a friendly, attractive bouldering area with an easy approach and a lifetime's worth of concentrated problems, look no further than the Gunks—especially if your climbing tastes run beyond bouldering into the world of roped climbing. For decades, the Shawangunk Mountains (hereafter referred to as "the Gunks"), located in the Mohonk Preserve, have been a destination for technical climbers, featuring more than 1,000 established technical rock climbs packed along the uniquely featured quartzite conglomerate cliffs. Known for their incredible tiers of steep overhangs, horizontal cracks, and an unusually high concentration of top-quality easy and moderate rock climbs, the Gunks' cliffs draw huge numbers of rock climbers from around the country (and the world) eager to sample this classic roped climbing area. In addition to rock climbers, numerous other user groups, including mountain bikers, trail runners, and cross-country skiers, all enjoy the scenic recreational opportunities available within the Mohonk Preserve. Boulderers are among the more recent additions to the list of major recreational user groups.

Though climbers have played around for years on the boulders scattered along the carriage road that runs along the Trapps area, as well as on the boulders lying beneath other climbing areas, bouldering in the Gunks did not start to re-ally take off until the mid-1990s, right about when bouldering itself was starting

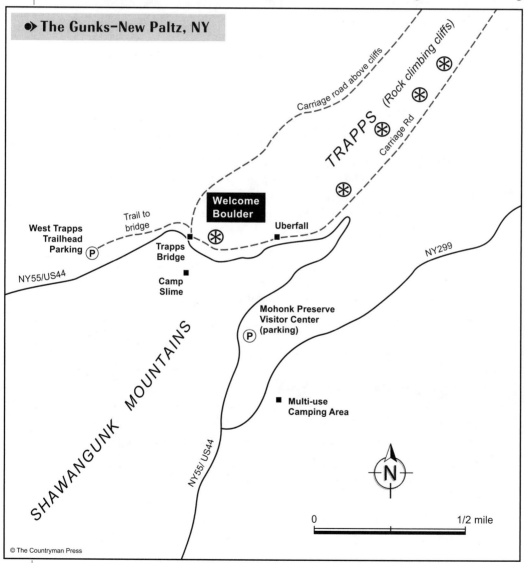

to explode onto the climbing scene as an end unto itself. As bouldering continues to expand within the climbing scene at large, attracting more and more devotees annually, so have the number of problems at the Gunks expanded—and consequently, the number of boulderers continues to grow. What used to be a rare sight along the carriage road—that of a crash-pad-toting boulderer or two—has become commonplace on any given day, especially on weekends, when crowds under some of the more popular boulders can reach 30 or more.

Don't let the crowds deter you, though—the climate at the Gunks is friendly and open, with people more than willing to spot you and allow you to use their pad or even going so far as to brush holds for you, point you in the direction of other good problems, or give you beta (most of the time only if you request it, though there are spraylords in every scene). If you have only a day or two, a simple saunter down the carriage road under the Trapps should provide more than enough material to keep you busy, with access to the problems right off the road (which is closed to vehicular traffic except for rangers' vehicles). Expect to find lots of slopers and some sharp crimpers, with angles ranging from slabby to steep, and some polish on the most traveled problems.

The Lowdown

➦GETTING THERE

Driving directions: From I-87, take exit 18 onto NY 299 toward New Paltz. Follow NY 299 west for a little more than 8.2 miles, traveling through the town of New Paltz. Turn right onto NY 55/US 44, and look for signs for the Mohonk Preserve Visitor Center. It will be on your right after 1.7 miles. The visitor center is free of charge and open Tuesday through Sunday from 9–5 except Thanksgiving, Christmas, and New Year's Day. Park your car in a valid parking area, not along NY 55/US 44. In addition to the parking at the visitor center, parking is available past the steel bridge entrance at Trapps Bridge, on the right at the West Trapps Trailhead Parking.

Nearest major airports: Half an hour from New Paltz is Stewart International Airport (845-564-2100; www.stewartintlairport.com; 1180 First Street, New Windsor). A little farther away (about 70 miles) is Albany International Airport (518-242-2200; www.albanyairport.com). Three major international airports—Kennedy, LaGuardia, and Newark—serve the metropolitan New York City area, about 90 miles from the Gunks.

Public transportation: New Paltz has an Adirondack Trailways bus station (800-858-8555; www.escapemaker.com/adirondacktrailways) located on the corner of Main Street and Prospect Street. From there, you can take a cab or walk a few blocks down Main Street to the local climbing shop, Rock and Snow, where it's likely you can hitch a ride to the boulders with another like-minded soul.

●▶CLIMBING CONCERNS

Cost: Entry to the Mohonk Preserve is $6 on weekdays and $8 on weekends and holidays. You can purchase a pass from a ranger at one of the entrances to the preserve or buy one at the visitor center. Children 12 and under get in free with an adult. Annual memberships are available for $85.

Hours: Dawn through dusk, 365 days a year.

Land manager: The Mohonk Preserve, Inc. (845-255-0919; www.mohonkpreserve .org; P.O. Box 715, New Paltz, NY), manages the Gunks. Encompassing 6,500 acres and only 90 miles from New York City, the preserve is the biggest member- and visitor-supported nature preserve in the state of New York.

Finding the boulders: Simply enter the preserve and walk along the carriage road below the Trapps. Entering via the steel bridge entrance at the Trapps Bridge (which, coincidentally, involves walking in either over or by the steel footbridge that passes over NY 55/US 44 before the West Trapps Trailhead Parking) will deposit you by some terrific warm-up boulders. Other boulders in the preserve lie scattered under the cliffs at the Near Trapps.

Type of rock: Shawangunk conglomerate, an extremely hard rock that contains quartz among other types of rock.

Five good problems: After you walk across the bridge, you can warm up at the Welcome Boulder (endless V0 variations) and Boulder of the Gods (many V0 variations; the beautiful boulder northeast of the Welcome Boulder) and then try The Lorax (V4, on the backside of the boulder southeast across the road from the Welcome Boulder) and Jackson Pollock (V8, on the boulder uphill from Boulder of the Gods) before exploring the boulders further down the carriage road.

Range of grades: From VB to V12.

Prime season: If you have any say in timing your visit, go to the Gunks in the fall when the leaves are changing and the weather can be crisp, sunny, and perfect, lacking the humidity and bugginess that can plague visitors in spring and summer.

Dogs: Must be on a leash and under direct supervision at all times. You are required to remove pet waste from trails and bury it or cover it with sticks and leaves in an area free of human traffic.

Special notes: Please respect the NO PARKING signs and park in designated areas only. The Mohonk Preserve gets extremely crowded on weekends and holidays, so if you want to park anywhere near the boulders, plan to arrive early.

Guidebooks to area problems: The book to buy is *Bouldering in the Shawangunks,* 2nd edition, by Ivan A. Greene and Marc E. Russo (Jefe Publications, 2003).

Online resources: The Mohonk Preserve has a section of its site specifically dedicated to rock climbing (www.mohonkpreserve.org/visit/climb). You can find additional information on Bouldering in the Gunks (www.boulderinginthe gunks.com), run by guidebook author Marc Russo; on the Gunks Climbers' Coalition site (www.gunksclimbers.org); and at Gunks.com (www.gunks.com), among numerous other climbing-related sites featuring the Gunks.

Other resources: New Paltz's climbing shop, Rock and Snow (845-255-1311; www.rocksnow.com; 44 Main Street), is a great place to gather beta or meet up with other boulderers—or to just pick up the guidebook or any other last-minute needs. If you want to climb some of the Gunks' bigger rocks but lack the technical knowledge and skills to do so safely, consider hiring a guiding service such as New Paltz–based Diamond Sports (800-776-2577; www.gunksguide .com) or Eastern Mountain Sports Climbing School (800-310-4504; www.em-sclimb.com/new%20paltz.htm). The Appalachian Mountain Club's New York–North Jersey chapter (212-986-1430; www.amc-ny.org) has offices in New York City and runs outdoor-oriented activities throughout the state.

Local climbing gyms: If you need to climb inside, check out the Inner Wall, Inc. (845-255-ROCK; www.theinnerwall.com; 234 Main St, Eckerd's Plaza, New Paltz).

The Boulder of the Gods, Gunks, New York.

Nearby bouldering and climbing areas of note: Peter's Kill, located in nearby Minnewaska State Park Preserve, offers more bouldering opportunities. In addition to the world-class route climbing at the Gunks, the nearby Adirondack Mountains offer classic traditional climbing and bouldering opportunities as well.

◆ OTHER IMPORTANT STUFF

Camping: There is a small, free (with entry fee to the preserve, of course) camping area near the steel bridge for rock climbers only that is located within the Mohonk Preserve. Known as "Camp Slime," this camping can be utilized only with permission from a ranger. About .5 mile from the intersection of NY 55/US 44 and NY 299, back toward New Paltz on NY 299, is a free, well-marked camping area known as "the multiuse area." Look for a small brown sign on the right (or the left if you're driving toward the Gunks), cars, and tents. Be sure to pitch your tent in camping limits and park only in marked spaces.

Nearby phone: New Paltz has numerous pay phones. The visitor center or one of the restaurants or stores located along NY 55/US 44 would undoubtedly help out by dialing 911 in an emergency situation.

Showers: The shower situation isn't entirely convenient, but if you're willing to drive 7 miles north out of New Paltz on NY 32, Creek View Campground (845-658-3949) will likely sell you a shower for a few dollars.

Water: Usually available to "drink at your own risk" at the Uberfall, where a pipe yields springwater (which can dry up at times). You can fill water bottles at the visitor center as well.

The Welcome Boulder, Gunks, New York.

In case of emergency: Call 911. Notify a ranger if possible, since they may be able to bring emergency services even faster.

North of New Paltz in Kingston are several hospitals, including the Kingston Hospital (845-331-3131; www.kingstonregionalhealth.org/kingston%5fhospital; 396 Broadway). From New Paltz, head north on I-87 for 15.6 miles (one exit). Take exit 19 and continue to go straight after the tollbooths. Follow signs for I-587/NY 28 East. Remain in the right lane and proceed to a traffic light. At the traffic light, continue straight onto Broadway for .7 mile. The hospital will be on the left.

Nearby Internet hookup: Elting Memorial Library (845-255-5030; http://elting .newpaltz.lib.ny.us; 93 Main Street, New Paltz).

Restaurants: New Paltz is a dining mecca, with an overwhelming selection of restaurants for such a small town. From sushi to pizza, fast-food joints to fancy sit-down establishments, you will have no problem finding a place that suits your tastes—and your post-bouldering attire.

To celebrate a successful send, dine at the Main Course Restaurant (845-255-2600; www.maincourserestaurant.com; 232 Main Street—in Eckerd's Plaza), where you will find perfectly prepared contemporary American cuisine. Whether you prefer a sophisticated twist on the ordinary, such as Asian grilled sirloin with wasabi mashed potatoes, or simply want to sample the extraordinary, such as a Chinese duck burrito, the Main Course will impress you not only with its service and comprehensive menu, but also with the preparation and presentation of its fabulous dishes. Vegetarians will find something to suit their palates here as well, as they will at most restaurants in New Paltz. Moderate to expensive, but it's well worth your cash for the pleasurable dining experience. Open Tuesday through Thursday 11:30–10; Friday 11:30–11; Saturday 9:30 AM –11 PM; Sunday 9:30 AM–10 PM; closed Monday.

If you're in the mood for something a little less pricey, try the Main Street Bistro (845-255-7766; www.mainstreetbistro.com; 59 Main Street), which serves up a variety of burgers, salads, burritos, wraps, quiches, and daily specials, as well as baked goods. Dinners are inexpensive to moderate. The bistro serves breakfast and lunch every day of the week year-round and serves dinner until 9 PM Monday and Thursday through Sunday (until 10 PM on Friday) from April through October; and Friday through Sunday the rest of the year. Hours vary according to season, but the restaurant is always open by 8 AM.

chapter 9

SOUTHEAST

BARBECUE RIBS WITH TENDER MEAT falling off the bones, warm peach cobbler so buttery and flaky that it practically melts in your mouth, blackened catfish coated with indescribable yet intensely delicious spices, and crispy hush puppies, those yummy fried cornmeal fritters—if you're a Yankee like me visiting the Southeast to boulder on its legendary sandstone, you might have to work hard not to be distracted by the fabulous regional cuisine, even if you can't stomach grits. Nonetheless, cuisine aside, the region's rock is well worth exploring, and it's best experienced at a time of year when most other areas are too cold. Given the humidity here, good friction is essential for success on many problems, and that friction declines rapidly with each degree of temperature gain. You might even hear local folks complaining on a sunny, 60-degree day in February that it's too hot for them to send their projects, while you're just happy to be bouldering outside without wearing a down jacket.

The Southeast has gained the respect of the worldwide bouldering community in the past few years, and for good reason. The two states covered here, Georgia and Alabama, are seemingly teeming with an abundance of sandstone perfectly formed to delight and challenge boulderers of all ability levels. And there's the likelihood of much more rock yet to be discovered—or at least made public by the local crowd, who must have some enclaves of bouldering badness that they are presently keeping secret.

Matt Wendling bouldering at Rocktown, Georgia.

That's fine, though, and perfectly understandable, given the popularity of Alabama's Horse Pens 40, perhaps the current crown jewel of Southeastern sandstone, known for its distinctive brand of slopers and slabby test pieces as well as horizontal roofs, not to mention boulderer-friendly camping with virtually all the amenities of home. Nestled a bit to the north is the more rugged bouldering of Sandrock, which, despite copious amounts of graffiti and broken glass, still manages to hold on as a worthy bouldering and sport-climbing area. Still farther north and east lies Rocktown, sporting its brand of the Southern sandstone experience, with its wildly featured overhangs, difficult top outs, and a smattering of slopers as well. And if you're in Atlanta for a couple of hours, or you live in the city, you can even find some bouldering right in town. Though not sandstone, the coarse-grained granite boulders of Boat Rock offer a great getaway from city life and an alternative to climbing indoors if the sun's out and you have time to spare.

Kate Reese bouldering at Horse Pens 40, Alabama.

Horse Pens 40— Steele, Alabama

On any sunny, winter weekend morning at Horse Pens 40, you might find yourself awakened to the thumping bass of your neighbor's gangsta rap at 7 AM, but don't be put off—it seems like most folks who come to boulder here are so eager to test themselves on the notoriously sloper-ridden sandstone that they can't sleep much later than that anyhow (myself included). The place receives so much traffic on those friction-perfect weekend days that the campground turns into a tent city, with clusters of both local and regional boulderers as well as travelers from distant places flocking to test themselves at one of the Southeast's premier boulder gardens. Thankfully, the number of problems and boulders in the park virtually ensures that you won't find yourself queuing up to try

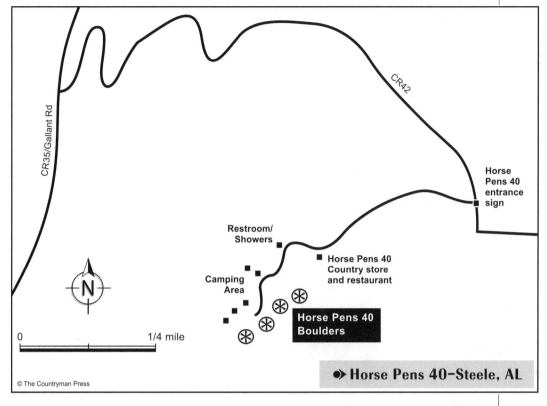

Restroom/Showers

Camping Area

Horse Pens 40 Country store and restaurant

Horse Pens 40 entrance sign

CR35/Gallant Rd

CR42

Horse Pens 40 Boulders

0   1/4 mile

© The Countryman Press

➤ **Horse Pens 40-Steele, AL**

problems or fighting through crowds on your way to the next boulder you want to check out.

Adjacent to the camping and the Horse Pens 40 Country Store you'll find the famous boulders, a tightly packed maze of rocks—some quite large—sporting problems of all angles, hold types, and difficulty levels. From the indescribably slopey slab problems, featuring bulbous blobs of sandstone that form the "holds" locals use to levitate up the slabs with ease (while the inexperienced like myself flail, curse, and slide back down to the ground), to horizontal roofs with virtual handholds that become usable once you solve the puzzle of the foot trickery, Horse Pens 40 as a whole is less about sheer brute pulling and more about figuring out how to use the unique features and formations that have made it such a destination. That's not to say you won't find yourself pulling powerful and straightforward problems on crimpers if that's what you like to climb. But to experience the full range of what Horse Pens 40 has to offer, you should expand your horizons and at least test your mettle on some of the problems that look like nothing you've ever attempted to climb.

After a day at the boulders, on weekends you can unwind at the Horse Pens 40 restaurant, where one of the friendly owners of the place, the Schultz family (Gina, Mike, and their three children), will take your order and prepare your food while you watch a video, play cards, or just hang out with other boulderers. When dinner's done, you can purchase a bundle of firewood at the camp store for $5, and a member of the family will deliver it directly to your campsite, saving you the hassle of carrying it there. The Schultz family has made a great effort to foster at Horse Pens a boulderer-friendly environment, and they offer pretty much every comfort and convenience a boulderer could dream of right on the premises—they even rent out crash pads for $5 a day.

The Lowdown

● GETTING THERE

Driving directions: From Birmingham, drive about 40 miles northeast on I-59. Take exit 166 for US 231 toward Oneonta/Ashville. Turn left onto US 231 and drive 3.3 miles (watch for obvious Horse Pens 40 signs). Turn right onto CR 35 and drive 1.8 miles. Turn right onto CR 42 and follow this to the top of the mountain, where you will find Horse Pens 40—look for a split-rail fence and a large gate on the right. Sign in at the country store.

From Atlanta, take I-20 west for about 115 miles. Take exit 158A for US 231 toward Ashville. Go 22.5 miles north on US 231 until you reach CR 35, where there will be a sign for Horse Pens 40. Turn right onto CR 35 and drive 1.8 miles. Turn right onto CR 42 and follow this to the top of the mountain, where you will find Horse Pens 40—look for a split-rail fence and a large gate on the right. Sign in at the country store.

Nearest major airports: Birmingham International Airport (205-595-0533; www.bhamintlairport.com; 5900 Airport Highway) is about 45 miles from Horse Pens 40. You might find cheaper tickets by flying to the Hartsfield-Jackson Atlanta International Airport (800-897-1910; www.atlanta-airport.com; 6000 North Terminal Parkway, Suite 435, Atlanta, GA), about 140 miles from Horse Pens 40.

Public transportation: None.

● CLIMBING CONCERNS

Cost: $3 per person per day.

Hours: 9 AM until just after sunset daily, but you can boulder any time if you're camping there.

Land manager: Horse Pens 40 (256-570-0076; www.hp40.com; 3525 County Road 42, P.O. Box 159, Steele, AL 35987) is privately owned and managed by the Schultz family.

Finding the boulders: Once you are in the park, you will have no problem finding the boulders. Trust me.

Type of rock: Sandstone.

Kenneth McGinnis, Horse Pens 40, Alabama. PHOTO BY MATT WENDLING

209

Five good problems: Five of my personal favorites include Ice Cream (V1, Slabolicious Block), The Crown (V3), Bumboy (Millipede Boulder, V3/4), Hammerhead (Front Slabs, V5), and Great White (HP Canyon, V7).

Range of grades: Hundreds of problems await boulderers of all levels with fairly even grade distribution and incredibly high quality and concentration.

Prime season: Winter is the time to make a visit, with spring and fall as runners-up. Don't bother stopping here in the summer unless you want to sweat profusely, slide off the slopers even more often, and curse your own stupidity.

Dogs: Allowed, but must be leashed at all times. You must pick up after your pet.

Special notes: You must sign a waiver before bouldering. Don't damage plants or the boulders in any way. No glass containers are allowed in the park. Do not consume alcohol openly outside of your campsite. The speed limit in the park is 5 miles per hour. For a detailed list of park rules (most simply involve using your common sense), see www.hp40.com.

Please keep in mind that Horse Pens 40 is not just a boulderers' park. It is an "Outdoor Nature Park" that also attracts hikers, picnickers, and nature lovers, and hosts many special events throughout the year, including bluegrass festivals, Native American festivals, Civil War reenactments, motorcycle rallies, and more.

For detailed historical information about the park, visit www.hp40.com.

Guidebooks to area problems: You can purchase a copy of the HP40 Bouldering Competition topo at the Horse Pens 40 store for $3. It includes easily understood descriptions of each problem and an overview map of the boulders.

Alli, Bum Boy, Horse Pens 40, Alabama.
Photo by Matt Wendling

Online resources: The official Horse Pens 40 Web site can be found at www.hp40.com. Visit Dr. Topo (www.drtopo.com) to download a free guide, *Bouldering at Horse Pens 40: One of Southeast's Finest*, written in collaboration with Adam Henry, Cooper Roberts, and Lee Payne. Both Flatliners Southeast Climbing (www.southeastclimbing.com) and the Southeastern Climbers Coalition (www.seclimbers.org) have excellent informational pages on Horse Pens 40. Visit the Alabama Climber's Association site (www.inline.com/aca/aca1 .html) for communion with like-minded locals. Modump Bouldering (www.mo dump.com) and HP Bouldering: The Southeastern Experience (http://freewebs .com/silveys) have more information as well as photos.

Other resources: The Horse Pens 40 Country Store (open Friday through Sunday, or if you ring the bell and someone's there) has a selection of camping supplies, basic meals and food, and chalk and chalk bags, as well as rental crash pads available for $5 a day. If you've never climbed or bouldered before and you want to hire a guide, try High Country Outfitters (205-985-3215; www.high countryoutfitters.com; 2000-147A Riverchase Galleria, Birmingham, AL) or GA-Adventures (404-630-7382; www.ga-adventures.com; 6851 Roswell Road, I-16, Atlanta, GA). In Birmingham you can shop for gear at Alabama Outdoors (205-870-1919; www.aloutdoors.com; 3054 Independence Drive; or at Urban Outpost (888-303-8850 or 205-879-8850; www.urbanoutpost.com; 1105 Dunston Avenue); both stores also have in-store climbing areas.

Local climbing gyms: See *Other resources* for Birmingham facilities. Located 70 miles away in Huntsville, you'll find Rock-it Sport Climbing Gym (256-880-0770; http://timym.com/rockit; 2100 Members Drive Southwest).

Nearby bouldering and climbing areas of note: The often-overlooked but decent bouldering of Sandrock (see pages 212–219) is less than 40 miles northeast of Horse Pens 40. About 100 miles northeast you'll find the well-known bouldering area of Rocktown, Georgia (see pages 219–226). Also in Alabama, you'll find Palisades Park (short routes and bouldering) and Little River Canyon (traditional climbing), among other climbing and bouldering areas. The Southeast has a vast quantity of additional excellent bouldering and climbing; check out the sites listed in *Online resources* for more ideas.

◆ OTHER IMPORTANT STUFF

Camping: Camping is available for $8 per person per day at the park (day-use fee of $3 is included in this fee). Each site can have only one vehicle and two adults. Electric and water hookups cost $5 extra per night.

Nearby phone: The Schultz family will gladly let you use the Horse Pens 40 phone to make brief calls, but they prefer that you use a calling card. (My cell phone got service at Horse Pens 40.)

Showers: Available in the park.

Water: Available in the park.

In case of emergency: Contact park personnel, on duty 24/7 in the store or the park office.

Drive to Riverview Regional Medical Center (256-543-5390; www.hma-corp .com/al1.html; 600 South Third Street, Gadsden). From the intersection of CR 35 and US 231, turn left onto US 231 and drive 3.3 miles. Merge onto I-59 via a ramp on the left. Go 15.2 miles, and then merge onto I-759 East via exit 182. Drive 4.9 miles. Merge onto US 411 North (Rainbow Drive) and go .8 mile. Turn left onto South Albert Rains Boulevard. After less than .1 mile, turn right onto Rainbow Drive. After .1 mile, Rainbow Drive becomes South Third Street. The hospital is .1 mile further.

Nearby Internet hookup: Nearby Steele has a public library, but it was slated to move in the near future and had sporadic hours at the time I visited. For a sure bet, head for the Attalla–Etowah County Public Library (256-538-9266; www.cityofattalla.com/html/library.html; 604 Fourth Street Northwest, Attalla). From the intersection of CR 35 and US 231, turn left onto US 231 and drive 3.3 miles. Merge onto I-59 via a ramp on the left. Drive 16.4 miles and take exit 183. Turn left onto Fifth Avenue Northeast and drive .8 mile. Turn right onto Fourth Street Northwest to find the library in less than .1 mile.

Restaurants: You can dine at the Horse Pens 40 Restaurant (and shop in the Country Store) Friday through Sunday, or just ask for a home-cooked meal during the week if you are craving something yummy. Selections include burgers (beef and veggie), grilled chicken, and tasty fried green tomatoes.

Great barbecue awaits you just down the road at Shaw's Hickory Smoked Barbecue (205-594-7801; Highway 231, Ashville). Choose from meaty barbe-cued ribs, catfish, or shrimp, among other selections, all of which come with a choice of two side dishes. Vegetarians will find slim pickings, such as a grilled cheese sandwich. Inexpensive. Open Monday through Saturday 8–8. From the intersection of CR 35 and US 231, turn left onto US 231 and drive about 3 miles (almost to the interstate), keeping an eye out for the restaurant on your left (it has a flashing sign).

For dessert or a treat on a rest day, head down the road from Shaw's for a couple of scoops of ice cream at the Rainbow Ice Cream Parlor, located inside the 24-hour Texaco gas station just off I-59 on AL 231. Try the Smokey Moun-tain Fudge—it rocks.

Sandrock—Leesburg, Alabama

Graffiti-covered boulders and broken glass aside, Sandrock offers up its own dis-tinctive brand of the Southeastern bouldering experience, from the impressive cave feature and highballs of the Fire Pit to the oddly formed Cannonball, which looks as though a perfectly spherical mass of matter simply popped out of the side of the short cliff band, leaving behind a spherical cave with problems exiting ei-ther side of it.

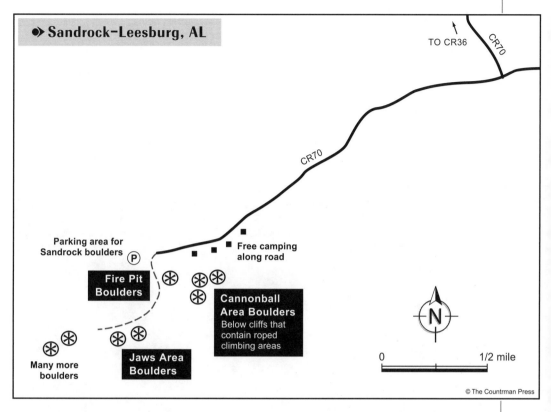

Abrasive in a not-so-subtle way, the pebbly, rough sandstone of Sandrock is like coarse-grained sandpaper when compared to its finer-grained cousin to the north, in Rocktown. This makes for great friction, of course, given the proper weather conditions, but it also can make for raw fingertips quite rapidly if you're not careful to pace yourself and to move precisely on the holds when you do climb.

Though I'd been warned about the potential for wild parties and hootin' and hollerin', on my visit to Sandrock I experienced only lovely roadside camping, quiet and removed, overlooking Weiss Lake and the surrounding area. I suppose it depends on the night you're there. In any case, you may find yourself surprised by the beauty this place has managed to retain in spite of all of the trash and graffiti—particularly if you're into climbing roped routes as well, since the bolted sport climbs made me wish I'd brought my rope and gear along. Either way, whether you're solely bouldering or climbing roped routes, too, you're likely to find enough climbable surfaces to keep you busy for at least a little while at Sandrock.

The Lowdown

➡ GETTING THERE

Driving directions: From I-59 between Fort Payne and Gadsen, take exit 205 onto AL 68. Go 1.2 miles, and stay straight to get onto AL 68/US 11. After .5 mile, turn left onto AL 68. Seven miles after the intersection of AL 68 and US 11, make a right onto CR 36 at the sign for Cherokee Rock Village. Continue 1.5 miles and then make a sharp left onto CR 70. Proceed .6 mile up a winding hill (the road soon turns to dirt) to a fork in the road. Take the right fork and follow this road 2.9 miles until it ends. Park here.

Matt Wendling bouldering at Sandrock, Alabama.

From Atlanta, you have a number of options. One involves driving north on I-75 for about 40 miles. Take exit 290 for GA 20 toward Rome. Turn left onto GA 20, heading west. After 2.4 miles, merge onto US 411 and continue for 21.6 miles before merging onto US 27 North toward Rome. After 3.2 miles stay straight to join GA 20 (Shorter Avenue Northwest). Stay on GA 20 for 17 miles; it becomes AL 9 in Alabama. Continue on AL 9 for 14.4 miles. Stay straight to join AL 68 (Cedar Bluff Road) for .2 mile. Turn right, continuing to follow AL 68/US 411 for 2.1 miles. Turn right onto West Main Street (still US 411), and proceed 3.3 miles. Turn right onto AL 68 (Industrial Boulevard) in Lees-burg, and drive 2.7 miles before making a sharp left turn onto CR 36 at a sign for Cherokee Rock Village. Continue 1.5 miles and then make a sharp left onto CR 70. Proceed .6 mile up a winding hill (the road soon turns to dirt) to a fork in the road. Take the right fork and follow this road 2.9 miles until it ends. Park here.

Nearest major airports: There are a number of major airports reasonably close to Sandrock, including Chattanooga Metropolitan Airport (423-855-2200; www.chattairport.com; 1001 Airport Road, Suite 14, Chattanooga, TN), 76 miles from Sandrock; Birmingham International Airport (205-595-0533; www.bhamintl airport.com; 5900 Airport Highway, Birmingham, AL), 90 miles from Sandrock; the Port of Huntsville (256-772-9395; www.hsvairport.org; 1000 Glen Hearn Boulevard, Huntsville, AL), 90 miles from Sandrock; and the Hartsfield-Jackson Atlanta International Airport (800-897-1910; www.atlanta-airport.com; 6000 North Terminal Parkway, Suite 435, Atlanta, Georgia), 115 miles from Sandrock.

Public transportation: None.

◆▶CLIMBING CONCERNS

Cost: Free.

Hours: Virtually no current regulations at Sandrock, meaning no hours, but you're best off bouldering only during daylight hours, since this is a favorite party spot for locals.

Land manager: The Cherokee County Parks and Recreation Board (256-927-8455; www.cherokee-chamber.org; Courthouse Annex, Centre, AL) manages Sandrock, also known as Cherokee Rock Village.

Finding the boulders: From the parking area, a short trail leads down to the boulders, which lie along the left side of the road as you are driving in and ex-tend beyond the parking area in the same line.

Type of rock: Sandstone.

Five good problems: Jaws (V0), Dial a Yield (V1, Fire Pit), Bread Loaf or Arrow Arête (V3, Fire Pit), Chinese Water Torture (V5, Fire Pit), and Cannonball (V8) are some of the best problems you'll find at Sandrock.

Range of grades: Whether you boulder V0, V5, or V10, Sandrock has enough problems to keep you busy for a day or two. Potential for further development exists, particularly for harder problems.

Prime season: As with all of the Southeastern bouldering areas profiled in this book, friction is the name of the game, and you'll find it to be at its prime in the cooler winter months, as well as in fall and spring. Summer can be out of hand with humidity and heat.

Dogs: Allowed, but please be a responsible pet owner.

Special notes: Cherokee County, where Sandrock is located, is a dry county. This means that possessing alcohol here could get you thrown in jail or slapped with a hefty fine, so leave the booze behind. Sandrock has received prolific amounts of abuse through the years, and you're likely to find trash or at least lots of graffiti. Please do your part by cleaning up not just after yourself, but also after the others who have left junk there—and if you happen to visit during the Southeastern Climbers' Coalition Annual Cleanup, take part in their efforts. Be aware that this is a favorite party spot for locals—you might have company, especially on the weekends, in the form of loud partiers and such. If you like bolted sport routes, bring your gear, or you'll wish you had.

Guidebooks to area problems: Nothing comprehensive; see *Online resources.* There is a small but helpful guide to bouldering at Sandrock in *The Dixie Cragger's Atlas: A Climber's Guide to Tennessee, Alabama and Georgia*, by Chris Watford (Market Place Press, 1999).

Online resources: Visit Dr. Topo (www.drtopo.com) to download a free guide, *Bouldering at Sandrock: Southeast's Most Underrated Bouldering Area*, written in collaboration with Adam Henry. Both Flatliners Southeast Climbing (www.south eastclimbing.com) and the Southeastern Climbers Coalition (www.seclimbers .org) have excellent informational pages on Sandrock. Trails Edge (www.trails-edge.com), the Alabama Climber's Association (www.inline.com/aca/sand rock.htm), and Climb Georgia (www.climbgeorgia.com/local/sandrock.htm) have helpful informational pages on Sandrock as well.

Other resources: If you've never climbed or bouldered before and you want to hire a guide, try High Country Outfitters (205-985-3215; www.highcountryout fitters.com; 2000-147A Riverchase Galleria, Birmingham, AL) or GA-Adventures (404-630-7382; www.ga-adventures.com; 6851 Roswell Road, I-16, Atlanta). If you need bouldering or camping gear, the closest outfitter is about 25 miles south on US 411 in Gadsden—Outdoor Supply, Inc. (256-543-7833; 414 Chestnut Street). Another option is to drive to Birmingham to find gear at Alabama Outdoors (205-870-1919; www.aloutdoors.com; 3054 Independence Drive) or at Urban Outpost (888-303-8850 or 205-879-8850; www.urbanout-post.com; 1105 Dunston Avenue); both stores also have in-store climbing areas.

Local climbing gyms: Your closest option for a full-scale facility is to head northeast to Chattanooga, Tennessee, to Grip City Climbing Center (423-894-3910; www.taggym.com/gripcity.htm; 6242 Perimeter Drive, #102). Or check out the Tennessee Bouldering Authority (423-822-6800; www.tbagym.com; 3804 St. Elmo Avenue, Suite 102).

Nearby bouldering and climbing areas of note: Less than 60 miles north of Sandrock on the northern end of Lookout Mountain you can find the amazing bouldering of Rocktown, Georgia (see pages 219–226). The world-class bouldering of Horse Pens 40 (see pages 206–212) is less than 40 miles southwest of Sandrock. Also in Alabama, you'll find Palisades Park (short routes and bouldering) and Little River Canyon (traditional climbing), among other climbing and bouldering areas. The Southeast has a vast quantity of additional excellent bouldering and climbing; visit one of the sites listed in *Online resources* for more ideas.

Matt Wendling bouldering at Sandrock, Alabama.

❧OTHER IMPORTANT STUFF

Camping: Camping is free around the parking area and the road leading to it, but beware the local party scene, especially on weekends. Use your discretion—this is an isolated area, and you're on your own. There may be a porta-potty and dumpsters in the parking area.

Nearby phone: From the intersection of AL 68 and CR 36, drive 2.6 miles on AL 68, where you will find a pay phone at Roadrunner Café (a gas station) or one of several other gas stations. (My cell phone got service at Sandrock.)

Showers: For $42, you and a friend can grab a room—with showers—for the night at the nearby Leesburg Lodge (800-209-3219 or 256-526-7378; 5915 Weiss Lake Boulevard, Leesburg). From the intersection of AL 68 and CR 36, drive south for 2.7 miles on AL 68. Turn left onto US 411 (Weiss Lake Road) and proceed about .1 mile to find the motel on your left. Otherwise, try your luck at one of the many RV parks and campgrounds lining US 411, or just wait and take a shower when you get to Horse Pens 40, if you plan to head that way.

Water: None available at Sandrock. Ask politely or purchase water at one of the nearby gas stations (see *Nearby phone*).

In case of emergency: Dial 911 for all emergencies.

Drive to Cherokee Baptist Medical Center (256-927-1382; www.bhsala.com/cherokee; 400 Northwood Drive, Centre). From the intersection of AL 68 and CR 36, drive south for 2.7 miles on AL 68. Turn left onto US 411 (Weiss Lake Road) and follow it for 3.3 miles. Turn left to continue following US 411 for another 2.2 miles. Turn left onto AL 68 (Cedar Bluff Road) and proceed .3 mile. Turn right onto Northwood Drive and go .4 mile to the hospital.

Nearby Internet hookup: Cherokee County Public Library (256-927-5838; www.cheaharegionallibrary.org; 310 Mary Street, Centre). From the intersection of AL 68 and CR 36, drive south for 2.7 miles on AL 68. Turn left onto US 411/AL 25 (Weiss Lake Blvd) and drive 5.1 miles. Turn right onto College Street. After .1 mile, turn left onto Second Avenue. The library will be on your right.

Restaurants: Get your belly filled at Starr's Real Pit Bar-B-Que (256-927-2400; 1464 West Main Street, Centre). This locally owned and operated restaurant offers an array of barbecue choices, from mouthwatering barbecued ribs to barbecued chicken. Here vegetarians will have to content themselves with an all-you-can-eat soup and salad bar or a grilled cheese sandwich. If cobbler is available, do not miss out—a warm and buttery fruit-and-crust paradise awaits your taste buds. Inexpensive. Open Monday through Saturday 10–9. From the intersection of AL 68 and CR 36, drive south for 2.7 miles on AL 68. Turn left onto US 411/AL 25 (Weiss Lake Road) and drive 3.7 miles to find the restaurant (the street name changes).

For breakfast, try Royal Waffle King (256-927-6555; www.royalwaffleking.com; 101 Piedmont Road, Centre), where you will find plentiful helpings of breakfast, lunch, and dinner food whenever you're hungry, from omelets served with grits and toast to an assortment of burgers, salads, and sandwiches, as well as a T-bone steak dinner. Inexpensive. Open 24 hours a day, 7 days a week. From the intersection of AL 68 and CR 36, drive south for 2.7 miles on AL 68. Turn left onto US 411/AL 25 (Weiss Lake Road) and drive 5.6 miles. The restaurant is on the right corner of US 411 and Piedmont Road just after a stoplight.

Rocktown—LaFayette, Georgia

As you drive the long, steep, winding, and rock-riddled road up the mountainside to Rocktown, you might start to wonder whether your destination is really worth the bumpy ride or whether your two-wheel-drive rental car will make it all the way. The answer to both of these questions is a resounding yes, as I found out when I visited Rocktown. Rocktown's bouldering features clusters of sandstone

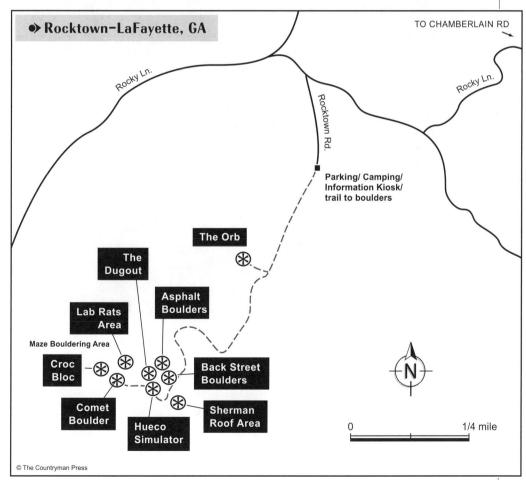

Matt Wendling bouldering at Rocktown, Georgia.

boulders or individual boulders strewn about in a Southeastern deciduous forest, with almost all perfect, sandy landings. The boulders are notable for their wild features, sculpted through eons of erosion. You'll find steep overhangs riddled with chickenheads (knobs of rock attached to the rock face by narrower "necks" of rock, hence the name) and protruding pieces of rock sort of like a jigsaw puzzle, particularly noticeable on the Sherman Roof (or like a crocodile's hide, such as on the aptly named Croc Block). Wildly wavy iron intrusions swirl up the over-hung faces of the rock, making perfectly positive crimpers such as those found on the Comet. You'll also find huecos, pockets, slopers, and shelves, as well as an abrasive, finger-eating rock masquerading as gentle, smooth sandstone. Honest top outs demand that you know at least a little bit about how to mantle on most problems, or you will find yourself groveling and beached-whaling it a bunch, should you succeed in getting over the top at all.

At Rocktown you really can feel like you've escaped from the rest of the world, high on the side of the mountain, camping and bouldering for free, yet the town of LaFayette is just a short drive away.

Never mind the town, though—if the sun gods choose to shine on your visit, you're likely to forget about civilization. You'll learn to really enjoy a daily lack-adaisical jaunt through the woods on a flat trail that takes you first to the classic Orb Boulder and its surrounding boulders, which resemble mushrooms—huge, top-heavy boulders balanced atop much smaller pedestals of rock—and then past the Sherman Roof to the Hueco Wall (a great warm-up area) and the Maze and its surrounding boulders.

At the end of the day you can wander back to camp and relax in one of the great, flat sites around the parking lot and cook up a little meal. Just cross your fingers that it doesn't rain while you're there—rain in Rocktown equals an un-welcome reality check when you're faced with either hanging out shivering in camp or making a slow drive down that road to go into the small town of LaFayette in search of entertainment.

The Lowdown

➡ GETTING THERE

Driving directions: From Atlanta, drive north on I-75 for about 70 miles (de-pending on exactly where you started). Take exit 320, the Resaca/LaFayette exit, onto GA 136. Turn left onto GA 136 and drive for a total of almost 26 miles, following the road through several turns (watch signs closely) as follows: Drive 6.5 miles to T-intersection and turn right onto GA 136. Drive 14.3 miles to another T-intersection where you will turn left to stay on GA 136. Proceed 1.3 miles, and then turn right to stay on GA 136 for another 3.9 miles. When you arrive at the intersection of GA 136 and GA 193/East Villanow Street, go straight. Follow GA 193 as it turns to the left at the third stoplight you encounter. Drive to the second stoplight and turn right, following GA 193. Remain on GA 193 for 2.7 miles before turning left onto Chamberlain Road (Uncle Jed's gas station and store will be on the right side of the road). Drive for 3.3 miles and then look for a small brown sign on the right indicating the road (Rocky

Alli, Croc Block, Rocktown, Georgia. PHOTO BY MATT WENDLING

Lane) for Crockford-Pigeon Mountain. Turn right onto this gravel road and proceed 4.8 miles total (passing the ranger station at .5 mile), taking the right fork (Rocky Lane) where the road splits. Turn left onto Rocktown Road (keep your eyes out—the sign is off to the left on Rocktown Road, below a DEAD END sign) and proceed less than 1 mile to the parking and camping area.

From Chattanooga, you can take Broad Street/TN 17 to the Georgia border and then continue on the same road, now called GA 193, for 23.4 miles to Chamberlain Road outside of LaFayette. Turn right onto Chamberlain Road (Uncle Jed's gas station and store will be on the left side of the road). Drive for 3.3 miles and then look for a small brown sign on the right indicating the road (Rocky Lane) for Crockford-Pigeon Mountain. Turn right onto this gravel road and proceed 4.8 miles total (passing the ranger station at .5 mile), taking the right fork (Rocky Lane) where the road splits. Turn left onto Rocktown Road (keep your eyes out—the sign is off to the left on Rocktown Road, below a DEAD END sign) and proceed less than 1 mile to the parking and camping area.

Nearest major airports: Chattanooga Metropolitan Airport (423-855-2200; www.chattairport.com; 1001 Airport Road, Suite 14) is the closest to Rocktown, about 40 miles away. You might find cheaper tickets flying to the Hartsfield-Jackson Atlanta International Airport (800-897-1910; www.atlanta-airport.com; 6000 North Terminal Parkway, Suite 435), a little more than 100 miles from Rocktown.

Public transportation: None.

❥CLIMBING CONCERNS

Cost: Free.

Hours: Dawn to dusk.

Land manager: Georgia Department of Natural Resources, Wildlife Resources Division (706-295-6041; http://georgiawildlife.dnr.state.ga.us; 2592 Floyd Springs Road, Armuchee, Georgia, 30105).

Finding the boulders: From the parking area, you can locate the trailhead to the boulders in the corner of the lot adjacent to the information kiosk. A flat, relatively short (less than 1 mile) trail leads to the boulders.

Type of rock: Sandstone.

Five good problems: Five classic Rocktown problems include the V2 on the left side of Croc Bloc, the Standard (V3, Comet), Lab Rats (V6), Sherman Photo Roof (V7), and the Orb (V8).

Range of grades: An array of problems to keep boulderers of all ability levels busy for at least a couple of days, from the novice to the expert (V10 and up), with the potential for greater development as well.

Prime season: Plan to visit in fall, winter, or spring, since summer can be unbearably hot and humid.

Dogs: Allowed, but must be leashed at all times, and you should be responsible for cleaning up after your pet.

Special notes: Obey the speed limits; there have been problems with climbers and boulderers speeding. The speed limit is 20 miles per hour on all of the roads in the Crockford-Pigeon Wildlife Area. Do not bring beer or other alcoholic beverages, since it is illegal to possess or consume alcohol anywhere in the Crockford-Pigeon Wildlife Area. You may not camp or have a fire in Rocktown or along the Lost Wall trail (see *Camping* for details). Be aware that hunters also frequent this area during hunting seasons; please check http://georgiawildlife.dnr.state.ga.us/content/displaywma.asp?areaid=28 for specific dates.

Guidebooks to area problems: None. There is a brief reference to Rocktown in *The Dixie Cragger's Atlas: A Climber's Guide to Tennessee, Alabama and Georgia,* by Chris Watford (Market Place Press, 1999). This guide has detailed information about the adjacent sport-climbing area Lost Wall, also on Pigeon Mountain.

Online resources: You can download *An Introduction to the Bouldering of Rock Town* for free at Dr. Topo (www.drtopo.com). Definitely visit Flatliners Southeast Climbing (www.southeastclimbing.com) and the Southeastern Climbers Coalition (www.seclimbers.org) before planning a visit for quality information about Rocktown bouldering. Also check out Climb Georgia (www.climbgeorgia.com). Go to HP Bouldering: The Southeastern Experience (www.freewebs.com/silveys/boatrockandrocktownga.htm) and www.crags.net/trips/uscrags/tr_rocktown.html to see photos of Rocktown bouldering.

Other resources: If you've never bouldered or climbed before and you want to hire a guide, nearby Chattanooga has a number of services, including Granite Arches Guide Services and Climbing School (423-413-1432; www.granitearches.com) and The Adventure Guild (423-266-5709; www.theadventureguild.com). If you need supplies, try the Wal-Mart in LaFayette (706-639-4900; www.walmart.com; 2625 North US 27) before you drive to Chattanooga or Atlanta in search of goods.

Local climbing gyms: About 40 miles away in Chattanooga, you can pull on plastic at the Grip City Climbing Center (423-894-3910; www.taggym.com/gripcity.htm; 6242 Perimeter Drive, #102). Or check out the Tennessee Bouldering Authority (423-822-6800; www.tbagym.com; 3804 St. Elmo Avenue, Suite 102).

Nearby bouldering and climbing areas of note: Lost Wall, a small top-roping and traditional climbing crag, is also located on Pigeon Mountain. Sunset Rock, one of the Southeast's longest established traditional climbing areas, lies north about 40 miles on Lookout Mountain near Chattanooga. Less than 60 miles south of Rocktown on the southern end of Lookout Mountain you can find the often overlooked but decent bouldering of Sandrock, Alabama (see pages 212–219). The Southeast has a vast quantity of additional excellent bouldering and climbing; see one of the sites listed in *Online resources* for more ideas.

❖OTHER IMPORTANT STUFF

Camping: Camping is free, but do not camp in Rocktown. Rather, camp in the woods around the parking area, anywhere along Rocktown Lane, or on the top of Pigeon Mountain. There are no facilities, so come prepared. The camping limit is 2 weeks.

Alli, Lab Rats, Rocktown, Georgia. PHOTO BY MATT WENDLING

Nearby phone: You'll find a pay phone at Uncle Jed's (706-639-3330; 23617 Highway 193) at the corner of Chamberlain Road and GA 193. (My cell phone did not get service at Rocktown.)

Showers: Available at the LaFayette Parks & Recreation Department's Municipal Park (706-638-3908; 638 South Main Street). From Rocktown, head back into town on Highway 193. When you reach South Main Street, take a right and drive approximately 1 mile. Look for the Walker Senior Center and a sign that says "LaFayette Recreation Department & Golf Course." Turn right (Municipal Park Road), and follow the road around to the recreation center next to the playground. Inquire at the front desk about showers.

Water: Fill your water at the Crockford-Pigeon Mountain Checking Station, .5 mile after the turn onto Rocky Lane off Chamberlain Road. Please be sure to turn off the water completely.

In case of emergency: Dial 911 for all emergencies. The park rangers are trained for vertical rescue.

Head for Hutcheson Medical Center (706-858-2000; 100 Gross Crescent Circle, Fort Oglethorpe). From the intersection of GA 193 and Chamberlain Road, drive east on GA 193 for 2.7 miles. Turn left onto South Main Street (still GA 193). Drive .2 mile, and then turn right onto East Villanow Street (still GA 193). Drive .4 mile and turn left onto US 27. Continue on US 27 for 2.4 miles, and then turn right onto North Main Street (still US 27). Continue 11.3 miles. Turn right onto US 27 (LaFayette Road) and continue 4.2 miles. Turn left onto Thomas Road and proceed .2 mile to find the hospital.

Nearby Internet hookup: LaFayette-Walker Public Library (706-638-2992; www.walker.public.lib.ga.us/index.html; 305 South Duke Street). From the intersection of GA 193 and Chamberlain Road, drive east on GA 193 for 2.7 miles. Turn left onto South Main Street (still GA 193). After less than .1 mile, turn right onto Cooper Street. Proceed less than .1 mile to find the library on the corner of Duke and Cooper.

Restaurants: For dinner, eat at Don Lolo's Mexican Restaurant (706-638-3761; 315 North Main Street, LaFayette). There you'll find heaping platters of delicious Mexican food priced right for the traveling climber. Entrées are inexpensive and range from combo platters to a steak dinner or shrimp fajitas. Vegetarians will find plenty of options here. Open Monday through Friday 11–10; Saturday and Sunday 12–10. From the intersection of GA 193 and Chamberlain Road, drive east on GA 193 for 2.7 miles. Turn left onto South Main Street (still GA 193) and proceed .5 mile to the restaurant.

You can always grab a bite to eat at Uncle Jed's, too (see *Nearby phone* for contact information). They have subs, burgers, fries, and even chicken on a stick. While you're waiting for your food to be prepared, you can look at the shop's impressive collection of pipes and other needs catering to smokers of all kinds. Open 7 days a week from 5:30–midnight.

Boat Rock—Atlanta, Georgia

In between housing developments that are multiplying like rabbits, you'll find the relative sliver of land upon which sit the remaining boulders of Boat Rock, saved from imminent destruction (like so many of their adjacent kin) thanks to the efforts of the Southeastern Climbers Coalition (SCC) and the Access Fund. When the cacophonic echoes of the last power tool die away and the nearby housing developments are finished, you will likely still be able to enjoy this urban escape in its shrunken but hopefully permanent state, as the boulders contained within the 7.8-acre tract of land purchased for preservation are slated to remain au naturel, regardless of the encroaching suburban sprawl surrounding them. During a visit in early 2004, however, it was hard to put aside thoughts of the recent destruction of the many historic boulders nearby, as constant construction noise resonated around the remaining boulders as I explored the area.

Despite this, Boat Rock still has something worthwhile to offer in the way of bouldering, particularly for local Atlanta boulderers eager to climb on real rock during the workweek, or for visitors who have only an hour or two to spare. Coarse granite boulders, some quite noteworthy in size, offer up challenging problems that often require more brains and balance than brawn—you can pull all you want on a slab, but it won't get you anywhere but on the ground unless

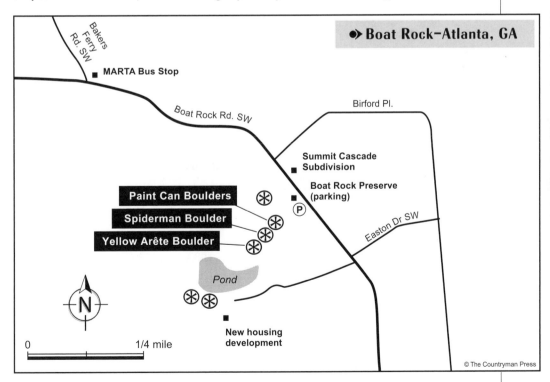

you weight your feet correctly! A lot of care and effort has gone into cleaning up this place and maintaining it—no trash can be seen around the boulders, and helpful signs identify most of them, making it easy to navigate even if you've never been to Boat Rock before. This lovely wooded boulder garden, which even includes a little "lake," stands as a testament to the dedication and passion of the bouldering and climbing community in Atlanta, for without its efforts, Boat Rock would probably be just a footnote in the pages of Southeastern climbing history.

The Lowdown

➨ GETTING THERE

Driving directions: From I-20 East or West, take exit 49 (GA 70/Fulton Industrial Boulevard) toward the Fulton County Airport. Stay left at the fork in the ramp, turning left onto Fulton Industrial Boulevard. Drive for 3.7 miles. Turn left onto Bakers Ferry Road Southwest. Drive .5 mile and turn left onto Boat Rock Road Southwest. Drive .4 mile, keeping an eye out for a sign reading "Boat Rock Preserve." Park in the small gravel lot on the right at 1221 Boat Rock Road Southwest, across from the Summit/Cascade subdivision. Please carpool if possible.

Nearest major airports: The Hartsfield-Jackson Atlanta International Airport (800-897-1910; www.atlanta-airport.com; 6000 North Terminal Parkway, Suite 435) is less than 15 miles from Boat Rock.

Public transportation: Bus Route 73, run by the Metropolitan Atlanta Rapid Transit Authority (MARTA; 404-848-4711; www.itsmarta.com), stops at the corner of Bakers Ferry Road Southwest and Boat Rock Road Southwest, .4 mile from the boulders. Head east on Boat Rock Road after debarking to reach the parking area at 1221 Boat Rock Road Southwest.

➨ CLIMBING CONCERNS

Cost: Free.

Hours: Dawn until dusk. Do not climb after dark.

Land manager: The Southeastern Climbers Coalition (www.seclimbers.org; 1936 Wellona Place, Atlanta, GA 30345).

Finding the boulders: A small informational kiosk in the parking area will help guide you, as will helpful signs labeling many of the boulders. A trail leads up from the parking area to the main area; the lake area is located a few hundred yards southeast.

Type of rock: Granite.

Five good problems: Spiderman Boulder (numerous V0s), Lost Digits (V3, thin crack down the hill from Paint Can), Fire Woman (V4, down the hill from Paint Can), Yellow Arête (V4), and Paint Can (V5) are a few of the fun problems you'll find at Boat Rock.

Range of grades: An ample assortment of beginner-friendly problems as well as a plentiful selection of intermediate and advanced problems. Elite boulderers (V10+) will find little to challenge them after a couple of days, as the problems at Boat Rock top out at V9.

Prime season: Locals climb here year-round, but summers can be miserably hot and humid. Fall, winter, and spring are better times to visit.

Dogs: Due to all of the access issues, it is recommended that if you bring your dog, you keep it on a leash and under your direct supervision at all times, cleaning up after it as well. If you have a pesky or noisy dog, leave it at home.

Special notes: Boat Rock's very existence was threatened until 2002 with the urban sprawl of Atlanta reaching out its arms to try and embrace and devour this historic bouldering area. Though some of the boulders have been destroyed and still more are likely to face destruction in the future, efforts by local climbers, the Southeastern Climbers Coalition, and the Access Fund secured the purchase of a 7.8-acre tract of land along Boat Rock Road Southwest that is now open to the public and slated to be turned into a park in the future.

This is a local, urban bouldering area, not a world-class destination, though it's a great place to stop by if you happen to be in Atlanta. Maintain a low profile, and if you arrive and can't find parking, return on another day. Be careful not to trespass off the 7.8 acres, even if other boulders call out to you—they are not open to the public, and trespassing could

Matt Wendling samples the granite of Boat Rock, Georgia.

cause future access issues. Be aware that the landowner on the far west side of the 7.8-acre tract is not climber friendly, so stay clear of his land and house. Be conscientious and courteous to all area landowners. Park only in the gravel parking lot off the road, and carpool if necessary. Do not clean the ferns off the tops of boulders. This area has also seen heavy use by nonclimbers, and the result has been an accumulation of trash, so help show that the bouldering community has environmental awareness and wants to keep the area clean. Do not climb after dark.

Guidebooks to area problems: There is no published guidebook; see *Online resources* for more information.

Online resources: You can download *An Introduction to the Bouldering at Boat Rock*, by Alex Gerrits and Cooper Roberts, for free at Dr. Topo (www.drtopo.com). Definitely visit Flatliners Southeast Climbing (www.southeast climbing.com) and the Southeastern Climbers Coalition (www.seclimbers.org) before planning a visit to Boat Rock for the latest information and updates on any access issues or concerns, and also for information on the annual Float the Boat outdoor climbing competition, usually held in December or January. Also check out Climb Georgia (www.climbgeorgia.com). Go to HP Bouldering: The Southeastern Experience (www.freewebs.com/silveys/boatrockandrocktownga.htm) to see photos of Boat Rock. To meet other like-minded souls in Atlanta, check out the Atlanta Climbing Club (www.atlantaclimbingclub.org).

Other resources: If you've never bouldered or climbed before and you want to hire a guide, Atlanta is home to several services, including the Challenge Rock Climbing School (888-312-5462 or 404-237-4021; www.thechallengerock.com; 1085 Capital Club Circle, Atlanta) and GA-Adventures (404-630-7382; www.ga-adventures.com; 6851 Roswell Road, I-16, Atlanta). If you need bouldering supplies, Atlanta has a number of outdoor retailers, including two REIs (www.rei.com): REI-Atlanta (404-633-6508; 1800 Northeast Expressway Northeast) and REI-Perimeter (770-901-9200; 1165 Perimeter Center West, Suite 200). Also in Atlanta, you'll find a Galyans (404-267-0200; www.galyans.com; 3535 Peachtree Road) and High Country Outfitters (also a guiding service; 404-814-0999; www.highcountryoutfitters.com; 3906 Roswell Road).

Local climbing gyms: Atlanta has a number of indoor climbing facilities, including Atlanta Rocks! Intown (404-351-3009; www.atlantarocks.com; 1019-A Collier Road), about 15 miles from Boat Rock and Escalade Rock Climbing Gym (770-794-1575; www.escaladegym.com; 2995 Cobb International Boulevard, Kennesaw), about 30 miles from Boat Rock.

Nearby bouldering and climbing areas of note: A little more than 100 miles to the north, you will find the boulders of Rocktown (see pages 219–226), and the crag of Lost Wall. A little more than 100 miles northeast lies the roped climbing area of Yonah Mountain. If you live in or around the Atlanta area, you should ask around to find out more information about other little local bouldering spots. The states surrounding Georgia contain numerous notable climbing and bouldering areas as well, from the sport climbing and bouldering of the Obed Wild and Scenic River in Tennessee to the bouldering of Horse Pens 40 (see pages 206–212) and Sandrock in Alabama (see pages 212–219).

◆▸OTHER IMPORTANT STUFF

Camping: No camping at Boat Rock. One option is to make reservations at Stone Mountain Family Campground (800-385-9807 or 770-498-5710; www.stonemountainpark.com; US 78 East, Stone Mountain). From Boat Rock, head west on Boat Rock Road Southwest for .4 mile. Turn right onto Bakers

Matt Wendling, Boat Rock, Georgia.

Ferry Road Southwest. After .5 mile, turn right onto Fulton Industrial Boulevard Southwest (GA 70). Drive for 3.7 miles and then merge onto I-20 East. Follow I-20 East for 18 miles. Take I-285 North via exit number 67 toward Greenville. Take exit 39B off I-285, the US 78 East (Snellville/Athens) exit. Drive 7.7 miles and take exit 8 for the Stone Mountain Park main entrance. Follow the exit ramp to the East Gate entrance of Stone Mountain Park. Expect to pay $23 to $38 per night for a site, which comes with hot showers, laundry facilities, and more.

Considering the steep price of camping, you might also try your luck bidding on hotel rooms for a night or two through Priceline (www.priceline.com). I nabbed a three-star, $110 per night room in Atlanta for four nights for $35 a night.

Nearby phone: You can find a pay phone at the Quick Trip on Fulton Industrial Boulevard. From Boat Rock, turn left onto Boat Rock Road Southwest and drive .4 mile. Turn right onto Bakers Ferry Road Southwest and go .5 mile. Turn left onto Fulton Industrial Boulevard and go one block—the Quick Trip is on the right. (My cell phone got service at Boat Rock.)

Showers: Atlanta Rocks! Intown (404-351-3009; www.atlantarocks.com; 1019-A Collier Road) has showers. From the parking area of Boat Rock, head west on Boat Rock Road Southwest for .4 mile. Turn right onto Bakers Ferry Road Southwest. After .5 mile, turn right onto Fulton Industrial Boulevard Southwest (GA 70). Drive for 3.7 miles and then merge onto I-20 East. Drive 7.9 miles and then merge onto I-75 North toward Chattanooga/Greenville via exit 57. After 6 miles, take exit 252B, the Howell Mill Road exit. Take a right onto Howell Mill Road Northwest. Drive .2 mile and then turn left onto Collier Road Northwest. Go for .4 mile; the gym is located in Collier Industrial Park on the right.

Water: Ask politely to fill your water at the Quick Trip (see *Nearby phone*).

In case of emergency: Dial 911 for all emergencies.

One option is to head for Piedmont Hospital (404-605-3297; www.piedmont hospital.org; 1968 Peachtree Road Northwest). From Boat Rock, head west on Boat Rock Road Southwest for .4 mile. Turn right onto Bakers Ferry Road Southwest. After .5 mile, turn right onto Fulton Industrial Boulevard Southwest (GA 70). Drive for 3.7 miles and then merge onto I-20 East. Drive 7.9 miles and then merge onto I-75 North toward Chattanooga/Greenville via exit 57. After 3.4 miles, take exit 250 toward Georgia Tech. Turn right onto Tenth Street Northwest. Go .2 mile and then turn left onto West Peachtree Street Northwest. Proceed 1.3 miles to the hospital.

Nearby Internet hookup: Try the Southwest Regional Library (404-699-6363; www.af.public.lib.ga.us/loc/southwest/index.html; 3665 Cascade Road Southwest, Atlanta). From Boat Rock, drive .6 mile east on Boat Rock Road Southwest and then turn left onto Bruce Place Southwest. Go .3 mile and then turn left onto New Hope Road Southwest. Drive 1.5 miles. Turn right onto Danforth Road Southwest. Go 1.3 miles. Turn right onto Cascade Road Southwest. Go .6 mile to find the library.

Restaurants: Close to Boat Rock, you'll find some fast-food joints by the Quick Trip (see *Nearby phone*).

For fancier fare, sample unique takes on traditional flavors of the South—or totally wild and innovative entrée combinations—at the Feed Store Restaurant & Bar (404-209-7979; 3841 Main Street, College Park). The restaurant actually used to be a feed store owned and run for 75 years by the grandmother, Ada Estelle Smith Harris, of one of the current co-owners, Celita Bullard. From salmon with potato gnocchi to Feed Store fried steak—plus a number of vegetarian options—you'll find something palatable on the menu. Moderate to expensive. Open daily 11–10. From Boat Rock, head east on Boat Rock Road Southwest for .8 mile. Turn left onto Campbellton Road Southwest and proceed 3.6 miles. Merge onto I-285 South toward Montgomery. After 2.2 miles, take exit 2, the Camp Creek Parkway exit, toward the Atlanta airport. Take the ramp toward the airport. Turn left onto Camp Creek Parkway and drive 2.7 miles. Take the US 29 North/GA 14/GA 139 ramp. Turn left onto US 29/GA 139/Roosevelt Highway, following it for .4 mile to find the restaurant (the street name changes when you cross Camp Creek Parkway). Total driving time is about 20 minutes.

For tighter budgets, consider feasting at one of the many Waffle Houses (www.wafflehouse.com) around Atlanta. Sure it's a chain, but the whole shebang started in a suburb of Atlanta in 1955, so Waffle House still retains its local flair, not to mention serving darn good food—not only waffles, but also breakfasts, lunches, and dinners—prepared to order at great prices (most menu items are under $5). All of the restaurants are open 24 hours a day, 7 days a week, 365 days a year. To get to the Waffle House closest to Boat Rock (404-699-0130; 4120 Fulton Industrial Boulevard Southwest), from Boat Rock, turn left onto Boat Rock Road Southwest and drive .4 mile. Turn right onto Bakers Ferry Road Southwest and go .5 mile. Turn right onto Fulton Industrial Boulevard Southwest and drive 4 miles to find the restaurant (just off I-20).

Glossary
OF BOULDerING Terms

THIS COMPILATION of commonly used bouldering terms should help you get started understanding the lingo when you're out at the boulders. Many of the terms described will make much more sense with a visual demonstration, so don't be shy and ask someone to show you what a drop knee or finger lock is if you can't quite picture the move.

add-on: A climbing game in which a group of two or more boulderers make up a problem together, taking turns adding moves (usually two to five apiece), thus creating one problem for all to work on sending together once it is deemed finished.

backstep: Using the outer edge of your climbing shoe to step on a hold. (See photo on page 43.)

beached whale: A particular type of groveling, most commonly experienced during the top out of a boulder problem, involving the flopping of the stomach region onto the top surface of the boulder, usually accompanied by frantic pawing with the hands for a tangible hold and repeated desperate kicking of the legs and feet, which often are no longer in contact with the rock.

beta: Information, usually about how to do specific moves or about specific holds on a problem. For example, "Backstep with your left foot on the small edge, and then fire for the jug with your right hand." Also used more generally by climbers and boulderers to refer to any sort of information, climbing-related or otherwise.

campus; campus board: To execute a move from one handhold to another without using your feet. The campus board is a training device on which people do multiple campus moves, up and down. The board usually over-hangs about 30 degrees and has one or more columns of up to 10 uniform wooden rungs spaced the same distance apart (each set of rungs is usually different in size, making for harder or easier campusing). The first rung is usually about 5 or 5½ feet off the ground, allowing for easier lift-off so that you can start moving up the board without using your feet.

chipping: A much frowned-upon practice of altering the rock's surface with the use of any sort of tool in order to create or enhance the holds, making a problem or route easier (and ruining it for everyone else).

choss; chosspile; chossy: Terms used to describe less-than-perfect rock. Rock that is crumbly and possibly breakable under the pressure of weight from a climber's hands or feet, or that has visible loose components, such as flakes or even bone-crushing blocks that could break off.

circuit: A series of any number of problems, indoors or outside, that you routinely visit. Circuits can be a great training tool—for example, you might have a warm-up of 5 to 10 problems that help you assess how you're feeling on a given day.

clean; cleaning: Clean rock is rock with no choss, moss, lichen, or plants. Cleaning is sometimes required in order to render a problem or route safe. At a basic level this involves knocking off loose pieces of rock that would likely come off under a climber's body weight. A fine line exists between aggressive cleaning and chipping; different people have different ethical standards dictating how much cleaning they do, and this ethic can vary drastically from area to area as well. Before climbing a problem or route for the first time, a good rule is to first check on the established ethical standards for an area before doing any sort of cleaning, and then to attempt to remove anything from the rock's surface that could potentially harm the climber or on-lookers.

contrived: A term used to describe a problem in which some natural feature or hold, or even a particular movement or way of grabbing a hold, has been declared to be off-route.

crank: Not to be confused with the drug! *Crank* refers to performing a move or problem and is often used as a term of encouragement ("Crank this problem!") or as an expression of admiration (i.e., "Wow, you just cranked on that little crimper like it was nothing and sent the problem").

crash pad: A padded mat, usually from 1 to 4 inches thick, designed specifically to cushion the landing areas of boulder problems. Most crash pads are designed to be folded up into somewhat odd-looking backpacks into which bouldering gear can fit, thus allowing for easy transport of pad, food, clothing, and climbing necessities from boulder to boulder. Often used as a sleeping pad.

crimp; crimper: A way of gripping a hold, a full crimp involves placing the fingertips on a hold and then bending all of the finger joints and wrapping the thumb over the first two fingers—almost like making a fist on the hold. A crimper is a small edge used as a handhold (and often as a foothold). Oddly enough, not all climbers will crimp a crimper—some can pull on these holds just fine with the less injury-provoking open-handed grip. (See photo on page 40.)

crux: A distinctively harder move or series of moves surrounded by more moderate moves on a problem. Problems can have more than one crux, and you may also hear people refer to a "pump-crux," meaning that one of the difficulties on the problem involves having the stamina to complete all the moves without falling (due to pumped muscles) instead of simply executing one or a couple of particularly difficult moves.

deadpoint: A dynamic motion in which one or both feet remain on the footholds. You push with your feet and pull with your arms in one smooth, precise motion, grabbing the next handhold at the "deadpoint" in your movement—that point where you are no longer upwardly mobile but have not yet begun your downward motion.

diet: Also called weight-off, the diet is a technique used by boulderers that involves asking a partner to give you a little push or lift through a difficult move or series of moves that you cannot execute yourself. This helps you to learn and catalog the movement, and to train your muscles to execute it.

dirtbag: Used to describe climbers and boulderers who value inexpensive resources above all else, whether you're talking cheap (or free) camping, food, showers, or any other relevant expense. For example, "I am such a dirtbag that I'd rather jump into an icy cold river than pay $5 for a hot shower, and I do most of my grocery shopping at the dollar store."

down climb: Often the only way to get down off the top of a boulder after topping out, a down climb usually involves an easy or relatively easy way to climb down the boulder and is often specified on topos or in the problem descriptions in a guidebook.

drop knee: A drop knee usually involves having one foot stably positioned with your big toe on a hold. The other foot is then placed on another hold to the side of the stable foot, toe up. You then pivot that toe so that it is partially or fully turned downward, depending on the drop knee that is necessary, and you can sometimes push off it as well, as there is a ton of power stored up in that bent leg. (See photo on page 44.)

dyno: Much like a deadpoint, except that your feet leave the starting footholds—it's essentially jumping up the wall. (See photo on page 42.)

eliminate: An eliminate is a contrived boulder problem in which certain holds have been designated as off-route (despite their proximity to the holds on the route), usually to increase the difficulty of the problem.

feeling the love; feeling it: A term used to describe your general state of being on a given bouldering day, often in negative terms. For example, "I'm just not feeling the love on the crux of this problem today."

fingerboard: A single, somewhat large, injection-molded piece of plastic featuring a variety of climbing grips, usually hung at about the same height as you would hang a pull-up bar. Used for a variety of training exercises from pull-ups to grip-strength training.

finger lock: A technique often used by crack climbers that can also be applicable to bouldering, this involves sinking your fingers into a narrow crack in the rock and then twisting your hand so that you "lock" your fingers into the feature securely.

fire: To go for a hold quickly, or to send a problem with authority—"She just fired my project in a couple of tries and made it look easy."

flag: Dropping one foot off the wall entirely and moving it to the side or behind your other leg to find an effective balance point that enables you to better move to the next hold. Think of the leg off the wall as similar to a cat's tail, helping achieve a better, more balanced position than you would have by forcing yourself to always have both feet on the wall. (See photo on page 44.)

flail: To experience marked and most often repeated difficulty on a problem or a particular move, usually involving an utter lack of success. For example, "I flailed and flailed on the opening moves of that problem, but never even managed to get my butt off the ground."

flake: A somewhat flat piece of rock that is partially separated from, but still attached to, the main cliff or boulder face. If attached solidly, flakes often provide good handholds, allowing you to wrap your fingers or hands around their edges for great purchase.

flash: Doing a problem on your first try without any kind of beta (whether from watching another boulderer, having another boulderer describe the problem to you, or some other foreknowledge of the moves).

gaston: Usually use on a vertically facing hold, this is a way of taking a hold that involves turning your hand so that your pinky is above your thumb on the hold and your elbow is pointing outward from your body. Very shoulder-intensive.

gripped: A state of being extremely scared for one's safety, whether perceived or real—"I was way too gripped to top that problem out, since I was 15 feet above the crash pad and I didn't have a spotter."

grovel: Used to describe a particularly unaesthetic mode of ascent. In bouldering, often used to describe a difficult top out that forces most boulderers to flop about ungracefully and use any and all body parts to achieve success (see *beached whale*).

hand-foot match: A move in which you place your foot on the same hold on which you have your hand.

hand jam: A technique often used by crack climbers that can also be applicable to bouldering, this involves placing your hand in a crack feature and then using your thumb and the shape of your hand to gain secure purchase on the hold. People who are good at hand jams can find great rests utilizing them, so be sure to ask someone to show you how to execute a hand jam properly.

heel hook: A move in which you place your heel on a hold, either to take some weight off your upper body (enabling you to move your hands) or to actively pull yourself with your leg to the next holds. (See photo on page 41.)

highball: A problem that tops out above a comfortable level from which to take a fall. Depending on who you ask, a highball could be a 10-foot boulder problem or a 30-foot boulder problem, since everyone has a different comfort zone.

high step: A move in which you bring your foot up to a high foothold, often near your waist. This move requires good active flexibility. (See photo on page 45.)

holds; also handhold and foothold: Terms used to describe rock features or the bolted-on sculpted hunks of plastic at the climbing gym that boulderers and rock climbers use to ascend the rock or the climbing wall. A dead giveaway that someone is not a climber or boulderer is if they describe holds as "grips."

hueco: A pocket, often used as a handhold or foothold, that is larger in circumference than a mono, two-finger, or three-finger pocket. Though often fist- or grapefruit-size holes in the rock, huecos can sometimes be large enough to accommodate double knee bars or even an entire body. Often found at Hueco Tanks, but also seen in other areas.

intermediate: A hold in between the normally used or more positive holds on a boulder problem, often stopped on only briefly before you fire for the "real" hold.

jib: Small footholds, also called screw-ins, used on indoor climbing walls and recognizable by the fact that they are screwed to the wall with small screws instead of the standard bolts used to affix holds to the walls. Many gym problems will specify that the allowed footholds include jibs as well as the marked handholds.

jug: A large hold.

knee bar: Finding a position in which your bent knee pushes into a feature in the rock while your foot on the same leg is set on a feature in opposition. The resulting tension transfers much weight off your arms (sometimes resulting in a no-hands rest). Knee bars can often be found in a hole (hueco) or similar feature that has a lip under which you can slide your bent knee and a ledge or edge for your foot of the same leg.

knee scum: Any usage of the knee to assist in ascending a boulder except for a knee bar; often involves pressing the inside portion of the knee against the rock to gain purchase.

landing: The area in which you will hit the ground if you fall off a problem. A good landing is generally clear of uneven ground, rocks, logs, vegetation, and other potentially injurious objects.

lock-off: A position in which you can hold on to one hold with your arm bent and tensed and let go with the other hand to reach statically to the next hold. Also used as a verb, for example, "He could just lock off that tiny crimper and grab the awful sloper with his other hand."

mantle: A move that is like getting out of a swimming pool without the helpful buoyancy of the water. When you encounter a mantle while bouldering, most of the time it will be part of topping out the problem—and sometimes, mantling can be the crux. As you pull up on the holds to top out the problem, at some point you will need to transition from pulling on the holds to pushing them down, while often at the same time bringing up a foot onto which you can rock your weight. (See photo on page 38.)

match; matching: Using the same hold with any two distinct body parts—you can match your hands or your feet or do a hand-foot match.

mono: A one-finger pocket—very injury-provoking.

mutant: An inconceivably strong boulderer.

no-hands rest: A rest in which you figure out a way to take both hands off the rock, thus allowing for a more complete rest of your shoulders, arms, and hands.

off; off-route: Terms used to describe holds or areas of a wall or boulder that are not considered a part of a particular problem.

one-move wonder: A boulder problem that involves literally a single hand movement, or a boulder problem that gets its difficulty rating due to one singularly hard, stopper move of much greater difficulty than any other move on it.

onsight: Doing a problem on your first try without any beta—meaning that you didn't watch anyone else attempt the problem, nor did anyone give you any information about the problem beforehand.

open feet: A term usually used to describe a gym problem in which you must use the marked handholds for your hands, but you are permitted to utilize any of the holds on the wall as footholds.

open hand: A grip that looks just like it sounds—instead of balling up your hand into the fistlike position of crimping, in the open-handed grip your knuckles will be barely bent, just enough to maximize the surface area in contact with the hold. (See photo on page 39.)

overgripping: Gripping handholds with more force than necessary, resulting in more rapid fatigue.

plateau: A significant period of time in which you can discern no noticeable improvement in your bouldering ability.

pockets: Features found in rock that climbers and boulderers use for handholds and footholds. Pockets vary in size from shallow, one-finger monos to deep, double-handed jugs (huecos). Two-finger and three-finger pockets are quite common.

problem: The term commonly employed to describe bouldering routes. A problem can involve 1 move or 50 . . . or more.

project: If a problem is listed in a guidebook as a project, it means that no one has yet been successful in climbing that particular set of holds. Boulderers also uses the term to describe established problems that they are working and trying to send.

pull down: Similar to *crank*, *pull down* refers to performing a move or problem and is often used as a term of encouragement.

pump; getting pumped; pumping out; flash pump; pumpfest: A pump happens when a boulderer can no longer hang on to the holds or continue to progress on a problem due to excessive upper-body fatigue, usually in the forearms. This leads to a painful state of not being able to even close the hands on the holds or execute what would otherwise be easy moves. A flash pump often occurs when a boulderer gets on a problem that is too hard too early in the workout and gets pumped where he or she normally would not get pumped. A pumpfest is a route or problem that most climbers or boulderers (with the exception of endurance freaks who never get pumped) find exceptionally pumpy.

reach; reachy: A long move, usually between handholds; often, the shorter you are, the more difficult or reachy it is perceived as being. For example, "That 6-foot-tall guy just reached past the bad hold and grabbed the good hold, but it was way too reachy for me to do it that way. I had to use those really bad intermediate holds."

redpoint: Any send of a problem that takes multiple attempts, whether it takes you two tries or 200.

rest day: A day off from bouldering or any sort of physical activity.

send: To successfully complete a problem or route. Also used as a noun.

session: Commonly used to describe any period of time spent bouldering ("We went to the gym for a short session today"). Also used to describe working a particular problem or boulder ("I sessioned the challenging problem to no avail—even after an hour, I couldn't put more than two moves together at a time, and then some local guy came up and did some laps on it").

shake out: A way in which climbers try to recover strength in arms and hands that involves dropping one hand off a hold and shaking the hand and arm to try and decrease the pump, and then switching hands to repeat the process for the other arm, if possible.

sidepull: A handhold that affords the most efficient and sensible usage when pulled at from a sideways angle, rather than straight down or from another angle.

sit-down start (sds): Beginning a boulder problem by pulling onto the rock surface from a sitting position; usually adds difficulty to the problem. (See photo on page 37.)

sketchy; sketch: A catchall term used to describe either components of a boulder problem that are inadequate for some reason or another ("The footholds are really sketchy on that problem" or "That problem has a sketchy landing") or one's own shaky performance, either mentally or physically, on a particular problem ("That problem sketches me out because it's a highball" or "I get really sketchy with my hands during that section of the problem").

slab; slabby: Less-than-vertical rock, though some boulderers will deem vertical or even slightly overhanging rock as slabby.

sloper: A true sloper is a handhold that is smooth and usually somewhat rounded, devoid of any bumps, edges, or positive features that would enable a climber to utilize any sort of crimp grip on it. Slopers are true open-handed holds for everyone.

spot; spotter: To spot, those who are not bouldering stand with palms facing the boulderer on the rock, arms out in readiness to make an effort to ensure that in the event of a fall, the boulderer lands on the pad unhurt. Just like in gymnastics, spotting can help prevent injuries. Becoming an adept spotter requires practice and experience, so be sure to observe others, ask plenty of questions, and practice before attempting to spot others yourself.

spray; spraylord: Bragging or sharing extensive information about your (or someone else's) accomplishments or specific moves on a particular route, or providing other super-detailed and usually unsolicited information related to bouldering or climbing. While most boulderers and climbers can't help but spray every so often, spraylords show no discrimination about their spraying, sharing intricate and unasked-for beta about routes—even those they have never been on—and extensive information about their sends, and perpetually namedropping all of the names of "famous" boulderers and climbers they know or have ever encountered.

squat-down start: A ridiculous takeoff on the sit-down start, used when you cannot start from a sitting position, yet can start squatted down on handholds lower than those reachable from a standing position.

static: A term used to describe a climbing move made without any dynamic motion.

stopper: Used to describe a move or sequence of movements that prevent you from sending a problem.

system board: A uniformly angled, flat, overhanging climbing surface with a variety of holds bolted onto it, possibly with large, identical square holds that each feature a number of different grips. Usually there will be several sets of the same types of holds lined up in columns, allowing people to design exercises that work specific grips, such as pinches, crimps, open hands, slopers, and the like.

test piece: A problem that represents a standard in both quality and difficulty for an area, often of a relatively hard or extremely difficult grade.

tick: A mark that boulderers make with chalk to indicate a particular hand or foothold or a desirable spot on a hold to fire for. It is polite and looks better to brush off ticks when you are finished trying a problem.

tick list: A list of problems that a boulderer would like to send, or a list that has been sent, or a list in a guidebook of recommended problems that shouldn't be missed.

toe hook: Toe hooking involves turning your foot sole-up so that you can latch a feature or hold it with the top of your shoe in the toe area, either to hold yourself in place while you move your hands or to pull yourself with the top of your foot and your leg to the next hold or holds.

top out: The finish to most boulder problems involves a top out, or standing on top of the boulder. Guidebooks will usually indicate if a particular problem does not top out.

tracking: In gym climbing, a problem that requires you to use the same holds marked for your hands for your feet.

traverse: A boulder problem that spans the face of a boulder in which you climb right-to-left or left-to-right instead of climbing up. Sometimes traverses top out, and sometimes they simply stop at a randomly appointed hold or else roll around a corner of the boulder and stop.

treed: Being stuck on top of a boulder with no feasible down climb or walk off in sight.

undercling: A hold best used by turning your hand palm upward and pulling in and up; very bicep-intensive.

walk off: As opposed to a down climb, a walk off allows you to simply walk down a part of the boulder to regain terra firma.

weight-off: See *diet.*

work: If you work a problem, you spend time figuring out each of the individual moves and then strive to put those moves together. People can work a problem as little as one time before sending or for several years before sending.

QUICK REFERENCE LIST OF BOULDERING GUIDEBOOKS

I'VE CHOSEN TO LIST guidebooks and their authors separately from the index to make for easier referencing if you're seeking a particular guidebook to one of the destinations in this book. For each book, I've given the name of one online merchant who sells it, if possible. If I've failed to include a better or more recent guidebook for any of the 25 included areas that you know of, please let me know. Many of these works proved to be invaluable resources and references in my travels to research this work, and as far as I know, they represent some of the best comprehensive published works on the areas included. If you plan to spend any significant time at one or more of the areas in this book, I highly recommend that you support these local guidebook authors by purchasing their books.

Northwest

SINKS CANYON

None. Some bouldering included in *Lander Rock*, by Greg Collins and Vance White (2003), $20. Available for purchase online at www.wild irisclimbing.com.

Sinks Canyon Bouldering, by Steve Bechtel, out of print.

CODY

Cody Bouldering, by Mike Snyder and Jeremy Rowan (due out summer 2005).

DIERKES LAKE

None. Route climbs indexed in *Basalt Climbs of South-Central Idaho*, by Mark Weber (1995). Available for $12.95 online at www.chesslerbooks.com.

California

CASTLE ROCK STATE PARK

Bouldering Guide to the Castle Rock Area, by Bruce Morris (MorComm, 2002), $16.95. Available for purchase online at www.rei.com.
The Buttermilks (Peabody Boulders area)
The Bishop Bouldering Survival Kit, 2nd edition, by Mick Ryan (Rockfax, 2003), $18. Available for purchase online at www.rockfax.com.

JOSHUA TREE NATIONAL PARK

A *Complete Bouldering Guide to Joshua Tree National Park*, by Robert Miramonte (2003), $34. Available for purchase online at www.fixeusa.com.

Utah and Colorado

IBEX

Bouldering Guide to Utah, by Mike Beck, Jeff Baldwin, and Marc Russo. (Springhill Press, 2003), $34.95. Includes more than 5,000 problems in 22 areas. Available for purchase online at www.rei.com.
Utah Bouldering, by Chris Grijalva, Noah Bigwood, and Dave Pegg (Wolverine Publishing, 2003), $19.95. Includes Little Cottonwood Canyon, Joe's Valley, Ibex, Big Bend, and Ogden. Available for purchase online at www.rei.com.

JOE'S VALLEY

Bouldering Guide to Utah, by Mike Beck, Jeff Baldwin, and Marc Russo (Springhill Press, 2003), $34.95. Includes more than 5,000 problems in 22 areas. Available for purchase online at www.rei.com.
Utah Bouldering, by Chris Grijalva, Noah Bigwood, and Dave Pegg (Wolverine Publishing, 2003), $19.95. Includes Little Cottonwood Canyon, Joe's Valley, Ibex, Big Bend, and Ogden. Available for purchase online at www.rei.com.

LITTLE COTTONWOOD CANYON

Bouldering Guide to Utah, by Mike Beck, Jeff Baldwin, and Marc Russo (Springhill Press, 2003), $34.95. Includes more than 5,000 problems in 22 areas. Available for purchase online at www.rei.com.

Utah Bouldering, by Chris Grijalva, Noah Bigwood, and Dave Pegg (Wolverine Publishing, 2003), $19.95. Includes Little Cottonwood Canyon, Joe's Valley, Ibex, Big Bend, and Ogden. Available for purchase online at www.rei.com.

FLAGSTAFF MOUNTAIN

Rock & Ice: The Boulder Bouldering Map, compiled by a number of Boulder-area climbers (Rock & Ice, 2001), $4.50. Available for purchase online at www.rei.com.

Best of Boulder Bouldering, by Bob Horan (Falcon Publishing, 2000), $18. Available for purchase online at www.rei.com.

Colorado Bouldering, by Phillip Benningfield (Sharp End Publishing, 1999), $28. Available for purchase online at www.rei.com.

Colorado Bouldering 2, by Phillip Benningfield and Matt Samet (Sharp End Publishing, 2003), $28. Available for purchase online at www.rei.com.

CASTLEWOOD CANYON STATE PARK

Colorado Bouldering, by Phillip Benningfield (Sharp End Publishing, 1999), $28. Available for purchase online at www.rei.com.

Colorado Bouldering 2, by Phillip Benningfield and Matt Samet (Sharp End Publishing, 2003), $28. Available for purchase online at www.rei.com.

Southwest

PRIEST DRAW

None. Check for possible topo brochure at Vertical Relief Climbing Center, (928-556-9909; www.verticalrelief.com; 205 South San Francisco Street, Flagstaff). See Dr. Topo (www.drtopo.com) for free online guide.

BOX CANYON

None. See *Socorro Bouldering Guide*, by Bob Broilo, available free online at www.nmt.edu/~bob/boulder_guide/socorro_boulder_guide.html.

HUECO TANKS STATE HISTORIC SITE

Hueco Tanks Climbing and Bouldering Guide, 2nd Edition, by John Sherman (Falcon, 1995), $30. Available for purchase online at www.amazon.com.

Midwest

MOUNT BALDY

No published guidebook available at press time, but local boulderer Dan Dewell plans to have one out in both written and online formats by spring of 2005. Check Climbing Black Hills (www.climbingblackhills.com) for details and more information.

Northeast

RUMNEY

Rumney, by Ward Smith (Ward Smith, 2001), $25. Available for purchase on-
line at www.nerock.com.

HAMMOND POND RESERVATION

Boston Rocks, 2nd edition, by Richard Doucette and Susan Ruff, $25. Avail-
able for purchase online at www.rei.com.

LINCOLN WOODS STATE PARK

A Bouldering Guide to Lincoln Woods, RI, by Joe McLoughlin (Joe McLoughlin,
2002), $14.95. Available for purchase online at www.newenglandbouldering
.com.

THE GUNKS

Bouldering in the Shawangunks, 2nd edition, by Ivan A. Greene and Marc E.
Russo (Jefe Publications, 2003), $22. Available for purchase online at
www.rocksnow.com.

Southeast

HORSE PENS 40

No comprehensive published guidebook. See Dr. Topo (www.drtopo.com) for
free online guide.

SANDROCK

None, but a small guide appears in *The Dixie Cragger's Atlas: A Climber's
Guide to Tennessee, Alabama and Georgia,* by Chris Watford (Market Place
Press, 1999), $32. Available for purchase by e-mailing callwild@atlanta.com
or by calling 770-992-5400. See Dr. Topo (www.drtopo.com) for free online
guide.

ROCKTOWN

No comprehensive published guidebook. See Dr. Topo (www.drtopo.com) for
free online guide.

BOAT ROCK

No comprehensive published guidebook. See Dr. Topo (www.drtopo.com) for
free online guide).

Selected Bouldering Web Resources

BY NO MEANS INCLUSIVE, this list of links should guide you to some of my favorite online merchants and resources, many of which proven to be fantastic general resources and references in compiling this work. I'm not into chat rooms and such, so you're on your own finding sites where folks like to while away their workdays sharing beta or spray with other like-minded people. For regional and local Web resources (also indispensable research aids in my efforts) see *Online resources* in each area's individual profile.

0Friction (www.0friction.com) offers up eye candy galore minus the spray that so often accompanies bouldering Web sites. Understated and mature, it allows you to surf through a ton of great photos and find destinations that call to you.

The Access Fund (www.accessfund.org) helps preserve access to climbing areas and conserve climbing environments around the country.

The American Alpine Club (www.americanalpineclub.org) provides rescue insurance to members and tons of additional resources, as well as working to conserve climbing environments.

American Bouldering Series (ABS) (www.rockcomps.com) lists information about upcoming bouldering competitions around the country, most of which are redpoint format (meaning multiple attempts on each problem) and include a beginner category.

The American Mountain Guides Association (www.amga.com) lists qualified climbing guides.

Dr. Topo (www.drtopo.com) is the first site I usually visit when I'm planning a short jaunt to a bouldering area, in hopes of a free, downloadable guide that will suffice for one or two days in lieu of purchasing a tome.

Galyans (www.galyans.com) has numerous stores around the nation that have in-house climbing venues as well as retail products for climbers.

IndoorClimbing.com (www.indoorclimbing.com) contains a comprehensive listing of gyms around the country, as well as training advice and other useful information.

Mountain Gear (www.mgear.com) offers terrific package deals, as well as the Hot Sheet, a weekly e-mail listing the latest bargains.

The Online Climbing Guide (www.onlineclimbing.com) is striving to build an enormous database of information about climbing areas around the world.

Priceline (www.priceline.com) is the first place to go if you're planning a climbing trip that involves flying, hotel rooms, and rental cars, so long as your dates are flexible. You can snag plane tickets and such for ridiculously low prices if you're lucky, and you get a "yes" or a "no" answer to the price you name in seconds.

Public Lands Information Center (www.publiclands.org) provides extensive information, including maps and detailed write-ups, of all the public lands in an assortment of Western states.

REI (www.rei.com) tops the list as a nationwide online retailer of adventure goods as well as being one of the premier resources for climbing gear, climbing-related clinics and shows, and in-store walls around the United States. Log on and use the nifty store-finder tool to find the location nearest to your home.

RockClimbing.com (www.rockclimbing.com) has a vast amount of information about various climbing and bouldering areas around the country, and it is almost always a good place to start if you are seeking area-specific information or the latest spray about an area.

Sierra Trading Post (www.sierratradingpost.com) might just be the kingpin of closeout deals, not just for climbing gear, but also for all sorts of athletic outerwear. This is a great place to start if you're looking for clothes, shoes, chalk bags, and so forth.

Wal-Mart (www.walmart.com) has a store-finder feature online and is a great resource for travelers, both for inexpensive camping supplies and groceries as well as in being a place to park the car and grab some sleep should other camping options elude you.

index

T

U